Staten Island in Fiction 1896-2015

Jeffrey Coogan

Castleton Press
Staten Island, New York

First Edition

Published by:
Castleton Press
www.castletonpress.com

Library of Congress Control Number: 2017910292

ISBN: 0692828583
ISBN-13: 978-0692828588 (Castleton Press)

Cover image from George A. Ward's *Description of New Brighton, on Staten Island, opposite the city of New York* (1836).

"All events and experiences are local, somewhere. And all human enhancements of events and experiences -- all the arts -- are regional in the sense that they derive from immediate relation to felt life.

It is this immediacy that distinguishes art. And paradoxically the more local the feeling in art, the more all people can share it; for that vivid encounter with the stuff of the world is our common ground.

Artists, knowing this mutual enrichment that extends everywhere, can act, and praise, and criticize, as insiders -- the means of art is the life of all people. And that life grows and improves by being shared. Hence, it is good to welcome any region you live in or come to, or think of, for that is where life happens to be, right where you are."

— William Stafford, poet

Contents

Acknowledgements

I would like to acknowledge several people without whom this book wouldn't have been written. First, my mother, Joan, who imparted her love of reading to me from my earliest years. Second, my wife Divonne who provided invaluable feedback, encouragement and endless patience with a project that must have seemed never-ending and bizarrely arcane. And third, Dr. James A. Kaser, Professor and Archivist of the College of Staten Island, whose work in building a collection of Staten Island fiction was an invaluable resource and whose own scholarly, yet endlessly entertaining studies of Washington D.C., Chicago and New Orleans fiction were the direct inspiration for this work.

Introduction

"Men of Letters have lived upon the Island, but their labors have not been especially identified with it and we are not aware that any of its local traditions have been commemorated in song or in story."

—George William Curtis in "Literature on Staten Island" from
The Staten Island Magazine, Vol. 1, No. 1, 1888.

When I was a child I somehow came into possession of a second-hand Phyllis Whitney novel (*Step to the Music* I believe) and I can still recall the bewildered shock of recognition I felt as I noticed all the references to Staten Island places and historical figures in the book. A story about Staten Island?? Inconceivable! My family and friends were just as surprised as I had been to learn that a published novel actually took place on Staten Island (in our own neighborhood, no less.) It wasn't as if we thought that our fair island wasn't a rich and fascinating source of stories; after all, the real-life dramas we pored over every day in the *Advance* were fit subjects for a thousand novels, and the minutiae of our island's exciting history was, and is, an endlessly popular subject for native Staten Islanders. It's just that, as engrossing as we found our hometown, decades of contempt from metropolitan tabloids and popular culture (not to mention ill-usage and neglect by our political overlords in Manhattan and Albany) had internalized in us the attitude that no real author (a high and mighty type of personage that existed somewhere far across the bay) would ever deem our community interesting enough to utilize as a fictional setting. It was as if one were to turn on the TV and see one's grandmother profiled on the 6:00 news; as beloved as she might be to us, widespread media attention would seem somewhat puzzling and incongruous.

Nevertheless, the findings of this project reveal that the corpus of Staten Island literature does indeed contain a surprising number of volumes. Identifying them required some detective work however. I was fortunate, in working for the Archives and Special Collections at the

College of Staten Island Library (CUNY), to be able to draw upon its nucleus of a local literature collection, without which I probably would never have discovered relatively unknown, older works like *Dear Guest and Ghost*, *Alfie and Me and the Ghost of Peter Stuyvesant*, and the novels of Theodora DuBois and John Sampson among others. Published sources of information on local literature, however, were few and far between.

Our island's primary reference work, *Staten Island and its People*, contained only a very few tantalizing mentions of fictional works when its five volumes were published in the early 1930s. The *Staten Island Historian* contained reviews of only a few novels over the course of its many decades. The lack of a publicly available index for *The Staten Island Advance*, let alone a searchable database for issues before 1991, precluded me from mining that undoubtedly valuable resource. The various reference works that have examined literature set in New York City have never been able to cite more than a mere handful of Staten Island fictional works, if they even took note of any at all. When City University of New York (CUNY) Professor John P. Martin wrote a journal article on the subject in 1992 (*Community Review*, Volume XII, Numbers One and Two) he was only able to spotlight five written works that had a Staten Island setting, concluding that the constant theme of Staten Island literature has been to depict the island and its wild natural areas as metaphors for untamed, violent adolescence, eventually tainted and subdued by contact- through the Verrazano Bridge- with the rest of "civilized" New York.

The general obscurity of the subject can partly be attributed to the literary world's lack of interest in an unfashionable, under-populated outer borough that is almost universally regarded as *terra incognita* by the rest of the city. But trends in library cataloging played a role as well: it was only relatively recently, as library catalogs became increasingly computerized and publishers began providing more information electronically, that geographic designators for fictional works began to be incorporated into catalog records. The growth of the internet made such information even more widely available, so that in 2000 an official geographic descriptor for fictional works was created in cataloging rules. Nevertheless, inclusion of such information still depends on the human cataloger, and I've discovered that the majority of the Staten Island works I've identified, including the more recent ones, are not cataloged as such. Therefore I was in a unique position, working for the CSI Archives, to cultivate our collection of local fiction, identify new works, and write this book.

Utilizing library catalogs, online resources, obscure local histories and word-of-mouth, I've been able to identify over 140 fictional works, including novels, plays, short stories, and children's books that are set, in whole or in some significant part, on Staten Island. The island's rich history, particularly from the Revolutionary era, is an inspiration for a number of works of historical fiction. Mysteries and police procedurals abound. Pulitzer Prize-winning local author Paul Zindel used his hometown for a number of his successful and influential juvenile and young adult novels. Best-selling authors Phyllis Whitney and Theodora DuBois used the island as the locale for many of their respective works in mystery, sci-fi, historical fiction, and novels for young people. The modern, award-winning novels of Tracy Brown are unique in this category for their focus on the island's contemporary African American community. Genres of other novels run the gamut from Lovecraftian horror, gay romance, dystopian sci-fi, Socialist agitprop, humor and gothic supernatural, with plenty of crime and coming-of-age stories thrown into the mix. Some themes stand out: from the earliest works, the rural isolation of the island is often depicted as an Arcadian retreat but, more frequently, as a useful base for criminal, conspiratorial or even occult acts, with the latter trope enduring to the present day. More recent works almost invariably depict the island as a paradise lost that was forever destroyed by the opening of the Verrazano Bridge and the physical connection to New York City, but it may surprise the modern reader to find out that even in the early 1950s novels of Theodora Dubois, the themes of overdevelopment, ugly architecture and the encroachment of outsiders upon the "natives" can be found. The constant impression, however, is that Staten Island was and still is a place apart, with a location and culture that are unique and distinct from the city with which it is connected, and a place where things can happen and people can exist that can't happen or exist in the wider metropolis.

I've written this book in the form of an annotated bibliography, listing the bibliographic citations for each book and including an annotation that explores the plot, the characters, themes and specific local settings.

Due to the relatively limited number of works examined, the obscurity of many, and the practical unavailability of some, my annotations were more detailed than is usual in this type of project. I felt that this level of description would be both informative for the scholarly researcher and entertaining for the general reader. I've included a biographical section for the authors and a short appendix that briefly discusses some works that didn't quite merit inclusion in the bibliography but that deserve to be noted. Another appendix lists the works in chronological order so that researchers can quickly identify the output of a particular era.

As academia in recent years has taken a strong interest in regional literature and the "Literature of Place," this book will hopefully be one of an increasing number of studies that document and analyze those works of the imagination that were inspired by New York City.

Annotated Bibliography, 1896-2015

1. Abbruzzi, Patrick. *Nothing to Report.* CreateSpace, 2012. 327pp.

   Written by a retired NYPD Lieutenant, this novel of police life is based on real incidents that occurred in New York City from the 1960s through the 1980s. Charlie Goodheart is a forty-six-year-old driver for the veteran Lieutenant John Audenino at the 120th precinct. Interspersed with the story of Charlie's torrid affair with the counter girl from the Dunkin' Donuts on Victory Boulevard near Bay Street are Lieutenant Audenino's tales of the sensational cases he'd been involved in through his career. Filled with the intimate details and minutiae of a police officer's life, the novel takes place entirely on Staten Island, mostly within the confines of the 120th precinct, and contains a wealth of local settings, history and description. Among the pseudonymous figures who populate this novel, one who can be identified is the pastor of St. Stanislaus Kostka church on York Avenue, who is clearly based on Polish priest Monsignor Artur Rojek (1906-1988), a survivor of the Dachau concentration camp and well-known figure in the Polish-American community.

2. Adinolfi, JoAnn. *Tina's Diner.* New York: Simon & Schuster Books for Young Readers, 1997. 29pp.

   This picture book for children depicts the trouble that ensues when the sink at Tina's diner on Staten Island became clogged. Tina placed a call to J.P. Pettifog, the best plumber in New York City, but only reached her voicemail. As the dirty dishes piled higher and higher, the little boy who is narrating the story decided to take the ferry to Manhattan and find Ms. Pettifog. Following the sound of her banging on pipes, the young narrator chases Ms. Pettifog through the skyscrapers and sewers of Manhattan and finally brings her back to Tina's diner, where she unclogs the sink. Unfortunately, a few sewer alligators snuck back to Staten Island with them and seem to be scaring the customers.

3. Ambrose, Dominic. *Nickel Fare.* New York: Ferrandina Press, 2012. 225pp.

   This gay *bildungsroman* tells the story of Nicangelo Bello and his journey into and out of addiction and degradation. Bello, a young man from Brooklyn who is a dilettante film student at Staten Island

Community College in 1971, decides to look up a charismatic and imposing acquaintance, Ned Hartland, who lives at the top of Brighton Avenue and attends classes at Richmond College. Their get-together almost leads to a sexual encounter but Nicangelo is turned off when he sees the marks of Ned's heroin addiction on his body. Soon after this meeting, Ned pays a visit to Nicangelo's Daniel Low Terrace apartment with a certain Jansen, a former inmate from the special section for the insane at the Greenbelt Hospital for the mentally retarded, where Ned and Nicangelo used to work. Jansen is obviously sleeping with Ned, but Jansen and Nicangelo later hook up at Silver Lake Park, where they achieve an emotional connection in addition to having a sexual encounter.

Nicangelo's semi-stable existence begins to unravel when he is questioned at the 120th Precinct in connection with a check-stealing scheme at his night job, but he is released after enduring anti-gay and anti-Brooklyn insults. After viewing a film at SICC and taking a horse tranquilizer pill from another hippie, he staggered away stoned and was picked up by a man (later revealed to be one of the police officers who had interrogated him) who brutally rapes and beats him. Nicangelo endures further tragedy when he finds out that Jansen hung himself in his parents' Eltingville home. He takes the SIRR down to the funeral home there to pay his respects but is literally stoned by Jansen's family, who believe that Nicangelo was his drug supplier. The police rescue Nicangelo from the mob but take him down to the docks where they sexually abuse him and insult both his sexual orientation and his Brooklyn origins. They express the belief that both of those aspects of his personality threaten the quiet and moral Staten Island that they deem themselves to be protecting. They drive him over the Verrazano Bridge and order him never to return to Staten Island under threat of physical violence, false arrest or death.

Now homeless, Nicangelo looks up one of Ned Hartland's Brooklyn addresses, which turns out to belong to an aged transvestite prostitute named Manette, who gives him shelter and a cut of "her" business selling fake subway tokens. The rest of the book relates Nicangelo's descending spiral into drugs and degradation. Ned Hartland, who is himself a prostitute, gets Nicangelo addicted to cocaine and heroin and pimps him out for gang bangs in Times Square porno theaters. In search of money and shelter, Nicangelo takes up with an older German man who ends their arrangement when he discovers Nicangelo's drug use. The German man puts him on a plane to Puerto Rico (mistakenly believing that Nicangelo is Puerto Rican) where he finds himself a married lover and takes up with a hippie community. Returning to New York, Nicangelo begins to clean up his life and find some stability but Ned reappears, more strung out than ever. When Nicangelo discovers that Ned beat up Manette (who, it is revealed, is Ned's own grandfather) in his search for drug money, Nicangelo disguises himself as Manette and stabs Ned in the movie theater where he turns tricks. Ned survives but is arrested and imprisoned for various parole violations.

The book contains a description of the Mayfair Bar on Hyatt Street, Staten Island's one gay establishment at the time. Nicangelo didn't even consider going into the "Mary-Fairy," as the bar and its clientele were too "laughably old-fashioned" for him. Richmond College is described as an "...experimental college, the type of place where people got degrees in things like 'The American Dream' and 'Comparative Aesthetics', -vague, undisciplined disciplines that seemed designed to make idle inquiries about 'majors' pointless." A student at the college says that everything is bigger and better there, even the drugs. Nicangelo's roommate on Daniel Low Terrace is a self-styled revolutionary from Richmond College. One character is described as living an openly gay lifestyle, flamboyant and militant, on Staten Island, but one of extreme poverty in a slum house on Bay Street. The novel presents a detailed portrait of both the hippie and gay subcultures of early 1970s New York.

4.   Amessé, Susan. *Kissing Brendan Callahan*. New Milford, Conn.: A Deborah Brodie Book, Roaring Brook Press, 2005. 149pp.
      In this book for young people, Sarah Olivia Simmons is a soon-to-be seventh grader and aspiring writer whose mother is an editor for the Staten Island Courier. Sarah is excited to discover that her mother's preservation group is sponsoring a play-writing contest for teens, on the subject of Staten Island history, but is dismayed when her mother forbids her from participating because of ethical considerations. Sarah's friend, the free-spirited Brendan Callahan, advises her to enter the contest under an assumed name, so Sarah begins riding her bike to many of Staten Island's historic places- Snug Harbor, Richmondtown, the Alice Austen House- to find inspiration, but is unsuccessful. Meanwhile, Sarah learns that her favorite writer, the romance novelist Antonia DeMarco, has been chosen to be the judge of the contest.

Sarah is inspired to impress DeMarco with a play about a girl who had lived in Sarah's house in the 19th century. Sarah's life is further complicated when, after having pizza with Brendan on Forest Avenue, he suddenly kisses her.

When Sarah is tasked by her mother to bring the contest entries to DeMarco at the South Beach bungalow she's renting, she gets herself recruited by her idol as her personal assistant. Sarah, now aping her hero in dress and mannerisms, helps the author do a book signing at Barrett Books. They then tour St. Andrew's Cemetery, where DeMarco reveals that she came to Staten Island in order to try and get through her writer's block. When DeMarco invites Sarah to an evening get-together at her bungalow, her mother forbids it but, following Brendan's rebellious advice, Sarah sneaks out of the house.

When she arrives at the bungalow she is introduced to several figures from Hollywood who are demanding to see DeMarco's promised script. Sarah begins to see that her hero has serious flaws, as DeMarco lies to them about how close she is to finishing her screenplay. Furthermore, Sarah discovers that DeMarco had also lied about her hard-luck upbringing and the fact that her last novel had been ghost-written. Sarah subsequently realizes that she had left the plays in the back of DeMarco's rental car, which had already been returned. The next morning, Sarah and Brendan discover DeMarco hiding from the rental company owner, who refuses to give back the plays until someone pays for the damage done to his car. DeMarco admits to the children that she is flat broke due to alimony for three ex-husbands and plans to skip town without paying for the damages or judging the contest. The children arrange to have DeMarco stay with Georgina, the nanny for Sarah's baby brother, in order to hide her from the rental car owner. DeMarco is inspired anew by watching Georgina's dancing and flies to Fiji to finish her screenplay. Sarah tells the truth to her mother, who had wisely copied all of the plays before sending them to DeMarco. Her mother consoles Sarah by telling her how she had once trusted a local politician who sold parkland to developers. Her mother ends up judging the writing contest and, although Sarah's pseudonymous play did not win, her mother thought it showed promise if not great historical accuracy. Sarah's disillusionment with DeMarco teaches her to find inspiration in the people she knows. She takes the independent Brendan's advice to heart and sneaks out of the house to see him perform standup comedy at the Java Cup coffeehouse in Stapleton.

5.   Baker, Etta Anthony. *Captain of the 'S.I.G.'s'*. Boston: Little, Brown and Company, 1911. 323pp.

    Lindsay Carteret Carroll (otherwise known as Carter) is the leader of a group of neighborhood boys on Staten Island. They want to form some sort of club and eventually decide on a baseball team, which they name the Staten Island Giants, or S.I.G.'s. Their dream is to become good enough to beat the Stars, a team of older boys who are rather boastful about their baseball prowess. Carter's best friend is Sid Armstrong, who, to the great disappointment of the S.I.G.'s, is going to have to stay with relatives in Manhattan and Newport, R.I. for the summer, because his parents will be traveling in Europe seeking a health cure for Sid's sickly mother. After being away for a while, Sid returns to Staten Island for a short visit, but refuses to leave Carter's house. Mr. and Mrs. Carroll agree to let Sid stay with them until his parents return from abroad.

    The book is episodic, didactic and rambling, but consistently shows Staten Island to be an idyllic wonderland of boyhood adventure. The boys adopt a small dog named Dixie Doodle; they witness the burning of the St. George Cotton docks (presumably, the 1908 fire at present-day Bay Street Landing); they train with their company of the UBBA (United Boys' Brigade of America) and Sid wins a competitive rifle drill against the captain of the Stars. The boys start a circus in order to raise money; they go to the beach; they team up to protect Dixie Doodle from the dog catcher; they help the neighborhood girls with their bake sale for the Sunshine Society, a charity which aids shut-ins. Finally, after arduous practice and some much needed coaching by Johnny Porter's uncle Sidney, who played ball for Princeton, the S.I.G.'s are ready to face the Stars. The Giants are trailing by a run with two outs in the ninth when Carter comes to bat with the bases loaded and smacks a double to win the game. The rest of the summer proceeds with similar joyful fun. The boys go fishing at Clove Lake, they pick apples in Bulls Head and, in one of their most exciting adventures, Carter and Sid are given a ride on a fireboat, *The New Yorker*, and an ocean-going tug boat, *The Invincible*. The boys witness the wreck of *The Molly Pitcher* and its attempted rescue by the crew of the Sandy Hook life saving station. Upon their return to shore, they enter a story contest sponsored by one of the New York newspapers and both win prize money. Mrs.

Armstrong regains her health and so she and her husband return to Staten Island. Mr. Carroll is able to foil a business rival's sinister machinations and enjoys a financial recovery. The Carrolls are then able to build a new home, whose garage will be the S.I.G.'s future clubhouse.

The book includes this epigraph- "Rome, with her seven hills is quite thrown in the shade by the Island's uncounted heights", and indeed the Island is described with loving affection. This book takes place mainly on Staten Island and includes numerous references to places and institutions. It is particularly detailed with regard to some of the issues of the time, such as the strict new dog law, and various aspects of middle class life and leisure activities.

6.   Baker, Etta Anthony. *Miss Mystery.* Boston: Little, Brown & Co., 1913. 370pp.
       This novel of mystery, amnesia, thwarted lovers and sudden windfall takes place in St. George, which is portrayed as a judgmental and gossipy small town where everyone knows the business of everyone else. Sedate and lethargic St. George is described as an unexciting place, but "...it was near enough New York to make excitement of its own unnecessary. Conservative schedules placed it twenty-five minutes distant from the city, but enthusiastic commuters unblushingly reduced the time to fifteen, and these same enthusiasts were wont to boast that it formed a part of the great metropolis, even though a league or so of sparkling sea-water separated it from that delectable expanse of sky-scraper-crowned, theater-crowded territory." Despite its parochialism, it is a "...pretty suburb, with many hills and wide, tree-shaded avenues. More than one stately, pillared mansion graced the water front or stood out commandingly upon the surrounding heights; but these relics of a long-gone colonial period were mere shells of a departed grandeur....The homes were, for the most part, roomy frame houses set in a liberal allowance of well-kept lawn."

In one of those homes dwelt the Porter family, whose domestic tranquility was disturbed one day when a meeting of Mrs. Porter's *Women's Philanthropic Club* was interrupted by moaning coming from the room of sixteen-year-old Chester Porter. Upon investigating, the ladies discovered an unconscious young girl who had wandered into the house after being hit in the head by construction debris from a nearby work site. Mrs. Porter declares her intention of caring for the young woman until she is recovered, a decision that some of the members of her club find unseemly, because of the possibility that the girl may be a lunatic or a prostitute. The girl, now known as "Miss Mystery," awakens but is suffering from amnesia from the blow on her head. The Porters' neighbor, Marjory Chamberlin, goes out of her way to investigate the origins of the mysterious boarder, but to no avail. When Marjory's fiancé, Winthrop (the Porters' oldest son, who had at first taken no interest in his mother's mysterious guest), finally sees Miss Mystery, he is taken by her beauty and spends a small fortune and many hours of his own time trying to find out her identity. The jealous Marjory breaks off their engagement, which begins a whole series of misunderstandings: Marjory believes that Winthrop then immediately proposed to Miss Mystery, while Winthrop believes that he had been thrown over by Marjory in favor of his best friend Arthur Courtland. A further mix-up ensues when younger brother Chester ends up taking Marjory to a dance at the Lyceum when he had actually intended to take her younger niece of the same name. It is at this event, in which dancing and social rituals of the time are described in detail, where all is made clear and Winthrop and Marjory are reconciled. However, both Arthur Courtland and the forty-year-old doctor who tended to Miss Mystery begin to pursue her.

It is at this point that Mrs. Porter receives an attorney's letter notifying her that she is to receive one million dollars from the will of Walter Warren, a childhood friend of Winthrop's whom Mrs. Porter had taken in as her own son after his parents died but who disappeared years before without a trace. According to the letter, Walter had become the heir of a wealthy, childless man (the terms of the adoption forced Walter to call himself William Husted) through whom he had come to great wealth in Australia. However, Walter recently died in a shipwreck, leaving his entire estate to Mrs. Porter, the woman who had been like a mother to him. Even before they are in possession of the fortune, the money turns the heads of the family, with the two boys planning to adopt a luxury lifestyle. Most notably, Mrs. Porter's socialist sister-in-law starts wearing French fripperies and makes plans to buy a new house and hire an army of servants. Their Irish maid mocks their newfound status by saying that she expects them to join the fashionable Church of the Ascension now instead of their Reformed Church (presumably the one in St. George). Before they can spend the money, a woman shows up claiming to be Walter's widow. Mrs. Porter agrees to relinquish any claim on the estate but before the woman can get anything in writing, Walter Warren shows up alive, and denounces the woman as an imposter, identifying her as a famous Australian vaudeville actress known as the Enchantress. Meanwhile Miss Mystery, her memory jogged by a brooch that had gone astray while she had been unconscious and finally been returned, enters the parlor and recognizes Walter as her husband, the both of them thinking the other had perished in the shipwreck. Mystery (real name Winsome) had been trying to find her way to Mrs. Porter's house when she was struck by the brick. Reunited, Winthrop and Mrs. Porter help the couple become integrated into St. George society. The wealthy Walter funds the construction of a boys' club, a project dear to the hearts of the *Women's Philanthropic Club*.

Dr. Guthrie makes pejorative reference to the "hatless brigade" of women in St. George. The characters observe the Lusitania passing through the Narrows.

7. Bauch, Jonathan. *Permanent Record*. (Master's thesis). Las Vegas, Nev.: University of Nevada, Las Vegas, 2006. 150pp.
    A copy of this master's thesis could not be obtained for review, but an online description says, "Permanent Record is a collection of loosely connected short stories, told primarily in the first person (framed by a prologue and epilogue in other points of view), taking place on Staten Island, New York, during the 1980s. Tracing the character's development from his bar mitzvah through college, the stories deal primarily with a young man's attempt to reconcile his feelings of rebellion---against his parents, teachers, tradition, etc.---with his growing awareness of the Judaism instilled in him as a child. As much as the character tries to distance himself from his parents and their religious values, he becomes increasingly aware how much his own beliefs were influenced by being brought up Jewish in the specific milieu of Staten Island. Through his interaction with family and friends---most specifically, girlfriends, both Jews and non-Jews---he gains a greater awareness of his own prejudices and need for reconciliation." (Google Books).

8. Bettinger, Keith. *Fighting Crime with "Some" Day and Lenny; or What Happens When Dragnet Meets Car 54 Where Are You?*. Taylorville, Ill.: Oak Tree Press, 2006. 115pp.

    This collection of humorous stories focuses on the adventures and hijinks of NYPD Detective Sergeant Robert "Some" Day and his partner Detective Lenny Birnbaum, who work the Major Case Squad on Staten Island where, according to the book's narrator, Det. Sgt. Day, every case is a major case and every shift is the graveyard shift. Other rules that one must know about police work are that real cops drink black coffee, get in early for work and bosses don't drive. Officers Day and Birnbaum are dedicated policemen who are devoted to solving the exclusively petty crimes which plague their "beloved island," including the theft of a birdbath, a lawn ornament and a sprinkler head, the burglary of a mime school, graffiti tagging, and a breach of promise case involving a pilfered dowry. To these detectives, Brooklyn is considered a foreign country, and the world outside Staten Island is so exotic that Detective Birnbaum falls for the story that eastern half of Long Island has its own currency. Det. Sgt. Day notes that Staten Island was never invaded except by Brooklyn. Staten Island is a place of small-time criminals and penny ante crimes, but its police force takes their duties seriously, even if said police force can sometimes be a bit bumbling. Staten Island settings abound and reference is made to the landfill, which in this book is being renamed the Jimmy Hoffa Memorial Park and Recreation Center.

9. Bowles, Jane. *Two Serious Ladies*. New York: Alfred A. Knopf, 1943. 271pp.

    Wealthy lady Christina Goering sells her home and moves, with her companion Lucie Gamelon and a ineffectual male hanger-on named Arnold, into a ramshackle house on the rural southern end of an unnamed but unmistakable Staten Island: "...not far from the city by ferryboat...One end of the island is very well populated, although you can only buy third-rate goods in any of the stores. Farther out the island is wilder and more old-fashioned; nevertheless there is a little train that meets the ferry frequently and carries you out to the other end. There you land in a little town that is quite lost and looks very tough, and you feel a bit frightened, I think, to find that the mainland opposite the point is as squalid as the island itself and offers you no protection at all." In a narrative that moves in no discernible direction, Miss Goering takes the train to the southernmost stop, during which she is reprimanded by the conductor for talking to strangers. She takes the ferry there to the town across the river, where she falls into strange relationships with two odd men.

10. Brett, R. *Hypocrisy*. College Station, Tex.: Virtualbookworm.com, 2013. 244pp.

Apart from this novel's setting on Oakwood Avenue, there are no other named local settings or descriptions of Staten Island. After his little sister went missing, Jack Franks mistakenly stabbed an innocent neighbor in a drunken haze and was sent to prison. Now being released early, Franks returns home determined to confront and implicate another neighbor, Denis O'Mally, whom Franks is convinced killed his sister. After a bloody altercation between the two, police discover the corpses of eight children concealed on O'Mally's property, with physical evidence confirming O'Mally's guilt beyond all doubt. With the guilty party revealed early in the novel, it might be said that this book aimed to be more of a character study and courtroom procedural than a mystery or suspense novel.

11. Brown, Tracy. *Aftermath*. New York: St. Martin's Griffin, 2011. 452pp.

This sequel to *Snapped* begins in the Staten Island mansion of Camille Bingham when her sister Misa murders her brother-in-law, Steven, because Misa believed that Steven had sexually molested her son. Although this book's two most significant events occur on Staten Island- Misa Atkinson's murder of Steven Bingham and her subsequent trial- the location is incidental to the plot and hardly mentioned at all, beyond naming two restaurants (Against Da Grill and R.H. Tugs) and Silver Lake Park as the backgrounds for several get-togethers of the characters.

Much of the book focuses on the troubled relationships among the characters: their abusive fathers, incarcerated boyfriends, cheating husbands, romantic entanglements and financial problems. Camille discovers that she's pregnant soon after her crime boss husband, Frankie, leaves her for Gillian, the daughter of his deceased criminal overlord, the murdered Doug Nobles. Frankie cuts off all financial support for Camille on Staten Island when Misa murders his brother Steven. Gillian's half-brother, Baron, a murderous criminal in his own right, is confined to a wheelchair from a shootout and is estranged from Gillian and Frankie due to his irresponsibility and his inadvertent role in causing the death of his father, Doug Nobles. Although Misa was only a sexual plaything to Baron before his shooting, her loyalty to him through his convalescence leads him to hire one of New York's best defense lawyers for her trial. Record executive Dominique pines for her convict boyfriend Jamel, but ends up cheating on him with Archie, a marijuana dealer, shortly before Jamel's release from jail. Dominique's teenage daughter Olivia gets pregnant. Tough-as-nails real estate agent Toya reunites with her abusive father and finds love with a man so ugly that she nicknames him "Shrek," but who compensates for his looks with his bedroom skills.

Misa's trial takes place at the St. George courthouse, where the prosecution exposes her poor mothering skills. However, when Frankie's mother tells him that Steven was beaten and sodomized by their father, he finds himself on the witness stand unable to categorically state that he believed in his brother's innocence. The jury finds Misa not guilty.

12. Brown, Tracy. *Black; A Street Tale*. Columbus, Ohio: Triple Crown Publications, 2003. 182pp.

Four-year-old Kaia Wesley lives in a Mariners Harbor housing project with her alcoholic father Maurice, her abusive mother Janice, and her older sisters, Asha and Nubia. Although a mean drunk, Maurice loves Kaia deeply, which her mother takes as a personal affront, and reacts to by tormenting Kaia. One night, when Maurice comes home drunk, he and Janice begin to argue violently. When Kaia runs to her father's defense, Janice strikes her, causing Maurice to attack Janice, who then stabs him to death, not in self defense (as he was incapacitated by alcohol) but out of opportunity. However, her claim of self-defense is believed by all, except Kaia, whose mental and emotional abuse by Janice becomes even greater.

Kaia grows up with three best friends: the beautiful Giselle Murphy, the fashionably-dressed fighter Symphany James and the quiet but tough Talia Hampton. At the end of her Junior year at Curtis High School, in the Spring of 1991, Kaia is sitting in the park when she is approached by Aaron Banks. Aaron, who had been interested in Kaia for years, finally earns her attention by being genuine and polite. They smoke pot there and begin secretly seeing each other, going to the zoo, hanging out in the park on Grandview Avenue, and reading *The Autobiography of Malcolm X* together.

After Kaia finds herself pregnant, Aaron pledges to stay with her and support her. When they break the news to Kaia's mother, Janice responds with incredibly abusive language and, when Kaia refuses to get an abortion, throws her of the house wearing nothing but the clothes on her back. She moves into the Westervelt Avenue apartment that Aaron shares with his older brother Keith. At a loss as to how he was going to support a family, Aaron reaches out to his friend Sean from the Stapleton projects and gets back into the crack-dealing business. Unlike other dealers, Aaron operates his business through a pager system, and not by standing on the street corner.

Years earlier Aaron had snitched out a friend, Wayne, rather than do time for a robbery that Wayne had committed. Now, in the parking lot of the Bay Street McDonald's, Sean warns Aaron that Wayne is out of jail and looking for him. On the day that Kaia is in the hospital giving birth, Aaron goes to use the phone at the gas station on Targee and Vanderbilt and encounters Wayne, who pulls a gun on him. In self defense, Aaron manages to shoot and kill Wayne, but gets sentenced to five years in jail.

Having to support herself and her daughter, Phoenix Grace, Kaia gets a job as a receptionist at the Teleport and an apartment on Trantor Place. Although her sisters attempt a reconciliation between Kaia and her mother, Janice refuses to have anything to do with her, and walks out of Thanksgiving dinner.

Symphany, in the meantime, reveals that she had been a drug dealer with Aaron and Sean, but was leaving the business and buying a house now that she had accumulated a sizeable nest egg. Kaia is upset that Symphany never told her, but her friends retort that she should be mad at Aaron instead.

When Kaia meets a handsome man, Eric, who works in the mailroom at another Teleport company, her friends all encourage her to sleep with him, reasoning that a woman is entitled to her fun and that Aaron surely wouldn't remain faithful to her if she were the one in jail. When she does sleep with him, she gets an angry phone call from Aaron, who somehow found out and is calling to break up with her. Kaia laments what a small world Staten Island is. When she visits him in prison, he grudgingly meets with her and reveals that it was her friend Giselle who told him. Giselle was always jealous of their relationship, since her promiscuous ways ensured that no man would ever love her or treat her with respect. In addition, Giselle was hoping to hook up with Aaron after he gets out of jail, in order to get her hands on the crack wealth he is rumored to have. To avenge Kaia, Symphany sends two of her cohorts to beat Giselle. In addition, Aaron's brother Keith, who was friends with Eric, tracks him down to the Rendezvous bar on Targee Street (the place where "Shaolin's Who's Who" gathers on weekends) and knocks him out for his betrayal.

When Aaron is released in 1996, the devious Giselle pursues her dream of snaring him, by lying about Kaia's continued relationship with Eric, and by lying to Kaia about her own relationship with Aaron. When Janice has a heart attack after her daughter Nubia repeats Kaia's assertion that she intentionally murdered their father, Kaia goes to visit her in the hospital and attempts to reconcile. The hate-filled Janice summons up all her strength to tell Kaia that she should have killed her as well as Maurice. With Kaia alone in the world except for her daughter, Aaron begins to relent and treat her less harshly than before, with the couple eventually reconciling. After Symphany has a seizure and falls into a coma, it is revealed that she had been secretly dealing with epilepsy. When she dies, Kaia and Symphany's mother, Monique, develop a mother/daughter-like relationship.

The funeral takes place at the First Central Baptist church on Wright Street in Stapleton, with the Rev. Calvin Rice officiating. The book mentions the hymns and details the order of service for a modern African-American Baptist funeral.

The book wraps up with the reconciliation of Kaia and her sister, Asha, who reveals that Janice finally admitted the murder of Maurice. Symphany's will is read, in which she left sizeable bequests to Talia, Kaia and her daughter Phoenix. Giselle receives nothing in the will except a posthumous denunciation. Aaron and Kaia are engaged to be married, Talia has found a man, and Giselle has five children with three different men.

13. Brown, Tracy. *Criminal Minded.* New York: St. Martin's Griffin, 2005. 292pp.
　　　Sixteen-year-old-year-old Port Richmond High School student Lamin Michaels enjoys a carefree life of drugs, drinking and sex. He lives on Grandview Avenue in Mariners Harbor with his mother, a

welfare cheat and government dependent, who uses the proceeds of her public assistance to shower Lamin and his sister Olivia with all the material goods they could desire. Her more responsible sister Inez, over on Continental Place, has a son Curtis, with whom Lamin is close. When Curtis has to attend summer school at New Dorp High School, he starts getting tormented by a bully, who threatens him with a gun. Before Lamin and his friends can come to Curtis' aid, Curtis went to school and shot the bully to death, earning a prison sentence. With Curtis in jail upstate, Lamin's grandmother starts dragging him to church, where he meets Zion, a street-smart, incipient drug dealer who has bounced around institutions and foster homes since his mother died of a crack overdose. Lamin quits school when a "racist" teacher tells him that the ancient Egyptians weren't black and, on the same day, gets thrown out of his house when he beats up his mother's abusive, live-in boyfriend. He moves in with his grandparents in Park Hill and starts selling drugs with Zion, the pair of whom come to dominate the crack trade on Staten Island.

One day in the Sneaker Asylum on Canal Street in Stapleton, Lamin meets and begins seeing Laila (Lucky) Matheson, a beautiful, bi-racial Notre Dame High School student. They attend her prom at the Staten Island Country Club, after which Lamin brings her to a borrowed yacht docked off of Manhattan, where they make love. Zion and Lamin begin having trouble with a group of Jamaican drug dealers from Park Hill, and while partying with Lucky, Olivia and Zion at the Consequences night club on Bay Street, Lamin is shot by one of the Jamaicans after they had spiked his drink. Although he survives, he falls into a coma and even after waking endures a lengthy recuperation. Meanwhile, Lucky's father disowns her for consorting with a dangerous drug dealer, so she moves into the Brooklyn apartment that Lamin and Zion share. Zion begins a sexual relationship with Lamin's sister Olivia, but his friendship with Lamin prevents him from making any commitment to her. When he exacts revenge on the Jamaicans who shot Lamin, and leaves their bodies in the woods off of Travis Avenue, the subsequent police crackdown forces Zion to conduct his business out-of-state and the only person he can trust to take Lamin's place on these trips is Olivia. First, Zion takes the inexperienced Olivia to the Staten Island Expressway to teach her not only how to drive on a highway, but how to do so without exciting police suspicion. They make frequent trips to Maryland and Virginia to keep the money and drugs flowing.

Lamin is discharged from the hospital and rethinks his thug life. He starts a film production company, named *Shootin' Crooks*, and tries to convince Zion to go straight, but Zion has no further ambition than controlling the streets and therefore limits himself to an investment that makes him a silent partner in Lamin's company. Lamin uses some contacts to hook up with the Wu Tang Clan and began working in the business. He filmed his first video for one of his dealers who had signed a recording contract, and drew industry acclaim for his work. Soon, Lamin was one of the most sought-after producers in the rap music industry. He made Olivia his chief stylist and, when his cousin Curtis was released from jail, he was made head of security. Curtis, however, was jealous of Zion's close friendship with Lamin and his immense wealth and power that Curtis felt should have been his had he not gone to jail. His resentment builds when he goes back to jail after getting mixed up in a shooting at the Island Room nightclub. Meanwhile, Lamin and Lucky start to grow apart. Among Lamin's many other women is Dream Biggs, a sexually-inventive recording industry executive. Even though Lamin broke off the relationship, a picture of them canoodling is published in the Daily News, causing Lucky to leave him and reject his marriage proposal. Devastated, he takes the engagement ring right over to Dream's house and proposes to her instead.

When the Staten Island police arrest Zion's lieutenant, Doug, they turn him into a snitch in order to bring down Zion, but when Zion finds out that Doug is hiding at 150 Brabant Street, he tracks him down and executes him. Zion also later murders Doug's girlfriend, who had witnessed the original hit. The police are also interested in Zion in connection with the murder of Olivia's abusive boyfriend, the manager of a rap group. When the feds start looking into Zion's connection with *Shootin' Crooks*, Lamin turns his back on his friend. After Curtis is arrested for drug dealing, Lamin is brought to the 120th precinct and is pressured to help them bring down Zion. A final showdown ensues at the W Hotel club in Manhattan when Curtis shoots and wounds Zion while Lamin shoots Curtis, who later dies of his injuries. By the end of the book, Lamin has been acquitted of murder, his mother has died of AIDS, and he has divorced the adulterous Dream but still not reconciled with Lucky.

14. Brown, Tracy. *Dime Piece*. Columbus, Ohio: Triple Crown Publications, 2004. 186pp.

In 1992, Celeste Styles goes out on the town with college classmates to Staten Island, the so-called "other borough." By chance, she gets out of her car on Targee St. to use a pay phone and is approached by Raheem "Rah-Lo" Henderson, a major Staten Island drug dealer and gangster, with whom she then begins a relationship. The married Rah-Lo keeps Celeste in a Howard Avenue house and bankrolls the purchase of a Brooklyn hair salon for her which she names *Dime Piece*. When Rah-Lo is shot at, he and his crew go to Stapleton and massacre a rival gang in front of 212 Broad St. A few days later Rah-Lo and his crew are arrested and sent to prison, with only his friend and second-in-command, Ishmael, remaining at-large and running the business. Ishmael sleeps with two of three of Celeste's hairdressers, Robin and Charly, and begins a serious relationship with a third, Nina, while trying to avoid the mutual attraction that he and Celeste are feeling. The women's jealousy over Ishmael proves to be *Dime Piece's* undoing. When Rah-Lo is released from prison, Celeste reluctantly comes to the conclusion that he will never leave his wife or the hustler's life. After *Dime Piece* burns to the ground in a mysterious act of arson, Celeste decides to move to Atlanta with her mother, a story which is continued in *Twisted* (St. Martin's Griffin, 2008).

15. Brown, Tracy. "Flirting with Disaster" in *Flirt*. New York: St. Martin's Griffin, 2009. 195pp. pgs 6-72.

While riding the morning ferry to Manhattan, twenty-one-year-old journalism student Chloe Webster meets Trey, a handsome, slightly older man. Trey, who just moved to St. Mark's Place from the Bronx, claims to be a college student by day while working on the subways in the evening. The two hit it off and start seeing each other, with Trey lavishing expensive gifts upon Chloe while receiving no physical reciprocation, to his increasing frustration. In a revealing conversation with her friends, Chloe admits that she has an advanced strategy for using men and getting all the money she can out of them, by looking good and flirting and withholding sex until her boyfriends are quite tame. She's currently having sex with such a man, Jason, while she's working Trey for all that he has. When Jason is found murdered in the woods of Grymes Hill, Trey consoles her and they develop a closer relationship. Despite her little sister's suspicions that Trey isn't what he seems, Chloe sees Trey as a harmless and likeable ATM machine, and finally decides to reward all his patience.

She goes to his obsessively neat apartment for dinner after which she plans a special evening of physical intimacy. Misunderstanding follows misunderstanding and when Chloe openly disdains Trey's spartan furnishings (having spent all his money on her) and laughs when he experiences a sexual misfire (having been kept on the boil for months from Chloe's teasing) they argue and Chloe goes to storm out. Trey beats her into near death and dumps her body into the waters off St. George. Trey, in fact, was a deeply disturbed man who was not a college student studying psychology, but had been taking antidepressants and seeing a therapist to try to work through his issues of violence towards women. Having been abandoned by his mother when he was a boy, Trey reacts violently towards the women in his life who leave him. It is revealed that Trey had been stalking Chloe and recording her every move. He knew about her affair with Jason and had killed him. He is surprised to read in the *Advance* that Chloe had survived the vicious attack. Knowing that he will be implicated, he tries to fade away into the anonymity of Manhattan.

When Chloe and Trey first meet, Chloe admits that she lives in federally owned housing on Jersey Street, but hastens to add that she lives in the two story houses (nicknamed "McDonald houses" for their resemblance to the fast food restaurant) and not the projects, as she feels that will elevate her status in his eyes.

16. Brown, Tracy. *Snapped.* New York: St. Martin's Griffin, 2009. 361pp.
    Although Staten Island is hardly mentioned in this book, several major characters and events are connected with the island. Camille Bingham and her husband Frankie, a high-ranking member of the Nobles crime family, live in a mansion in Annadale on the edge of Blue Heron Park. Frankie starts developing a closer relationship with Gillian Nobles, the daughter of Doug Nobles, the head of the organization. Gillian's half-brother, Baron, is starting to harm the family business with his irresponsible behavior, and when he murders a rival to whom he owed money, the man's brother, Jojo, is determined to make Baron pay with his life.

Camille's sister, Misa, has a lifestyle that couldn't be more different than her sister's. Although they both grew up in the Stapleton projects,

Misa graduated from the College of Staten Island while her sister became a fashion model and then the wife of a wealthy drug lord. Misa is a single mother who works as a dental assistant in Graniteville. When she catches Baron's eye at a party and begins a sexual relationship with him, she starts abdicating her parental responsibilities and habitually leaves her young son Shane with Camille while she parties. Although the sadistic Baron beats and degrades her, Misa stays with him out of a desire to improve her material circumstances.

As Camille begins noticing Frankie's burgeoning relationship with Gillian, she starts drinking more and gaining weight. Her distraction leads her to pass off Shane to the care of Frankie's brother Steven, a freeloading man-child who lives in their backyard rental cottage.

Dominique Storms is a friend of Camille's from the Mariners Harbor apartments, who has become a successful music industry executive in Manhattan. While she pines for Jamel, a drug dealer who is doing time in an upstate prison, her thirteen-year-old daughter Octavia is losing her virginity to a boy from the projects.

Their mutual friend, Toya, a successful real estate broker, is a hard-edged woman who is surprised when her hated father reappears in her life.

The book ends when Octavia becomes pregnant and runs away from home. Dominique's father passes away at Staten Island Hospital. Camille discovers evidence of Frankie's unfaithfulness and confronts him, which pushes him into a full-blown affair with Gillian. Jojo and his gang assassinate Doug Nobles and seriously wound Baron, leaving Gillian and Frankie in charge of the crime family. And when Misa's ex, Louis, discovers that someone had been sexually molesting their son Shane, Misa deduces that it was Steven Bingham and murders him inside Camille's house.

In addition to mentioning Alfonso's bakery, *Snapped* makes reference to Staten Island's racial boundaries, when Camille notes that when she was a kid, you wouldn't see a brown face anywhere near their side of the island in Annadale. She notes that they are still the only black family on the block, but there's also an Indian family who live there now. The story concludes in *Aftermath* (St. Martin's Griffin, 2011).

17. Brown, Tracy. *Twisted.* New York: St. Martin's Griffin, 2008. 338pp.

In this sequel to *Dime Piece*, in which Celeste Styles burned down her own hair salon, she breaks up with Rah-lo and moves to Atlanta, where four years later she is pursued by both Rah-lo and Ishmael, who in turn are pursued by their jealous women, Asia and Nina, respectively. Certain characters still reside on Staten Island and it is the scene of several peripheral incidents, but it is hardly mentioned in this book.

18. Brown, Tracy. *White Lines.* New York: St. Martin's Griffin, 2007. 497pp.

Jada and Ava Ford live with their parents, Sheldon and Edna, in Brooklyn in 1990. When Sheldon unexpectedly abandons his family and is murdered by the husband of the not-quite-divorced woman he had taken up with, Edna began a relationship with J.D., and lets him move into her apartment. J.D. proves to be an abusive bully who beats Edna and her daughters. A weak and easily manipulated woman, Edna never stood up for her daughters and didn't believe Ava when she revealed that J.D. had been making sexual advances towards her. Feeling that she had no way out, Ava attempted suicide. She survived, but was sent by the state to a group home for girls on Maple Parkway in Staten Island. When J.D. died in a drunk driving accident, Edna and Jada moved to the Markham homes on Wayne Court in West Brighton (where everyone lived in "Section 8 houses or rent controlled apartments") to be closer to Ava. Both Jada and Ava were running with a bad crowd and smoking a lot of marijuana, but Jada's life took a turn for the worse when she experimented with a "woolah", a hollowed-out cigar filled with marijuana and crack. Declaring that she would never become an addict, she soon became heavily addicted to crack. Her mother's new boyfriend, Charlie, discovers her addiction but, instead of helping her, facilitates her habit, takes sexual advantage of her and eventually turns her out as a prostitute at his Harlem brothel.

Finally finding the strength to leave the brothel, Jada only survives by freelance prostitution, armed robbery and crack dealing, which leads to her arrest and enforced drug rehabilitation. After her release, she went to visit her sister in Mariners Harbor and met Born, Staten Island's biggest crack dealer.

Born- whose "government name" was Marquis Graham- was the son of Leo Graham, once one of Staten Island's most notorious drug dealers, pimps and gangsters. In 1980, the eight-year-old Marquis

watched his father shot by a rival in front of the Zebra Lounge on
Targee Street. Leo survived to exact revenge on the man who shot him.
His charisma, power and money made him an idol to his son. Leo took
Marquis to one of his brothels for an orgy on his thirteenth birthday,
cementing his reputation with his son. However, Leo began to be an
absent presence in Marquis' life. He ran around with women and
fathered other children. His power and street credibility suffered as he
became addicted to crack in the 1980s. Marquis, used to having all the
best things in life, easily fell into the business of crack dealing, along
with a group of his friends known on the street as the *55 Holland niggas*
(in reference to the Arlington Terrace apartments at 55 Holland
Avenue). In addition to selling crack in Arlington and the Harbor
Houses, they began killing rivals, taking hostages and committing
armed robberies. Meanwhile, Leo was so degraded by his addiction that
he began buying crack from his own son, who was so disgusted by his
father's weakness that he felt no compunction selling to him. By the
time Born had gotten involved with Jada, he had abandoned his crew to
work solo, and was living in a luxury apartment on Clove Road.

Born eventually made a deal with the Brooklyn kingpin, Dorian, to
take over the Staten Island drug trade. He used the Palestinian store on
Targee Street as a front, and began selling not only to Park Hill and
Stapleton, but to Rosebank, Grymes Hill and other White areas of
Staten Island. Jada meanwhile was living the life of a gangster's moll,
wearing the most expensive jewelry, clothing and making all the other
women jealous of her man, her lifestyle and her beauty. She was drug
free and happily living with Born in a house on Westwood Avenue.
When Born was brought into the inner circle of Dorian's crime family,
Jada became close friends with Dorian's wife Sunny, who proved to be
a bad influence when she encouraged Jada to do cocaine and steal
drugs from Born. When Sunny becomes pregnant, Dorian's jealous ex,
Raquel, barged into her baby shower to try to kill her, but Dorian took
a bullet and died in order to save his wife and unborn child.

Jada quickly falls back into her crack habit by surreptitiously
stealing Born's product from his Park Hill crack house. When he
discovers her betrayal, he throws her out in the street, where she takes
up with one of Born's enemies, his former friend Jamari, who both
hates and idolizes Born. Jamari feeds Jada's habit and eventually
impregnates her. The unscrupulous Jamari even tips off the police to
Born's activities, causing him to be arrested and imprisoned during a

time when the police were focusing on the crack trade on the island's most active spots: Jersey Street, Targee Street, Broad Street, Henderson Avenue and Broadway. Jada finally understands Jamari's disreputable motivations and decides to make her break with him, but not before stealing ninety thousand dollars worth of his crack and destroying his reputation on the street. Despite being pregnant, Jada went on a crack binge and was arrested buying her drugs in Brooklyn. She gave birth to her son- named Sheldon Marquis- in jail, and lost custody of the boy to the ever-devious Jamari who, while genuinely loving his new son, also resolved to defame and destroy Jada because of her betrayal and her crack habit.

Jada cleaned up her act in jail, for the sake of her baby, and fought Jamari in court for his custody. After being released, Jamari accosted Jada in Mariners Harbor and threatened her with a gun. Sunny snuck up behind him unawares and shot him to death when he resisted. With his father now dead (in a purported drug deal gone bad), a judge awarded custody of Sheldon to Jada, on the condition that she move in with her mother, Edna. The two women reconcile and renew their relationship while Jada cleans up her life, goes back to school and becomes an assistant editor at a premier magazine for Black women. She buys a house at 104 Christopher Lane and co-authors a best-selling novel with Sunny, who is now a successful fashion model. Her sister Ava, who had been inspired by her sister's plight to quit drugs and pursue an education, is a successful attorney in Philadelphia.

In the meantime, Born got out of jail and had a son, Ethan, with a woman named Anisa, whom he set up in a house on Bement Avenue. Like Jada, Born had grown as a person and realized that his extreme reaction to Jada's actions had their origin in his feelings about his own father's drug use and abandonment. He clears the air with his late father at his graveside in Frederick Douglas Cemetery and learns to forgive Jada, whom he had never stopped loving.

When Jada's mother dies of cancer, Born reaches out to her and reconciles with his only love, although their relationship remains platonic when the book ends.

Like other books by the author, Staten Island is a central scene of action, with place names extensively cited, but with slight physical description and with a Staten Island culture that resembles that of larger African American communities. However, it is noted that, as opposed to Brooklyn, everyone in Staten Island seems to know one another's business very quickly and that the island was so small that "parties were like minireunions."

19. Brown, Tracy. *White Lines II: Sunny*. New York: St. Martin's Griffin, 2012. 290pp.

In this sequel to *White Lines*, Sunny Cruz is pursuing her career as a high-end fashion model while Jada Ford, a successful writer and editor, is struggling to deal with her son Sheldon's ADHD, inappropriate outbursts and learning disabilities. Staten Island doesn't have the central role it did in *White Lines*, but several of the protagonists still live there. Born is living with Jada on Christopher Lane, while his "baby mama" Anisa and their son Ethan live on Bement Avenue. Born's mother Ingrid still lives in Arlington, which is described as a place of former affluence which degenerated into crime and mayhem. The book deals with the various romantic relationships among the characters as well as the repercussions of one's actions, particularly Jada and Sunny's past drug use.

Sunny goes to Los Angeles to negotiate a movie adaptation of the best-selling book that she and Jada co-wrote. Jada backs out of the deal, as she doesn't want her son knowing about her disreputable past as a crack dealer, addict and prostitute. Sunny retorts that it is well known that Staten Island is the most incestuous borough in the city and that her son will find out eventually. For that reason, Jada tries convincing Born to move them off the island, a plan which is rendered moot when Sheldon overhears his mother and Born speaking about Jada's arrests and crack addiction. He uses the internet to read old stories from the *Staten Island Advance* about his mother's arrests and his father Jamari's murder. He becomes more and more hostile to his mother for her notorious past, angry about the loss of his father and resentful of Born's relationship with Jada. When he acts out by drowning a puppy that his mother gave him for Christmas, he is forced to see therapists and begin taking Ritalin and Prozac. Anisa tells Born that she doesn't want Ethan to be around the unstable Sheldon anymore and subtly convinces Born that he should postpone his marriage to Jada. Distraught over all the emotions he feels but can't express, Sheldon overdoses on his prescription drugs. While her son is in a coma, Jada promises God that she will sacrifice her happiness with Born if He will let her son live, and curtly dismisses Born when Sheldon wakes up after three days. Their situation remains unresolved by the end of the book.

Meanwhile Sunny is pursuing a passionate relationship with Ivy League lawyer Malcolm, despite their different backgrounds. She hides her renewed cocaine use from him but eventually flushes away her supply out of love for him. While on vacation in Mexico, she nevertheless relapses when she realizes that everyone in her life, from her father to her late husband Dorian, seems to have used her for their own ulterior motives. When Sunny slits the throat of a cab driver that had attempted to rob them, she and Malcolm both realize that they are too different to be together. Unfortunately, the book ends when the TSA discovers a bag of cocaine in Sunny's luggage.

In addition to the Staten Island locales mentioned above, Sheldon is confined to South Beach Psychiatric after his overdose and Jada prays in the church on Fort Place, which can only be the Brighton Heights Reformed church. Jada runs into her former pimp, Mr. Charlie, and her former friend Shante- now a toothless crackhead and Mr. Charlie's primary woman- in the Forest Avenue Pathmark. Anisa is described reading *The Grain* by Shawn Berry, an autobiographical account of Staten Island's Wu Tang Clan.

20. Brown, Tracy. *Whites Lines III; All Falls Down.* New York: St. Martin's Griffin, 2015. 325pp.

This explosive finale in the *White Lines* trilogy ties up all the loose threads from the previous novels involving Sunny, Malcolm, Gillian, Frankie, Zion, Olivia, Baron, and Misa, and definitively resolves the relationship between Born and Jada. Although a good portion of the novel takes place on Staten Island, local description is minimal. After his rejection by Jada, Born falls back into the arms of his son's mother, Anisa, who lives on Bement Avenue. When a mysterious bombing attack puts Born in Richmond University Medical Center he and Jada rekindle their romance and join forces to fight an enemy from the past. Born has a man-to-man talk with Jada's son Sheldon at the McDonald's on Bay Street, where Born is confronted by the man who bombed him, after which he and Sheldon duck into the Next Level barbershop in Stapleton for safety.

21. Burdge, Anthony and Jessica Burke, eds. *Dark Tales from Elder Regions*. Staten Island: Myth Ink Books, 2014. 382pp.

Six of the stories of this anthology of horror and supernatural tales that take place in New York City have a Staten Island setting. In *E-ville* by Frank Collia, a man standing on the platform of the Eltingville train station is condemned to view his own life in a continuous loop, including his own death on those very tracks.

Rosebank NNL by Daniel Russo takes place in 1988 and makes reference to a notorious racist slogan that used to adorn a train overpass in the North Shore neighborhood. While examining the overpass' structural integrity, a two-man team of city engineers, one Black and one White, express disparate perspectives on their respective places in Staten Island. The White man, an Italian-American Staten Islander, talks about the glory days of the South Beach amusement area, and casually mentions how the Verrazano Bridge and the local housing projects caused the whole area to go downhill. The younger Black man, Milton, grew up in a St. George project and thinks back to how his mother always encouraged him to remember that, despite local racism, he "was a part of this place too." Milton then mysteriously finds himself on an early twentieth-century train filled with White families heading to the Happyland amusement park, who recoil in horror at the sight of a Black man, causing him to shout "I'm a part of this place too!"

The Mad Monk of St. Augustine's by Colleen Wanglund takes place at the former Augustinian Academy on Grymes Hill. In 1968, one of the monks, Brother Gabriel, began slaughtering his fellow brothers and sacrificing them to Satan. He was sentenced by the abbot to be sealed up in a cell for the rest of his life, but within a few days was found to have chewed apart his own wrists and killed himself, but not before writing "He is Coming" on the wall with his own blood. Moving forward to 1986, a group of New Dorp High School students go to the then-abandoned monastery for thrills and end up all being mutilated and murdered. Brother Gabriel may be dead, but the demon that inhabited his body had found a new vessel to inhabit when a homeless man came into the monastery to sleep. The dead teenagers have provided enough hearts for him to bring the "Dark One" into the world.

Remember Peter by Christopher Mancuso is narrated by Daniel O'Donnell, who was adopted by a supposedly infertile Staten Island couple who then proceeded to conceive a natural son, Peter, which made Daniel jealous. When he was fifteen-years old, Daniel left his Walcott Avenue home with a friend, Tommy, to explore the nearby Farm Colony. Seven-year-old Peter follows them, wanting to play hide and seek, but is driven off by the resentful Daniel, who chases his brother into one of the abandoned buildings where he injures the boy more than he intended and leaves him to die. Peter is forgotten by Daniel as the years go by, but in the week before his college graduation he learns that his parents were killed in an accident on the Staten Island Expressway by a driver who was high on meth. The driver is revealed to have been his friend Tommy, who had fled his home in a panic, screaming about being chased by an invisible assailant. Tommy died in the ambulance uttering Peter's name. After his parents are buried at Resurrection Cemetery, Daniel begins hearing Peter's voice, begging to play hide and seek. Daniel burns down his own house to escape the voice but finds himself in an eternal game of hide and seek with his vengeful little brother.

In *Ghosting* by Jessica Burke, a trio of 19th century ghosts at Snug Harbor haunts the premises and seeks to be released from their purgatorial existence there. Sean and Stefan were Irish and Danish sailors, respectively, while Bethany was a servant who arrived in 1833 but drowned herself in the Kill when Governor Melville dismissed her in her old age. When the modern day administrators start hosting paranormal tours in order to raise money, the ghosts discover that a young woman, Gwen, is able to hear them. Gwen returns with a team of ghost hunters, who are led into an attic where crowds of ghosts manifest themselves. Gwen channels the spirit of a murdered Snug and somehow opens up a portal that releases the ghosts from their captivity.

The Lonely Boat by Anthony S. Burdge takes place in 1984 and pays homage to the supernatural world of *The King in Yellow* by Robert W. Chambers (1865-1933). Twenty-two-year-old Daniel Scott had been admitted to Willowbrook after his parents' mysterious disappearance caused him to suffer a breakdown. As he showed improvement, he was allowed to work there as an orderly and then to move into his uncle Tim's basement in Tottenville and work with him on a clamming boat out of Lemon Creek. Daniel has strange visions and dreams, ever since reading a play called *The King in Yellow*, the same play that strangely affected his father and his cousin at an infamous Pouch Camp boy scout gathering some years back. During these visions, Daniel sees himself traveling through millennia, witnessing human sacrifice and death. One day while out clamming he pulls up a mysterious black stone with a strange symbol on it and starts seeing a vision of a boat that is a cross between an Indian canoe and a Viking longship. He blacks out and has to be taken to Richmond Valley Hospital. As he recuperates, Daniel wanders away and, somewhere near the Tottenville train station, he sees the strange boat of his visions moored to a private dock. He rows out to it and when he places his black stone in a similarly shaped recess, the accoutrements of Charon, the ferryman of Hades, appear to him and he finds himself taking on the identity of the immortal Boatman of the dead. When he awakes he is surrounded by his purported Uncle Tim, his psychiatrist at Willowbrook and the hospital EMTs who reveal themselves to belong to a cult that worships a god they believe has spoken through Daniel, his cousin and his father, the latter two whom the group murdered when they were found to be devoid of useful supernatural information. Daniel finds that he has actually been held in Willowbrook since 1977, drugged and in confinement.

22. Burke, Jessica and Anthony Burdge. *The Friendly Horror and Other Weird Tales*. Staten Island: Myth Ink Books, 2013. 146pp.

   The anchor of this collection of short stories and poetry inspired by the fiction of H.P. Lovecraft, and the only one to overtly incorporate Staten Island is *The Friendly Horror*. Taking up where Lovecraft's *The Shadow over Innsmouth* left off, the Deep Ones- the ancient race of sea-dwelling immortals who transform in adulthood from human shape to various aquatic forms- have been scattered from Innsmouth, Massachusetts by the federal raids of the 1920s, with the survivors starting a successful ice cream company headquartered in Staten Island. Narrated by the present day head of the family, Silas Billop Maxfield, who is in the process of undergoing his transformation, he tells how his grandfather, Fern Billop Maxfield, purchased the Seguine Mansion from Cornelius Kolff in 1940, and then proceeded to acquire more land and homes from Lemon Creek down to the Burial Ridge for the use of his dispossessed relations, who aided him in the increasingly successful family business. (In fact, these Deep Ones had roots on Staten Island going back 10,000 years, and even counted Captain Christopher Billop as one of their ancestors, helping him with his fabled boat race which won Staten Island for New York and won Billop a thousand acres of land on the island's southern tip).

Grandfather Fern, plotting revenge against the "primates" and dreaming of world conquest, had experimented with a concoction that, when introduced into Maxfield's ice cream, both addicted its consumers and effected a gradual metamorphosis in them, turning them into the same fish-frog people as the Deep Ones, with some of the transformed humans intended for inclusion in the race, and some marked as sacrifices for their angry gods. Grandfather Fern began his dream of world domination with a donation of ice cream to the sailors at Snug Harbor, some of whom already had fish blood. One of these Snugs informed Grandfather Fern that the government maintained secret facilities at Snug Harbor and at the Farm Colony where the last prisoners of the Innsmouth raids were the subjects of brutal experimentation. A secret map revealed that tunnels connected these places as well as the future Halloran Hospital. The prisoners were rescued and more tunnels were built by the Deep Ones through the years, connecting these places to the Seguine Mansion, Willowbrook State School, and the sea at various points. Ice cream donations were made to these institutions as well as to Fort Wadsworth and the Mount Loretto orphanage. Modern advertising techniques increased the consumption of Maxfield's ice cream and a nest of Deep Ones was established below the Farm Colony. Concocted legends about Satanic cults in the woods of the area kept prying humans away.

Back to the present day, Silas prepares for his final transformation and accompanying ceremony while noting the changes come over the local population on his ice cream route. Stereotypically Brooklynite Staten Islanders are described growing webbed hands, tentacles and gills. Finally, Silas is escorted to his people's command center beneath the Farm Colony, where he observes their growing army and is reunited with his father and grandfather. He goes down a tunnel to the shores of Conference House Park, where his people gather for a seaside ritual involving human sacrifice to their deities, Dagon and Mother Hydra.

23. Burleigh, Cecil [Harry Moore, pseud.]. *The Liberty Boys at Staten Island*. The Liberty Boys of "76", No. 900. New York: Frank Tousey-Publisher, March 29, 1918. 18pp.
    Dick Slater is the leader of the Liberty Boys, a group of young patriot irregulars engaged in active duty service for the American army

during the Revolutionary War. While on a mission in the southwest end of Staten Island, Slater notices a caddish young dandy purposely rocking a rowboat in order to frighten his passenger, a pretty, teenage girl. When the dandy accidentally capsizes the boat, Slater rows out to rescue the girl, but forces the young man to swim back to shore. Scorning the angry dandy's demands, Slater escorts the girl, Mildred Winters, back to her house. The dandy, revealed to be Harold Winters, Mildred's cousin and the scion of an influential Loyalist family, recognizes Slater as the notorious rebel and orders his men to beat and capture him. Instead, Slater beats them up and escapes to New Jersey. He reports to General Washington in Morristown, where he and the Liberty Boys are ordered to set up camp in Elizabethtown and spy on the British in Staten Island.

Slater and his 1st lieutenant, Bob Easterbrook, slip across the frozen Arthur Kill and head for the "more settled part" of Staten Island, where they follow a pair of British officers into the Red Bull tavern, hoping to pick up some information. Unfortunately, Harold Winters arrives and proposes a toast to King George but, noticing that the two quiet strangers did not join in the toast, approaches them and recognizes Slater. The Liberty Boys reveal themselves, insult the king and escape with guns blazing.

While riding their sleigh back to their camp in New Jersey, they come across a young woman and a baby lying in the snow. Once revived, she reveals herself to be the widow of the late Percy Winters, Harold's older brother who, though an English aristocrat, sympathized with the Revolution. The Winters family hates Percy's widow, because she was an American and a commoner, and they deny the existence of the baby, the true heir to the family title and fortune. Nevertheless, because of her poverty, Lady Winters was traveling to Staten Island to beg for help from her former in-laws. Slater vows to aid her cause, and goes with Liberty Boy Mark Morrison to the Winters' home in Staten Island to press her case. They end up in a fight with Harold, his father and another British officer, and escape with Mildred's help.

Slater and Morrison next go in disguise to Manhattan, where they again try to speak to the Winters in their New York townhouse, but another fight ensues. Thinking of his mission, Slater goes undercover in a tavern, where he hears Generals Clinton and Knyphausen planning an attack on the patriots in New Jersey. He reports this information to

General Washington, who orders a raid upon Staten Island, under the command of Lord Stirling. This attack, which included the Liberty Boys, was a failure. During another spying expedition to Manhattan, Slater comes upon an English lawyer who has come to handle the affairs of Lord Winters, who has died in England. Harold will inherit everything and is to marry Mildred. Slater tells the lawyer about the existence of the rightful heir in New Jersey. Another Liberty Boy gathers some valuable military information which is brought to General Washington. At the same time, the English lawyer investigates the claim of Percy Winters' son, and declares him the lawful heir. The Liberty Boys are next ordered to go to White Plains.

24. Burtone, Gaetano J. *Only a Prayer Away*. Victoria, British Columbia: Friesen Press, 2014. 214pp.

Although this nostalgic *roman à clef* of growing up in Staten Island in the 1960s and 70s reads like a straight memoir, the narrator is named Michael Parisi and the book is categorized as a novel. Parisi, born in 1964 to Italian-American parents -a policeman and a homemaker- who came over from Brooklyn, lived in a neighborhood (presumably Annadale or Eltingville, since he attended Holy Child school) where everyone knew everyone else, everyone was Catholic and where his entire extended family lived nearby. He lives an idyllic childhood of sports, bike riding with friends and numerous cousins, and a close relationship with his family. "Staten Island was a great place to grow up. It was not like anywhere else in the world." "The streets were tree lined and quiet, and at night we fell asleep under starlit black skies. Looking back on it now, it still feels safe. It was as perfect a place and time as I've ever known, and I thought it would last forever." Loving and detailed description of the traditional Italian-American family Sunday is included, as is the local celebration of the national bicentennial in 1976. Parisi takes part in an informal eight grade Catholic School football championship (which he tells us was started in 1967 by students from eight South Shore schools) in which he plays for his school, Holy Child, which wins the final championship of 1977. He bonds with his father over their love of the Oakland Raiders, but discovers his own tastes when he becomes a fan of K.I.S.S. Eighth grade is significant because he and his childhood sweetheart, Lauren Sedona, finally share their feelings for each other as well as a first kiss. His childhood ended however, when a favorite uncle died of a heart attack on Christmas morning.

25. Coston, Alicia. *She's Killin' Me.* Virginia Beach, Va.: Indigo Press, 2007. 381pp.

    Chris Balducci is a happily married thirty-six-year-old, successful restaurateur from Staten Island. Chris prides himself on his long brown hair and refuses to look like "the typical, spiky-haired young punks on Staten Island." Having grown up in poverty, Chris now lives in one of Staten Island's "swankiest hoods." On a trip to Virginia Beach to open up a new restaurant he begins an affair with an African-American stripper, Connie, who had also previously been sleeping with his cousin. His obsession with Connie leads him into all sorts of difficulties, including getting kidnapped, having his new restaurant burned to the ground and being manipulated into disposing of a dead body. When Chris attempts to break off his affair, Connie becomes threatening and violent.

    She stalks him to Staten Island, where she shows up at Chris' Richmond Avenue restaurant, near the Mall, during his anniversary party with his wife, Sylvia. She even drugs Chris and, with her lesbian lover, has sex with him against his will. When Chris received a ransom note with a picture of his kidnapped wife, he goes to his wealthy father-in-law, who lives in a fortress-like house in the hills of Staten Island, for the money. When he attempts to redeem his wife from captivity, he ends up being robbed of the money while discovering a horrible conspiracy against himself, perpetrated by those he loved best. His cousin Vinnie reveals that he and Sylvia were lovers and that he was really the father of Sylvia's baby. Connie and Sylvia had conspired to set up Chris and steal the ransom money. Apart from Chris killing Vinnie in the end, their plan worked and they got away with the money while Chris received fifteen years in jail.

26. Daulton, Agnes Warner McClelland. *Fritzi; or, The Princess Perhaps.* New York: Century Co., 1908. 417pp.

    Twelve-year-old Fritzi von Saal works as an artist's model and as an assistant in a performing cockatoo show in order help her struggling Manhattan family. When she was a small girl her mysterious birth mother was killed in a streetcar accident and Fritzi was subsequently adopted by the attending nurse and her husband. When her husband dies, Fritzi's adoptive mother leaves her with a neighboring fortune teller and goes back to her own family in Indiana. The fortune teller then goes on a national tour with the cockatoo show, leaving Fritzi to fend for herself. When a Mrs. Spear comes to have her fortune read, she is so filled with pity for Fritzi's situation that she takes the girl back to her home on Staten Island, which she shares with her sister-in-law, Mrs. Muldrow, and her children (all of whom, including the girls, have boys' names.) The aristocratic but financially embarrassed Southern family lives in their summer home on Staten Island, which is called the Eyrie, because it "...clings to the brow of a hill, and you can see miles and miles across the bay and out to sea."

Fritzi was taken in and embraced by the family, with the exception of John, one of the Muldrow girls, who chafed at Fritzi's talent, popularity and rumored descent from German nobility. Indeed, when the fortune teller forwards a package containing the diaries of Fritzi's birth mother, it is confirmed that she is the child of noble German parents. Mrs. Spear and Mrs. Muldrow determine to track down Fritzi's father in Germany, which they manage to do with the help of the U.S. Ambassador. The book ends with John and Fritzi reconciled, Fritzi reunited with her real father (a baron) and the Muldrows' financial situation improved.

Description of the island is almost non-existent, but the impression given is of an idyllic and bucolic refuge for a city orphan. The children put on a circus in a barn, play in an amateur symphony called the Dinkle-Dinkle-Dells and sled down Monroe Avenue in St. George in the winter time, a street described as being resplendent with blossoms and flowers in the Spring. The island is said to have particularly exquisite Autumns.

27. Davis, J.T. *New York Stories; And Other Potentially Libelous Tales of the 1970s.* CreateSpace, 2013. 504pp.
    This tale of gay life in post-Stonewall New York City focuses on the romances and sexual adventurism of a tight-knit group of gay men who joyfully sample everything the city has to offer. In 1972, Lieutenant Mike Myles, a physical therapist with the Coast Guard, is transferred from Cleveland to work at the U.S. Public Health Service Hospital in Staten Island, which was treating a lot of wounded veterans from the Vietnam War. Mike gets an apartment nearby and reunites with old friends in Manhattan while adding a few new friends to their fellowship. Much of the book deals with the various romantic relationships the men form, as well as their numerous one-night stands and more unconventional sexual experiences. The men go to

bathhouses, strip clubs, dance clubs, Broadway shows and wild parties, while dining and drinking establishments are described in detail.

Despite most of the story taking place in Manhattan (and Fire Island), Staten Island plays a significant part as well. Mike brings a lover, Lee, back to his apartment for a weekend, and the pair eat at Nunzio's Pizza on Hylan Boulevard and at the Bay Street Luncheonette, while visiting the Botanical gardens and taking a walk on South Beach. Despite having a wonderful time, one of Mike's friends declares that the only reason Lee went to Staten Island was because he wanted to avoid being seen by anyone, as no one goes to Staten Island unless they have to. As it turned out, he was right, since Lee was somewhat closeted and subsequently declares his intention to marry a woman (in order to please his parents) while discreetly having male lovers. When Mike finds out that his next boyfriend is cheating on him, he sequesters himself on the island in depression, causing his friends to break their record of never going to Staten Island and come across the bay to take him out to lunch at the Basilica Inn (a stand-in for the Basilio Inn of South Beach), the oldest restaurant on the island, located in an 1850s carriage house. Mike's next boyfriend is an injured sailor, in town for Fleet Week, who was being treated at the hospital. They eat at the Golden Dragon, an upscale Chinese restaurant located on one of the island's highest points, and at Kessler's Bierhaus, located in one of the island's oldest German breweries. They also go to a gay bar near the Paramount Theater on Bay Street.

One of Mike's circle of friends, Jim Bertagni, is from Staten Island and he invites Mike to Sunday dinner with his family, near Fort Wadsworth. Jim and his boyfriend are fully accepted by the traditional Italian-American family and, for the first time, Mike feels loved and accepted by a family that knew he was gay. On another Sunday, Mama Bertagni invites Mike, who only sometimes attends non-denominational services at Fort Wadsworth, to attend Mass at St. Peter's. And when Jim's brother Joey, a firefighter, comes out of the closet to Mike, he invites Mike to go meditate with him at the Tibetan Museum. The two men form a relationship which is only strengthened when Mike tends to Joey's wounds after he is injured on the job. Although Mike and Joey haven't yet made their romance public, it is widely suspected and Thanksgiving at the Bertagnis' house sees Mama and Papa Bertagni hatching schemes to get the two men into bed together, including turning down the thermostat for the attic room they shared so that they'd have to bunk up together. The family is overjoyed when they announce their love at Thanksgiving dinner, with Mama Bertagni revealing that she had been praying to Saints Raphael and Valentine to bring them together. Mike and Joey get an apartment together near South Beach, but don't get much time to enjoy it when Mike receives orders to be transferred to Savannah, Georgia. Joey realizes that he can never leave his family, so Mike resigns his commission and returns home to San Antonio, Texas where he discovers a new circle of friends who promise to introduce him to the gay social life of that city.

28. DeCandido, Keith R(obert) A(ndreassi) *Four Walls*. New York: Pocket Star, 2008. 334pp.

In this original novel based on the CBS TV series *CSI: NY*, a team of NYPD forensic crime scene investigators takes on a double murder case at the Richmond Hill Correctional Facility on Staten Island. At the same time as a skinhead inmate murdered a black Moslem inmate for a perceived slight, a respected ex-cop, doing time for vehicular homicide, is found dead in the ensuing commotion. Following the twists and turns of the case, the CSI team finds out that the victim had actually died of anaphylactic shock in reaction to a medication. There are only two references to Staten Island, about the intense loyalty and hatred it inspires in its native children. An Italian-American prison guard from Van Duzer Street was born on Staten Island and never wanted to live anywhere else. On the flip side, CSI team member Danny Messer hated coming back to his home borough, a "feeling he seemed to share with most people who'd grown up on the island and left it."

29. DeStefano, Anthony [Anthony John, pseud.]. *The Judas Voice*. New York: Jove Books, 1989. 329pp.

Detective Lieutenant Vincent Ciano is a *Dirty Harry*-style cop whose crime-fighting methods upset his by-the-book superiors in the NYPD. When he kills a perp in order to save a baby's life, he is punished with a reassignment to the quiet 122nd Precinct on Staten Island, his former hometown, where his ex-wife and son still live. On the first morning of his new assignment, he is called to Holy Cross church, just outside of the Richmondtown Restoration, where Monsignor Francis Bryan is found mutilated and crucified upside down. In the course of his investigation, Ciano is introduced to Ed Hanratty, a retired cop who offers his help in catching the murderer of his good friend Msgr. Bryan, who had saved Hanratty from suicide many years before. Hanratty also has a beautiful, but volatile daughter Erica, with whom Ciano soon begins an affair.

From an abandoned house in the hills above Richmondtown, a deformed and malevolent drifter named Joseph Steppe observes the police activity at the church. In his pocket he holds Msgr. Bryan's eyeball. Steppe is a laborer at Richmondtown and harbors an intense hatred of its director, Abigail West, whom he eventually kidnaps and murders in the basement of Holy Cross church. In the meantime, Father David Graff is also brutally mutilated and decapitated at Holy Cross, where he was preparing to give the eulogy for his friend Msgr. Bryan the next day. Acting on a tip he had received from Abigail West before she disappeared, Ciano tracks down Steppe and, after a brutal fight, drowns him in Richmondtown's millpond. Thinking the murderer is dead, everyone is shocked when another priest, Fr. Thomas McKenna, is mutilated and thrown from the bell tower of Sacred Heart Academy.

Interspersed through the story we read the inner thoughts of the murderer; about how he was sexually molested as a child by his drunken, promiscuous mother and her boyfriends, and how the traitor Apostle Judas came to him at the age of eight and made a covenant with him in blood, which gave him the power to kill his abusive mother when he was ten-years-old. The priests' murders were committed to fulfill his end of this demonic covenant. In an attempt to catch the killer, Ciano's partner Joseph Dugan disguises himself as a priest in the Holy Cross rectory, but is speared to death before he can react to the killer. Ed Hanratty meanwhile has hypothesized that the killer's pattern has been to kill the priests in the manner that the Apostles were martyred, and his own suspicions lead him to an abandoned house near Richmondtown where he is overpowered by the murderer, crucified and run through with a javelin.

When Ciano reconciles with his ex-wife, his lover Erica Hanratty abducts their son Vincent. When he calls Erica looking for his son, Ciano hears her speaking in two different voices, with two different personalities: Erica's and that of Judas. Ed Hanratty had suspected his daughter may have been the killer and gave a file with that information to Joseph Dugan, to be passed along to Ciano in the event of his death. The box is now opened and Ciano and his wife are able to track down Erica and save their son. Ciano chases Erica to the Richmondtown courthouse, where they engage in a brutal fight. Realizing that death is the only way to rid herself of the spirit of Judas, she hangs herself on the gallows. Judas then begins to appear to Fr. Thomas Layhe, the surviving pastor of Holy Cross, who has been committed to an insane asylum due to the horrors he's witnessed.

Staten Island is the setting for the vast majority of this story, with most of the action taking place in and around Richmondtown. There are numerous references to the various buildings in Richmondtown, as well as to other Staten Island streets and places. Snippets of Staten Island history are recounted, and reference is made to the radical buildup of the borough due to the Verrazano Bridge and the changing architecture of its neighborhoods.

30. De Sylvia, Josephine [Sylvia Dee, pseud.]. *Dear Guest and Ghost*. New York: Macmillan, 1950. 259pp.

In this comic novel, Staten Island is a bleak rural backwater, populated by backward eccentrics. When their Manhattan apartment building is sold, the Helmakobbler family move into a ramshackle "Victorian monstrosity" on Staten Island, because that is the only affordable place in the city with enough space for daughter Thelma's (a twenty-five year old bookish librarian) immense collection of books. On their ferry ride over, an old woman proudly declares that Staten Island will "...build you up real good" and "put roses in your cheeks." Mr. Helmakobbler, a traveling toothpaste salesman with a wealth of jokes and bawdy stories, declares that that they're living in "God's country" now and declares that their new house will give them "...some of the good old American values from which we've strayed so far." Mrs. Helmakobbler is not so enthusiastic.

On the train ride to their new home (identified by Virgil Markham as being near Richmondtown in the April-June 1957 issue of the Staten Island Historian) she observed "[m]ile after mile of bleak, flat landscape stretched to the left and to the right, sprinkled with gas stations and houses which looked as if they were inhabited by people who had moved to the Island in desperation." The taxi driver at the station, like all other islanders, refers to Manhattan as "New York City" and abruptly declares, apropos of nothing, that he hasn't been to New York City in twenty-two years. When they arrive at the house, sixteen-year-old Stevy declares it be something out of a Charles Addams comic. When decorated with their modern Swedish furniture, the nineteenth-century house looks like "an old lady dressed in a strapless evening gown," and is full of obsolete appliances that no one knows how to operate. The eminently domestic Mrs. Helmakobbler had visions of new friendships and stereotypically rural activities such as trading recipes with other housewives and gossiping while hanging out clothes to dry, but the neighbors prove to be American Gothic types and ready to lynch Stevy when an alarm he installed on his bedroom door wakes the whole neighborhood.

With her husband on the road most of the time, Thelma commuting four hours to work or with her nose buried in a book, and Stevy hanging out with friends or mashing on girls, the lonely and sad Mrs. Helmakobbler begins communicating with a handsome young ghost named Leiscester who inhabits one room of the house. She strikes up a valuable friendship with the ghost, who had died by falling in a paddle wheel in 1818. Leiscester, with his access to the omniscience of the "All-Knowing" and valuable afterlife social connections, helps solve all of Mrs. Helmakobbler's problems with advice that: gets Thelma engaged to the equally bookish local high school principal; helps find Stevy's true calling as an artist when Leiscester has his friend Vincent Van Gogh subconsciously inspire him; and rekindles the love life of Mr. and Mrs. Helmakobbler. When a doctor convinces Mrs. Helmakobbler that her ghostly friend is a mere menopausal hallucination, Leiscester disappears. She eventually realizes her error and causes him to return and even follow her to the family's next residence in Minneapolis.

31. Drew, K. *Wolf at the Door.* Tallahassee, Fla: Dreamspinner Press, 2013. 191pp.
    In this gay, gothic horror novel Nicholas Ashby finds a way out of desperate trailer park poverty in the Midwest by winning a nursing scholarship to Desentia College outside of New York City. His academic success and cultivation of professorial relationships earns him the prestigious internship at Blackwood Manor in Staten Island, on the fringe of Emerson Hill. His duty at the eerie gothic manor was to act as nurse, cook and servant for Lilith, an elderly woman who, strangely, is the wife of Sebastian Blackwood, the young and handsome lord of the estate. In this alternate Staten Island, the estate sits on hundreds of wooded acres, where Sebastian hunts game and whose environs seem to resemble the English moors. Nicholas isn't dismayed by his new assignment despite stumbling upon blood-soaked altars, undergoing

attacks from demonic succubi and discovering a hidden collection of decades' worth of student ID cards from the college he was attending.

He is eventually seduced by Sebastian but discovers that the college had been funneling students to the Blackwoods as food since the 1970s in exchange for sizeable donations and the hope that they could unlock the secrets of the Blackwoods' immortality. Sebastian has fallen in love with Nicholas and declares his intention to make him immortal. He explains that Lilith was actually the woman who, in Talmudic lore, was Adam's first wife before Eve. She had met Sebastian in pre-Revolutionary France and made him into a demon through worship of the serpent god, Gulgath. Sebastian and Nicholas go through the ceremony of immortality in the Blackwood mausoleum, but the jealous Lilith attacks them both, causing Sebastian to kill her.

Of Staten Island, one police detective says, "It's unlike any other part of the country I've ever seen. In the city everything is expendable-as soon as a building is complete, someone's tearing it down...But here...everything has a memory, every building, every person has a history, and it goes on forever, like a chain. People here are bound to the past. They may fight against it, but they're trapped by it nonetheless."

32. DuBois, Theodora. *Death Tears a Comic Strip*. Boston: Houghton Mifflin, 1939. 235pp.
    While visiting friends in Staten Island, amateur detectives Dr. Jeffrey and Anne McNeill become embroiled in a mystery when a young woman, Penelope Shepard, bursts into their dinner party seeking medical help for her stepfather Bigelow Dowd. Penelope, her brother Arthur "Sheppy" and their mother Nellie live with Bigelow, a wealthy wire factory owner, who is said to mistreat his stepchildren by stealing their inheritance, making them dress in rags and forcing them to attend school with Italians, Slavs and the children of ex-bootleggers. Although Jeffrey attends to Bigelow and gets him to a hospital for an appendix operation, he mysteriously drops dead after a successful surgery. Matters are complicated with the arrival of Bigelow's brother Lewis, who had received an anonymous note warning him about his brother's safety. Jeffrey decides to investigate, especially after Sheppy's friend Nick Maltby, a delivery boy and aspiring mandolin virtuoso, shows Jeffrey a salt shaker filled with lead sugar that Bigelow had used. Nick points a finger at the Mills, a married couple rumored to be working

below their stations as Bigelow's servants, owing to some mysterious hold he had over them.

Jeffrey further discovers that someone had been slipping morphine into Bigelow's quinine tonic, supporting his theory that Bigelow died of morphine withdrawal. Jeffrey and Anne also discover, using the McMorris method, an invisible list of twelve girls' names on Lewis Dowd's anonymous note.

Anne visits Bigelow's house to meet with Lewis and Mrs. Dowd in order to hear a promised revelation from Lewis about the case. However, before he can say anything Lewis is shot through a window while Mrs. Dowd is out of the room. Further complicating things, a comic strip of Sheppy's, an aspiring illustrator, is found in the bush outside the window. When morphine is discovered in one of Sheppy's puppets, Penelope takes the blame and is arrested, but it is later discovered that a certain piece of evidence (a piggy bank with a German coin in it) that implicated Penelope in a string of pharmacy robberies really came from Sheppy. Sheppy declares that he got the bank from Jenson, the household's Swedish masseur. In a final showdown with all concerned, Jeffrey ties together all the loose ends and solves the mystery. Jenson is shown to be the heroin addict (although Sheppy tried it a few times) and the person responsible for the pharmacy robberies. In the meantime, Anne McNeill had tracked down the list of girl's names to a local teacher, who admitted writing the anonymous note. The teacher's sister was involved with a man who admitted that he was poisoning Bigelow Dowd, because he disapproved of the man's romantic interest in Penelope and because of his frequent lectures regarding the man's moral failings. Furthermore, Sheppy's comic strip that was found at the scene of Lewis Dowd's murder was traced to the cobbler's shop of Nick Maltby's father, a fan of Sheppy's art. In addition, Nick Maltby was seen buying lead sugar at the pharmacy next door to his father's shop. Maltby is revealed to be a morphine addict and big time dealer and is arrested.

33. DuBois, Theodora. *The Devil and Destiny*. New York: Lancer Books, 1948. 271pp.

Although Staten Island is not mentioned by name in this book, internal references to ferry rides from the "island" to the city, as well as the testimony of the author's daughter (Theodora DuBois Papers, The College of Staten Island Library Archives) make the setting clear. Miles

Sparkman lives with his alcoholic wife, Antoinette, and his children from a previous marriage on a hilltop estate overlooking the lower harbor. When Antoinette drowns in their swimming pool, husband and wife detective team Dr. Jeffrey and Anne McNeill uncover a love quadrangle and mysterious goings-on.

Miles Sparkman and the singer Noel Edelfeld have long been in love, while Miles' secretary, Camilla Bohannen, is in love with Miles. Tom Taggery, the Sparkman children's tutor, is in love with Camilla. When Miles' impressionable Haitian servants accuse Noel of pushing Antoinette into the pool, the police begin to investigate. Having been educated in an Anglican convent school in Ireland, Noel has a strong belief in the supernatural, especially the devil, a belief which excites universal surprise and derision from everyone in America. When she dives into a frozen pond after mistakenly hearing what she thought was the Sparkman boy's shouts for help, and when someone matching Noel's description orders large shipments of linens and cookware from Manhattan department stores to the Sparkman house, Noel blames the devil, while everyone else questions her sanity.

Events come to a head when Noel shoots and wounds a "devil" in her apartment. The McNeills gather all the principals in one place and reveal that Camilla Bohannen and Tom Taggery, believing that Noel had actually killed Antoinette Sparkman, had conspired to make her appear insane so as to save her from the electric chair. Camilla had impersonated Noel in the department stores, while Tom had rigged up a hidden microphone in Noel's apartment to simulate the drowning cries of the Sparkman boy. Camilla had cut the electricity and invaded Noel's quarters dressed as a devil to further convince Noel of her insanity. The Sparkman children had been surreptitiously slipping the hallucinogenic drug scopolamine into Noel's food for the same reason. However, the McNeills reveal that it was Miles' good friend, Nicholas Poulos, who had killed Antoinette. He had drowned Miles' first wife, a rampant nymphomaniac, to save his friend from a bad marriage. When Antoinette, who had witnessed the murder, later married Miles, she began blackmailing Poulos. He drowned her to stop the blackmail and to save his friend from her destructive and socially embarrassing alcoholism as well.

Although description of Staten Island is nonexistent, the author's first hand familiarity with Staten Island makes the book of interest for its depiction of attitudes, mores and social culture of the time. The universal secularism of the authorities, the medical profession and the upper classes are of particular note.

34. DuBois, Theodora. *Fowl Play*. Garden City, N.Y.: Published for the Crime Club by Doubleday & Company, Inc., 1951. 189pp.

Dr. Jeffrey and Anne McNeill, the famed husband and wife team of amateur detectives, are- with their three boys- moving into their new home on Staten Island, overlooking the Narrows. A set of melodramatic, poetry-spouting teenaged twins come looking for a doctor because they fear that their elderly cousin, Louisa Santon- the matriarch of their family and the owner of the nearby High Battle estate- has died. When the McNeills go to High Battle (named for a battle that had been fought there between the Dutch and the Indians during the Pig War), they find out that Mrs. Santon had indeed died, of an apparent heart attack, when she mysteriously dashed up the stairs after hearing an unknown voice. They discover that High Battle, a mansard-roofed mansion from the 1870s, houses a motley collection of eccentric ne'er-do-wells and artistic dilettantes from the extended Santon family. It was Anne McNeill's private opinion that old brick, mansard-roofed mansions so often contained families and situations of "violent potentialities."

The McNeills' suspicions were raised when they learned that Mrs. Santon had told her family that she was selling the house, turning them all out into the street and moving to Florida with her precious mynah bird and her Irish maid Nora, but the victim's doctor confirmed that she died of coronary thrombosis. The family was terrified of having to make their way in the world, and were outraged when they learned that Mrs. Santon's had left everything to the mynah bird in her will. The maid Nora tells everyone that she believes Mrs. Santon was murdered, an accusation which seems to gain credence when one of High Battle's residents, Dan Santon, is sickened by ground-up glass that had been placed in his pudding. Suspicion was cast upon the young cousin Kit McCumber when a broken glass pitcher was found in her drawer. Nora the maid was then found dead from a gas leak, which Anne McNeill discovered had been perpetrated deliberately. Meanwhile, the two McNeill boys witnessed someone from High Battle throwing thirteen music boxes into Porridge Bowl Pond. When Jeffrey retrieves them, he finds out that they all play an old German tune that Mrs. Santon had liked. The mynah bird reacts strangely when he hears the tune and begins calling out for help to "Honey Lou," the name the late Mr. Santon had endearingly called his wife.

One day while Jeffrey and Anne are out, a disguised person claiming to be Kit McCumber takes the McNeill boys for a ride. She drives the boys to steep Hamilton Avenue in St. George, locks the boys in the car, removes the parking brake, and puts a big block of ice under the front wheel. Although one boy escaped in time, the car rolled down the hill into traffic when the ice melted. Luckily, he was not seriously injured. Jeffrey solved the mystery with the help of Anne's detective work when she found out which Santon had bought the music boxes and which had bought a block of ice that morning. Dan Santon believed he was the reincarnation of a Southern Colonel who had lost four sons and his plantation in the Civil War and was seeking vengeance for his loss. He had led Mrs. Santon to believe in reincarnation, and convinced her that her late husband had been reborn in the form of the mynah bird, which was easier to believe because he had trained the bird to respond to the German song Mr. and Mrs. Santon loved, and to shout for help using the pet name Mr. Santon had called his wife. Knowing that Mrs. Santon had a weak heart, he had indirectly but knowingly caused her to have a heart attack when she rushed to her "husband's" aid.

Among the references to Staten Island are Bay Street, Victory Blvd. Hamilton Avenue, the ferry and the Narrows. Descriptions are lacking, but the destruction of older homes on the island, a process which was already advanced in 1951, is mentioned. It is stated that there are only a few mansard-roofed mansion left on the island, and only three or four that are kept up. It was still a time of gracious living though, when upper class, old-stock Americans employed maids and nannies and lived in large homes and spacious estates in the hills of Staten Island, a life that somewhat reflects what the author knew.

35. DuBois, Theodora. *High Tension*. Garden City, N.Y.: Published for the Crime Club by Doubleday, 1950. 224pp.
    Down-on-his-luck Peter McVeigh and his young daughter Jane move to the Staten Island garage apartment of Mrs. Sprag, his mother's oldest friend, for the purpose of working as the gardener on her estate. No sooner does he move in than he is called to the neighboring house of Daniel de Rapellie, who is lying dead on his lawn. Mrs. Sprag's granddaughter, Celia, had been playing croquet with him when she stepped away to take a phone call. She claimed that he was dead when

she returned. However, the owner of the adjacent house, the popular radio personality Richard "Dick" Kutka, and his assorted hangers-on, all swore that they witnessed Celia kill de Rapellie with a croquet mallet. Celia's emotional trauma causes her to doubt her own innocence, and so she, her brother Sandy, and Peter McVeigh allowed the persuasive Mr. Kutka to "help her" by disposing of the body and promising that he and his friends would keep her secret.

The more Peter hears about Mr. Kutka, the less he likes. Kutka is a major figure on Staten Island. He not only enjoys widespread popularity through his lowbrow radio show, the *Joker Hour*, but he commands great loyalty due to the many charitable organizations and social events he personally sponsors, such as youth groups, rifle clubs and dances. In addition, even Peter has to admit that the man is naturally gifted with a voice and personality that are truly hypnotic. Indeed, he has mesmerized Celia, who declares herself prepared to dedicate her entire life to doing good through Kutka's Loyalty and Friendship Organization (LAFO).

The great homes of Staten Island, many of which were abandoned since the Depression, had been recently falling victim to destructive attacks by vandals. (Perhaps a reference to a real-life string of arson attacks against unoccupied mansions which occurred on Staten Island in the early 1930s). When Peter goes to investigate a break-in at the house of the late Daniel de Rapellie, he discovers the African American butler, Joe, badly hurt and claiming to have been attacked by men wearing hoods resembling welding masks. When Peter and Sandy go to visit Joe in the hospital, they also meet Mr. Kutka's African-American butler Roderick, who relates how he had discovered a secret plan of Kutka's which he showed to de Rapellie. He overheard de Rapellie confront Kutka about it and warn him to leave the country within a week or his plan would be sent to the FBI. Roderick later witnessed de Rapellie murdered by one of Kutka's masked men and further reveals that one of Kutka's men placed the phone call which drew Celia away at the time of the murder.

Peter and Sandy later come across a kind of coven of these masked men engaged in a sort of ritualized vandalism of a neighboring abandoned mansion, while chanting about LAFO and a new order in which the rich and upper classes would be overthrown. Peter and Sandy are captured and tied up while the mansion is set on fire. One of the members of the group, the local paper boy, feels a pang of conscience and frees them. Acting on a tip from the butler Roderick, Peter and Sandy search Kutka's boat and discover his secret plan for total world domination. In addition, Roderick tells the pair that Kutka brands his favored initiates on their hip with his initials and that Celia is scheduled to be branded. He suggests the ploy of allowing Celia to witness the branding of another girl before her turn to perhaps scare her straight. His plan works, she is disabused of her idol worship and she flees into the arms of Peter, who decides to finish off Kutka once and for all. With the help of Roderick, who drugs the drinks of the Kutka circle, Peter sneaks into the mansion, steals Kutka's personalized mask and branding iron, and brands one of the sleeping women on the neck while leaving the mask to make it appear to be Kutka's doing. The woman's husband then shoots and kills Kutka in a rage.

Although the location of the novel is not mentioned, the setting is obviously Staten Island, as the three homes at the center of the story are located on a hill overlooking the Narrows, the island is sufficiently undeveloped to afford space for forests and large estates, and a ferry is used to travel to Manhattan. In addition, Mrs. Du Bois' daughter listed this work as being set on Staten Island (Theodora DuBois Papers, The College of Staten Island Library Archives). Post-war unemployment, as reflected in Peter McVeigh's situation and the unrest of the lower classes, is a major theme, as is the encroachment of the lower classes upon the hill enclaves of Staten Island's old stock elite, as reflected in their vandalism of the their mansions. Socialistic ideology, represented by both Communism and Kutka's organization, is deplored and denounced. The book contains an interesting description of a ferry ride and notes that when the African American butler, Joe, was injured he had to be taken to a Catholic hospital as they did not discriminate.

36. DuBois, Theodora. *The Listener.* Garden City, N.Y.: Published for the Crime Club by Doubleday and Company, Inc., 1953. 192pp.

After her beloved fiancé Mark Leith is reported dead behind the Iron Curtain, Patricia Niall of Dublin, Ireland enters the Order of the Sisters of St. Ciaran as a novice nun. The Order, neither Roman Catholic nor Episcopalian, is a strict and ancient Irish order, dating from before the Council of Whitby, with chapters in several major world cities. The Order's Superior has ordered a new convent established in Staten Island, for the purpose of providing a school and convalescent home for underprivileged Puerto Rican children from Manhattan. Patricia Niall, now known as Sister Genevieve, is among the nuns who travel to New York to build up this new convent, which is located atop a hill (obviously Todt Hill), on the edge of the island's country club community.

Below the hill, on Richmond Road, are a "great block of low-rent apartments" from one of which Sister Genevieve hears the music of a recorder being played nightly. While sneaking out of the convent one night to mail a letter, Sister Genevieve lingers a moment to listen to the waltz music being played at the country club ball, when she witnesses the shooting death of a young woman who had arrived for the party. When Sister Genevieve later stumbles upon a dead owl and cat, she begins to make a connection between the recorder music from the Richmond Road apartments and the bloody deeds on the hill. The recorder player had played "Oh Dem Golden Slippers" before the golden slippers wearing girl was killed, and he had played a song about "The Owl and the Pussycat" before the animals were killed. The police suspect Sister Genevieve of the murder, while the convent's Superior, Mother Brigid, suspects her of frivolity, worldly thinking and disobedience as she begins to obsess over the murder and investigate. Subsequent songs from the recorder player result in corresponding deaths and injuries of humans and animals on Todt Hill. "Tom, Tom the Piper's Son" is a prelude to a vicious attack on the Piper boy on Buttonwood Rd. "Ach du Liebe Augustine" results in the death of a dachshund named Augustine. The song "Mrs. Bond" is played shortly before a Mrs. Bond is brutally beaten.

Sister Genevieve borrows some clothes from Sylvia Ammond, a sympathetic Todt Hill resident, and steals away from the convent in mufti in order to track down the musician in the Richmond Road apartments, who turns out to be a blind Korean War veteran who chooses his songs based on tunes his aunt whistles. His innocence apparent, she is alarmed when she finds out that he had recently been playing "Who is Sylvia?" When Sister Genevieve, still wearing Sylvia Ammond's clothes, goes to warn her of the danger, she is shot through the shoulder but survives. Sister Genevieve's own Mother Brigid (real name Helen McCrea) is the next target when "Mother Machree" is played by the recorder player, but she is saved when Genevieve shouts a last-second warning.

Mark Leith turns up alive and well, and takes charge of things at the convent. He orders a bust of Julius Caesar disguised as Sister Genevieve and tells the recorder player to play "Genevieve, Sweet

Genevieve" that night. He and the police wait in ambush for the killer, and apprehend a Todt Hill resident, Mr. Duchane, who had been in the French Resistance during the war. Directives from his superiors had been conveyed to him in musical code by means of flute music, and some subconscious flaw made him believe that he was still operating under wartime conditions. The mystery solved, Mark Leith whisks Sister Genevieve/ Patricia Niall away to be married.

Architecture and development are a noticeable theme, from the "low-rent" apartment houses on Richmond Road, to the feelings of Mr. Stockwell, a member of an old Staten Island family: "It used to be a far lovelier place twenty years ago before all these cursed housing developments and little tinderbox houses. There were a few handsome gentlemen's estates, and you could ride in the woods for hours and never see a soul or a house or hear those Boy Scouts yelling up in the woods and blowing their damn bugles...I swear I'd like to put a torch to all these houses, or wipe them all off the face of the island with a bomb; all the people too, myself included."

37. DuBois, Theodora. *Seeing Red.* Garden City, N.Y.: Published for the Crime Club by Doubleday & Co., Inc., 1954. 187pp.
Mysterious happenings ensue when Dr. Jeffrey McNeill and his wife Anne come across a murder victim on Swinburne Island in the Lower Bay. As the couple begins to investigate, they receive an anonymous call threatening to denounce Anne to the Senate Espionage Committee as a traitor and an atomic spy if she and Jeffrey persist in their inquiries. The basis of the threat went back to 1942 when Anne, while working in an atomic research unit, had been the recipient of unsolicited jewels and cash from a Nazi-sympathizing Spaniard named Zunyer, who was attempting to obtain a valuable scientific formula of which Anne had no knowledge. She had been kidnapped by Zunyer and threatened with death, but escaped from his clutches with the help of several wire hangers and the aid of Zunyer's pacifistic son. Now, the McNeills' investigation reveals that the same shadowy Spaniard, Zunyer, was somehow involved in the murder on Swinburne. When the McNeills do not cease their involvement in the case, Anne receives a summons to appear before the Senate Committee. Although she had dutifully turned over the jewels and cash to the FBI in 1942, her case was undermined by the fact that she had lost the receipt, and the FBI agent who handled her case was dead. By all appearances, she was guilty of treason and was expected to receive the death penalty. The

McNeills locate Zunyer but he refuses to help exonerate Anne, by feigning a faulty memory of the incident. However, induced by the McNeills' offer to help his son with his medical career and introduce him to some nice American girls, he reconsiders and appears before the committee at the eleventh hour. He has almost everyone- including Dr. McNeill- removed from the room, and explains away his gift of jewels and cash to Anne by claiming that they were lovers, leaving Anne both humiliated and relieved. It is revealed, almost as an afterthought, that the murder victim on Swinburne was killed by Butch Bergson of Front Street, in the course of his gang's narcotics trafficking.

This book includes perhaps the most extensive, if not the only, description of Swinburne Island in fiction, compared to which the description of Staten Island is almost non-existent. However, the island as a desirable suburb and comfortable home for the thoroughly admirable McNeills is an implicit subtext. An intriguing reference to a man who "seemed of Brooklyn origin" goes unexplained. As the author was herself a well-to-do, old-stock Staten Island resident, her descriptions of the attitudes and mores of the McNeills could perhaps be read as a first hand perspective of the island in the early 50s. As upper middle class professionals, owning a yacht was no remarkable thing, but using cream in one's coffee was an unimaginable extravagance. Mediterranean people were still thought of as "The Other" and casually referred to as "wops." The island still retained a sense of an enclave for the older WASP citizenry, but a dangerous and criminally-inclined ethnic class had already established a beachhead on the North Shore, in the form of Butch Bergson of Front Street. The book is noted for its early criticism of the McCarthy hearings and the anti-Communist crusade of the early 1950s.

38. DuBois, Theodora. *Solution T-25*. New York: Modern Literary Editions Publishing Company, 1951. 221pp.
    In this speculative sci-fi adventure, John Dean and his fiancée Joyce Van Pelt are attending a wedding in Connecticut when the United States is devastated by a nuclear sneak attack and lightning invasion by Soviet Russia and her allies. Radio reports say that Manhattan is destroyed and occupation troops in radiation suits are massacring Americans. When Oliver Dudley, a wedding guest who is a State Department official, explains that Staten Island was not important enough to be a target and was thus likely undamaged, Joyce goes back there to check on her grandparents. Dudley recruits Dean and some

other men to rescue a very important scientist, Dr. Sheridan, from Yale Medical School, and fly him to a safe house in the Florida Keys, since Sheridan is involved in research that might harm the enemy. With that accomplished, Dean goes to Manhattan, where he is convinced by Dudley to feign collaboration in order to more effectively serve the underground resistance, as Dudley himself has done. With Dudley's influence, Dean is placed on the staff of Commissioner Nicholas Charlov, who has chosen the Staten Island home of Joyce Van Pelt's grandparents as his headquarters.

Although the island suffered some bombing damage, the Van Pelts' High Street Victorian mansion was unscathed. However, an extermination camp, euphemistically called a "disposal center," has been set up in the southern part of the island. The occupation is brutal, with Americans being reduced to slave labor. A rump American government survives in Denver, but it is marked for destruction in good time. Dean curries favor with Charlov and is rewarded with a great deal of freedom of movement, which he uses to serve the resistance. When Dr. Sheridan sends word that he needs rhesus monkeys for his experiments, Dean tries the Staten Island Zoo, where the half-mad zookeeper explains that they don't have any monkeys, but he has managed to preserve the zoo's prestigious snake collection. Dr. Sheridan eventually gets his monkeys and successfully produces his secret weapon, a chemical called Solution T-25, which is smuggled to resistance leaders across the country, including John Dean. Dean connives to have the Solution slipped into Charlov's food, which soon renders him non-aggressive and child-like, a situation which plays out among much of the leadership of the occupying forces. The book ends with the expected American counter-attack, which the Soviets watch with passivity.

39. Du Bois, William Pène. *Call Me Bandicoot*. New York: Harper & Row, 1970. 63pp.
The narrator of this novel for young people is taking the Ferry to Staten Island to visit an exhibition in honor of his father, who was a famous Staten Island landscape artist. An oddly dressed boy with a rat-like face strikes up a conversation with him and proposes to explain, in exchange for some junk food from the ferry's snack bar, why the harbor is so dirty. The boy explains that his friend Ermine Bandicoot, who lives on a farm, "deep in the lush hills and woods of Staten Island"

(and whose physical description seems to match that of the boy) was responsible for the deplorable condition of New York harbor.

In his farfetched tale, the boy explains that the entrepreneurial Bandicoot started collecting half-used cigarette butts and eventually collected enough so that he was able to combine them all into a cigarette that was as big as the Statue of Liberty, which he erected on Liberty Island. He convinced the Mayor to give him permission because he argues that the stink of a giant cigarette would reinforce the city's anti-smoking and anti-pollution campaigns. At the same time, he obtains corporate sponsorship from Summertime cigarettes, which sees it as a great publicity stunt. When the fumes from the giant cigarette start choking downtown Manhattan, the cigarette company orders the half-lit tobacco-stick dumped into the harbor, which is why Ermine Bandicoot is responsible for the filthy water. After being conned out of several more dollars, the narrator bids the boy farewell, but sees him on the return trip pulling the same scheme with a different person, only with a different story, this time revolving around the "Cosa Nostril", an organization of large-nosed VIPs that seeks to further world peace.

The narrator follows the boy off the boat into Manhattan and witnesses a limousine pull up beside him, and a man inside offer him money and beg him to come home. The boy didn't even respond. A bystander tells the narrator that the boy is Hermann Vanden Kroote and his father is the owner of a huge cigarette corporation. Hermann lives at the YMCA and refuses to take his father's money because he believes that he is selling sickness. The narrator concludes with the observation that it's tough to be a kid with principles.

40. Earle, Olive L. *White Patch*. Illustrated by Olive L. Earle. New York: William Morrow, 1958. 64pp.
    In this naturalistic and unsentimental book for children a Battery Park sparrow named White Patch takes the ferryboat *Miss New York* to Staten Island in search of adventure and refuge from predatory falcons. He finds a hospitable home in a garden modeled after the author's own, at 66 Harvard Avenue, and eventually finds a mate and breeds.

41. England, George Allan. *The Air Trust*. Illustrations by John Sloan. St. Louis: Phil Wagner, 1915. 333pp.
    Dedicated to Socialist leader Eugene Debs, this anti-Capitalist novel of Socialist agitprop was conceived by its author as a thought experiment, a *reductio ad absurdum* of the monopolistic principle: to wit,

if the Capitalist monopolies of beef or coal or steel were right, then what would happen if someone decided to corner the market on oxygen? Wall Street billionaire Isaac Flint, with world domination as his goal, has that idea one day and commissions his chief R&D scientist to develop a machine that would extract 10% of the oxygen from the air, which would force the choking multitudes to buy back their clean air from him. Intending to visit their laboratories in Oakwood Heights, Flint and his partner Waldron take their limousine on the Staten Island Ferry, "...that glorious monument of municipal ownership wrecked by Tammany grafting," where a Socialist workman overhears their plans. The plutocrats visit their enormous self-contained research complex in Staten Island, which comprises a power plant, aviation field, proving ground, wireless plant, and numerous laboratories, all existing for the purpose of enslaving humanity. The same workman- Gabriel Armstrong- who overheard the billionaires' plans on the ferry- is an employee there and serendipitously obtains a notebook containing Flint's plans and resolves to thwart them. The rest of the book deals with Flint's brutal plan to imprison and destroy Armstrong, and the successful revolution that Armstrong initiates to overthrow the Air Trust and bring about Socialism in the United States, while simultaneously wooing Flint's daughter and converting her to the Socialist position.

42. Forgione, Louis. *Reamer Lou*. New York: E.P. Dutton, 1924. 279pp.
    This socially realistic novel brings to light the pleasure, pains and frustrations of immigrant workers on the New York waterfront. Although American born, Italian-American worker Louis Podesta has spent his entire life amongst immigrants, causing him to consider himself a "half-and-half foreigner." A brawling, hard-living man, he respects and idealizes physical strength and brutish aggression, although he also estimates himself to have a superior intelligence and perspective than his laboring peers.

    Originating in a Pennsylvania mining town, he finds a job as a reamer in a Mariner's Harbor shipyard before the First World War. Leisure time for Lou includes swimming at South Beach, movies in Port Richmond or carousing in Linoleumville or Mariner's Harbor. He rents a room in Arlington, which is described as being on the edge of "...as fine a stretch of woods as there is around New York..." through which he enjoys walking for relaxation. He starts dating his foreman's socially ambitious daughter, whose insistence that he go to night school and learn to enjoy high culture eventually drives a wedge between them.

When one of his two friends, a Lithuanian as strong as he is, starts wasting away after contracting a social disease, Lou bemoans the cultural dislocation and disorientation that leads immigrants to bad ends when they come to an unrestrained country lacking the stability and taboos of Old World villages. After Lou almost beats his boss to death during a fight, he flees the island via the Elizabethport Ferry, ending up working in a Brooklyn shipyard. He makes a return trip to Staten Island and kisses his best friend's wife on the swamp road from Arlington to Linoleumville. When he severely beats yet another boss in Brooklyn, he decides to go back to Pennsylvania, cursing and denouncing the cowardice, hypocrisy and cruelty of New York from the deck of the Staten Island Ferry.

While admiring the refineries and factories of Bayonne during a walk on Richmond Terrace, Lou reminisces how he once took a swim in the Kill van Kull and had to rub himself with kerosene for two days afterwards to get the fuel oil out of his pores. In contrast to the violence between workers and management in shipyards before World War I, Lou notes that the war caused special policemen and guards to be assigned to shipyards and that they brutally suppressed any resistance by workers, even killing a man on Shooter's Island.

43. Friedman, Robin. *The Importance of Wings*. Watertown, Mass.: Charlesbridge, 2009. 170pp.

Thirteen-year-old Roxanne Ben Ari lives with her father and her younger sisters Gayle on Brookfield Avenue in the late 1970s or early 1980s. Her mother has been in Israel for months caring for a sick sister, so the girls look after themselves as their father works long hours. Roxanne, who has to deal with issues of social awkwardness, self-image and identity, is also somewhat embarrassed about her Israeli heritage and intensely desires to be a real American like her peers, for whom the "wings" hairstyle is an especially important marker of belonging. As latchkey kids, Roxanne and Gayle watch endless hours of TV and absorb the assimilationist, all-American message of shows like *The Brady Bunch* and *Little House on the Prairie*. When an Israeli family moves into a "cursed" house on the block, Roxanne befriends Liat Asher, a girl her age who had lost her mother in a terrorist bombing in Israel. Liat is tough, proud and athletic. Her defiant attitude, which leads to her fighting and beating the popular girl in school, inspires Roxanne to be proud of her heritage and disregard what other people think of her. When Liat's house burns down, her father takes her back to Israel, but Roxanne has had her eyes opened and begins calling herself by her

Israeli name, Ravit, and living her life in a more independent and self-confident way.

44. Gallerne, Gilbert [Gilles Bergal, pseud.]. *Cauchemar á Staten Island.* Paris: Fleuve Noir, 1986. 156pp.

In this French-language horror novel, when the night watchmen of a Staten Island canned-goods warehouse begin disappearing, along with the merchandise, the head of the company hires Manhattan private detective Coogan (no first name) to solve the mystery. A thirty-seven-year-old ex-police inspector, Coogan had been fired from the force for a drunk driving accident which left his eight-year-old daughter in a coma. Needing money for her hospital bills, Coogan takes the case and immediately goes to the police station on Staten Island to read the reports. He tracks down the one night watchman who had any information, an alcoholic named Sullivan, and hears a bizarre tale about frog-like humanoids who emerged from the water and who were impervious to shotgun blasts. Before Coogan arrives for his first shift at the warehouse, an old enemy of his, Slim Cryde- a.k.a. the Monkey- lays in wait to murder the man who had put him in prison three years before. However, the frogmen ambush and devour Cryde before he can act, and steal more crates of food. Coogan discovers his remains and notifies the police. When the former night watchman, Sullivan, is found dead in the Hudson, exsanguinated and mutilated by human teeth marks, Coogan decides to conceal himself on the warehouse roof the next night and take pictures of the frogmen. He observes them stealing more crates of food and killing a fisherman who inadvertently espied them. When Coogan tells the police what he witnessed, and showed them his blurry photos, they mock his story but agree to send a ten man team into the sewer system beneath the warehouse to arrest what they believe will turn out to be a colony of pilfering hobos or hippies. Coogan accompanies them through the tunnel where their laughter turns to terror when they stumble upon a pile of mutilated corpses. The frog men attack the squad and kill all of them except Coogan and the chief lieutenant. The two later speculate as to the nature of the creatures and posit that they could be homeless people who mutated or they could be the mer-people of myth or a hybridization of the two. Whatever they were, the authorities covered up the story, despite the fact some of them were seen swimming towards Manhattan.

45. Gilman, Mildred. *Headlines*. New York: Horace Liveright, 1928. 309pp.

  Mary Pollock of Staten Island lives alone in her family's ancestral farmhouse whose "...meadows not so long ago had stretched down to the ocean on the east and back to the hills on the west..." As her father had been compelled to sell the land for fear of losing it for taxes, the family home now stood surrounded by hundreds of modern houses. Every morning Mary pores over the lurid stories of the tabloid newspapers which make her feel "thankful that she lived here sheltered and protected from all the sadness and cruelty of the world," ignoring all the equally tragic dramas being enacted amongst her immigrant neighbors. The unnamed neighborhood (New Dorp or Grant City, judging by the geographic description) consists of rows of two-story stucco houses along with hundreds of summer cottages "beyond the Boulevard." Some people had even built summer shacks on stilts in the swamp land. The grasping real estate broker, Morrison, and Mary's cousin from Brooklyn keep encouraging her to sell the house since the neighborhood had changed and filled up with foreigners. Nevertheless, Mary feels connected to the land and the old house and develops an interest in and connection with the tumultuous lives of her Italian, Irish, German and Finnish neighbors.

  Written in lapidary detail by an author who had an obvious familiarity with the daily lives of the immigrant communities that she covered as a newspaper reporter, the stories revolve around the problems and interactions of the different ethnic families of the neighborhood and the friction and occasional cooperation between them.

  Death and poverty are a constant presence. Almost every family has lost children and most are living on the edge of eviction. The Italian and Irish families have a plethora of children, a fact which is deplored by the supercilious Finnish housewife, who is literally driven mad by the fact that her husband will not move the family out of a neighborhood populated by those she views as social inferiors. The Irish Murphys are forced to put up extended family in their tiny home when a storm- the likes of which hadn't been seen in twenty years- caused the sea to come almost all the way up to "the Boulevard," destroying the unoccupied summer cottages near the sea, the winter cottages further inland and leaving many homeless. The German Ludwig runs a speakeasy, which is protected by the Irish cop, but is eventually raided by Prohibition agents and heavily fined. His wife dreams of a legal settlement for the death of their son. Madness, abortion, birth control, suicide, adultery and even parricide are situations and topics that come up in the lives of these people. The families quarrel and even brawl and ethnic slurs come easily to their lips, but they still help each other out with food and money in times of death and need. The old-stock American Mary Pollock grows emotionally involved with her exotic neighbors and eventually rejects her cousin's request for her to move across the Narrows, despite Mary always trying "dutifully to like Brooklyn".

46. Goldfarb, Aaron. "Health: Staten Island," in *The CheatSheet*. CreateSpace, 2010. 165pp. pgs 75-88.
     Arthur Lampkin is the sex education teacher for the Horatio Alger schools on Staten Island, a group of five middle and high schools ranging from middle lower class to lower middle class socioeconomically. He lives with his fiancée, assistant school superintendant Deborah Henke, in Manhattan but lack of sex is an issue in their relationship. Promising student Kendra Broyles comes to Lampkin and tells him that her mother is a prostitute at the corner of Broadway and Richmond Terrace. She asks him to try to talk to her mother. Since the public transportation system on Staten Island is bad he walks twenty five minutes to the corner where she solicits. When he introduces himself, she propositions him and the story ends with him laughing uncontrollably.

47. Goldsborough, Robert. *Silver Spire*. New York: Bantam Books, 1992. 216pp.
     One day a visitor comes to the Manhattan brownstone of world-famous detective Nero Wolfe. He is met by Wolfe's assistant and leg-man Archie Goodwin. The visitor is Lloyd Morgan, who works with the Reverend Barnabas Bay, the famous televangelist whose megachurch, the Tabernacle of the Silver Spire, is located on Staten Island. Morgan has come to hire Wolfe's services, because of some threatening notes that have appeared in the church's collection pouches over the past six Sundays. The anticlerical Wolfe rejects the opportunity, so Goodwin recommends another detective, Fred Durkin, for the job. The next that Goodwin hears of the situation is that Fred Durkin has been arrested for murdering the church's number-two pastor, Royal Meade. Durkin had gone to the church to investigate, and came to the conclusion that the notes were written by a church employee, an accusation that sent the church's executive committee

into a fury. Rev. Bay asked everyone at the meeting to cool off for fifteen minutes and retire to various offices to pray and reflect on the matter. When the fifteen minutes were up, it was discovered that Royal Meade had been shot and killed with Durkin's gun, which he had left unattended in his coat.

Archie Goodwin takes the ferry to Staten Island to investigate and describes St. George as a more like a "small harbor burg" that wasn't like New York City at all. Goodwin interviews the church's executive staff and discovers that Royal Meade had a nasty personality and was disliked by all. The breakthrough comes when Goodwin discovers some handwritten Bible verses in Meade's desk and shows them to Wolfe, who travels to the church on Staten Island to reveal his findings. He tells the staff that the verses were actually a code written by Meade to spell out the name "Morgan," as in Lloyd Morgan. Meade had discovered that Morgan was stealing money from the church and gave him a deadline to confess. Morgan then wrote the threats, in the hope that a private investigator could be called in, giving Morgan the opportunity to plant false evidence in Meade's desk. When Morgan saw that Durkin had left his gun unattended, he saw his chance to permanently remove the threat to his position, and implicate someone else in the murder.

48. Grayson, Richard. *Victory Boulevard.* New York: Art Pants, 2010. 110pp.
      The narrator of this work is a fifty-one-year-old gay man living in Los Angeles. A Staten Island transplant who grew up in a house that silent film star Mabel Normand once lived in, he sees parallels between himself and Normand, another Staten Islander turned Angeleno. The narrator relates his feelings about and experiences with his younger boyfriend, Jaime, and his sister Susan, and reminisces about life on Staten Island, where he attended P.S. 16, Curtis High School, Staten Island Community College and Richmond College. When a car accident gives him an epiphany, he decides to go back home and sell the family house on Staten Island. He drives past all of his old schools and recalls how Geraldo Rivera exposed the abuses at the Willowbrook State School. He eats at Lakshmi's Sri Lankan restaurant on Cebra Avenue, recounts the story of the Wu Tang Clan and goes to a Staten Island Yankees game. He makes a killing on the house sale and goes back to California to be with Jaime.

49. Gross, Andrew. *Everything to Lose.* New York: William Morrow; An Imprint of HarperCollins Publishers, 2014. 325pp.

Inspired by the real-life story of Susan Jacobson's 1976 murder, this thriller begins with the 1992 murder of eighteen-year-old Deirdre O'Byrne by an unnamed boyfriend in a desolate area of Port Ivory under the Goethals Bridge. Skipping ahead to the present day, financially strapped Westchester divorcée Hilary Cantor serendipitously comes upon a car wreck, from which she pilfers a satchel containing a half million dollars. The money comes as a godsend to the recently laid-off single mother facing foreclosure and the expulsion of her son (who has Asperger's Syndrome) from his private school. She begins to feel pangs of guilt when she hears from news reports that the driver of the car, Joseph Kelty, was a universally-liked city worker who lost his Midland Beach home from Hurricane Sandy. She attends his funeral there, where she hears his son Patrick, a retired NYPD officer, eulogize his father as an all-around great guy who selflessly helped his neighbors and spent all his money caring for his late wife in her dying days. When a hit man murders the only other witness to Joseph Kelty's car crash, and then invades Hilary's home in a search for the money, she goes to Patrick Kelty with the truth.

They uncover the fact that Joseph Kelty was helping his neighbor, Mrs. O'Byrne, blackmail an ascendant Connecticut politician, Frank Landry. Landry, originally from Staten Island, had unwittingly implicated himself in Deirdre O'Byrne's murder when he revealed his nickname, Streak, in a TV interview, which corresponded with information that Deirdre had left in her diary about her secret boyfriend. With Patrick Kelty's help, Hilary has to overcome first the murderous hit man and then the psychotic Landry, who not only killed Deirdre but also a prostitute and then his own wife. He murders Mrs. O'Byrne, Patrick Kelty and is on the verge of murdering Hilary when her son Brandon, who she fears may be violently psychotic himself, beheads his mother's attacker.

This book contains sensitive descriptions of the devastation inflicted upon Midland Beach and other areas of Staten Island by Hurricane Sandy, the drawn-out rebuilding process, the lack of concern by government entities, the feeling of abandonment by hard-hit residents and the illegal methods some felt compelled to resort to in order to get some financial relief.

50. Harper, Karen [Caryn Cameron, pseud.]. *Liberty's Lady*. Toronto: Harlequin, 1990. 297pp.

    This bodice-ripping historical romance follows the Revolutionary-era romance between patriot printer Elizabeth "Libby" Morgan and Cameron Gant, the youngest son of one of Staten Island's most prominent Tory families. The Morgans, who reside on Brady's Pond, were left in financial distress after the sinking of a ramshackle ferry owned by the wealthy Gants of Melrose Manor, which drowned both their paterfamilias and his partner in a Manhattan Whig newspaper, who was also Libby's godfather. Surprisingly, the newspaper was left to the free-spirited and independent Libby, who declared her intention of moving to Manhattan and managing it, rather than selling it. Cameron Gant, an ostensible loyalist, is actually a patriot sympathizer and spy, who is secretly working for General Washington to gather intelligence in the divided and soon-to-be occupied city. Maintaining his cover, Libby and Cameron trade heated political barbs that mask a blossoming attraction and when Libby finds herself in the middle of a skirmish at Turtle Bay, Cameron rescues her from certain arrest and spirits her back across to the harbor to Melrose Manor on Staten Island, where they begin a physical relationship.

    Most of the rest of the book involves their repeated romantic and political misunderstandings as each one doubts the other's true loyalties. Finally, as a patriot mob begins to tar and feather Cameron, General Washington himself comes to his rescue and publicly reveals the invaluable work Cameron had done for the American cause. He and Libby are married but before they can even enjoy their wedding reception, the British fleet is spotted coming through the Narrows. Expecting the occupation force to descend on Manhattan, Cameron sends Libby to Staten Island, where the army actually disembarks and occupies Melrose Manor. Not knowing that Libby escaped to the woods before she could be caught, Cameron goes back to Staten Island in disguise to rescue his bride, but is recognized and imprisoned in his own home. Concocting a plan, Libby and her sister disguise themselves as country girls and rescue Cameron, utilizing an angry hive of bees as a weapon.

51. Harrington, Joseph. *The Last Known Address*. New York: J.B. Lippincott, 1965. 190pp.

    In this police procedural mystery, Detective Frank Kerrigan was demoted to Sergeant and banished to foot patrol on Staten Island when he arrested a drunk driver with powerful connections. Kerrigan was transferred to the 122nd precinct in New Dorp, which is described (inaccurately) as "the farthest station in Staten Island" and "a sort of Siberia for Manhattan policemen." Kerrigan occupies his time with traffic summonses and tracking down stolen pigeons from a backyard coop. Called back into service in Manhattan for a hopeless case, Kerrigan and a female officer manage to locate a key witness and win official kudos. However, Kerrigan still cannot escape his exile and returns to New Dorp, which a colleague describes as having no bigger crimes than bicycle theft.

52. Hellstrom, Christopher. *Fresh Kills*. n.l.: Third Eve Books, 2009. 111pp.

This "genre defying experimental work of fiction" is a collection of interwoven short stories and poems that focus on a core group of Staten Islanders: Barry Starr, an amoral political operative; Mike Corona, an eccentric Futurist whose single good idea made him a millionaire by age twenty-nine; Dean Lopresti, an aspiring politician who pins his hope for office on his membership in the secret society, *The Secret Order of the Amoroc*; the author, Chris Hellstrom; and Max Bancroft, a slob of a bus driver who pines for his lost youth.

During a political fundraiser at Li Greci's Staaten, Dean Lopresti hires the services of Barry Starr who, with a phone call, promptly manufactures a scandalous drunk driving accident involving Lopresti's opponent. When Mike Corona, the bearded, vitamin-popping, paranoid millionaire, catches his wife cheating, he takes his infant daughter and moves into a fallout shelter on Todt Hill, where he takes to the airwaves to raise community awareness of nuclear disaster. He begins a relationship with the wife of his wife's lover. When she dies of cancer, Corona cryogenically freezes her in his facility bordering the Fresh Kills landfill. Max Bancroft, a sad-sack city bus driver whose only love is his TV, had dreams of being a rock star when he was a teenager in 1987. He had given a demo tape to his girlfriend, the Coney Island Snake Girl, but the tape was lost when she was murdered by a serial killer while hiking the Appalachian Trail. The tape had actually made its way into the hands of her infant niece, who rediscovered it in her college years, and put its hit song on the internet, where it went viral, ultimately bringing Bancroft fame and personal validation.

Starr quips that the Roman Empire moved to Staten Island and that a last name ending in a vowel is a prerequisite for political success here. He notes that although the dump made three-eyed fish, it also made hot Italian girls. Corona notes that everyone on Staten Island looks like they're going to the gym, what with the ubiquity of velvet track suits. Overdevelopment is a big political issue.

53. Hoff, B.J. *Winds of Graystone Manor.* Minneapolis, Minn: Bethany House Publishers, 1995. 318pp.

   In an isolated area of Staten Island, "[s]omewhere in the hills behind Fort Wadsworth and the place called the Haunted Swamp…" is located the stately old boardinghouse called Graystone Manor where, in the year 1867, the handsome and mysterious Irishman Roman St. Clare comes to take a room. A professional photographer who was a protégé of Mathew Brady and who was commended by President Lincoln, Roman has been traveling about the country for three years searching for the murderer of his wife Kathleen and their unborn child. Theirs was one in an apparently related series of murders in which the wives of prominent photographers were killed and, in a grisly twist, their photo taken and later mailed to the grieving husband. A crime of that description has recently taken place in Manhattan, which is what brought Roman to New York.

   Arriving at Graystone Manor in his wagon-cum-photography studio, accompanied by his wolfhound Conor, he quickly learns that Staten Island is in a state of panic due to a rash of mysterious crimes. Beginning with grave robberies near the old Quarantine hospital, Negro children from Stapleton have begun to disappear and later turn up murdered and mutilated. Roman goes into Manhattan to follow the leads related to his wife's murder, but quickly becomes preoccupied by the young and beautiful proprietress of Graystone Manor, Amanda (Andy) Fairchild. The attraction is immediate and mutual, but will remain unspoken for some time. Andy has another admirer, in the form of Dr. Niles Rutherford, a childhood friend with a tragic family history of insanity and suicide. Andy, however, loves him only as a friend and has rebuffed his marriage proposals, although she toys with the idea of becoming his wife.

   Christian themes are prominent: St. Clare met his late wife in a Washington hospital while recuperating from a wound at Gettysburg. She taught him about love and brought him to God. His relationship with God is evident and after a night of prayer it is revealed to him that Andy will be his wife. Before he can propose to an ailing Andy, she is surreptitiously drugged with laudanum by Dr. Rutherford and, under the pretense of taking her to the hospital, whisked away to a cell in the basement of his ostensibly abandoned family home in the woods near Tompkinsville. Rutherford is revealed to be the perpetrator of the grave robberies and the murders. With the goal of curing insanity and becoming a wealthy man from the sale of his new serum, he has been conducting medical experiments on his victims that would render useless the part of the brain that controls free choice and individuality. He has brought Andy to his lair to inject her as well and thus eradicate her "destructive independence" and resistance to marriage. St. Clare in the meantime has discovered that Andy never made it the hospital and tracks her down to the Rutherford house. With the help of his dog, he breaks in and rescues Andy from an imminent chemical lobotomy. Rutherford resists and in the struggle an oil lamp breaks, setting the house on fire. Rutherford's mind snaps in the chaos and he reverts to a childhood personality. He locks himself in a room and dies in the fire. The book ends with the engagement of Roman and Andy and reveals their plan to travel, pursuing Roman's photography business and searching for his wife's murderer.

This book was meant to be the first in a trilogy, but no sequels have been published. Most of the book takes place on Staten Island and a good many locations, landmarks and historical events are mentioned, including the Vanderbilt mansion, the Ward-Nixon house, the draft riots, the Civil War encampments, St. Patrick's church, Doctors' Hospital and others.

54. Holding, Elisabeth Sanxay. *The Unlit Lamp; a Story of Inter-Actions*. New York: E.P. Dutton, 1922. 334pp.
   In this fictional study of male/female relationships and the dangers for women in unfulfilling marriages, young Gilbert Vincelle, at the urging of a friend, travels from Brooklyn in 1890 to attend a dance on Staten Island in order to see the "prettiest girl there was to see." At the top of a hill lives the Mason family, whose bohemian home is a center of music, warm hospitality, intellectual and artistic pursuits. Daughter Claudine is wooed and won by Gilbert, who brings her to live with him and his domineering mother in their emotionally cold Brooklyn home. The exuberant and talented Claudine is gradually stifled in a loveless marriage. Years later one of their headstrong daughters, Andrée, finds herself in her own difficult marriage to a wealthy Christian Socialist. When Claudine falls ill, she goes to recuperate in her childhood home

on Staten Island, which serves as an almost magical restorative for her health, her daughter's marriage and for her own, as Gilbert comes to spend the summer with her there and they rekindle their youthful romance in the gardens of the joyful house in the Staten Island hills.

55. Hopkins, George R. *Letters from the Dead.* Outskirts Press, 2013. 304pp.

In this third of a quintet of novels featuring NYPD Detective Tom Cavanaugh and his half-brother Jack Bennis, a Special Forces soldier turned Jesuit priest, Cavanaugh is exiled to the Tottenville precinct on Staten Island (here called the 120th for unknown reasons) by his enemies in the offices of the Mayor and the Brooklyn D.A. Compared to his former precinct in Brooklyn, Tottenville is a sleepy backwater, where graffiti and missing cats are the most serious crimes occupying the police force. Meanwhile, Father Bennis has taken up temporary residence at "St. John Berchmann's" with a woman he brought back from his adventures in Cuba. Tempted by her attractions, he questions his priestly vows and obtains a six month leave of absence from the priesthood, during which he takes a teaching job at the prestigious Garfield Academy. Not long before a Garfield student took her own life in what was thought to be a case of cyberbullying. Detective Cavanaugh's testimony had been instrumental in undermining the case against the accused, another Garfield student. Nevertheless, the victim's father- calling himself the Lex Talionis (Law of Retaliation) killer- undertakes a murder spree against everyone he perceived as having killed his daughter or failed in giving her justice, bringing Cavanaugh and Bennis together in an investigation. The brothers eventually discover that the killer is the school librarian, who commits suicide on top of Moses Mountain rather than be arrested.

This novel contains a significant amount of Staten Island settings, such as R.H. Tugs, Duffy's and Ni Ni's restaurants. Cavanaugh and his pregnant fiancée are settling down to life on the island and buy an abandoned church on Arthur Kill Road to be converted into a home.

56. Hopkins, George R. *Random Acts of Malice.* Xlibris, 2014. 284pp.

This fourth in a quintet of mystery and adventure novels featuring NYPD detective Tom Cavanaugh and his half-brother Father Jack Bennis, revolves around a series of mysterious Staten Island murders. When an upright local judge, Carlo Abbruzza, finds out that Tamika Washington, a woman he had sentenced to prison for child abuse, was threatening his life, he turns to an old friend, Tom Cavanaugh, for help.

Cavanaugh, still in exile at the 123rd precinct, dismisses the threats as jailhouse boasting, but when other key figure from Tamika's trial start turning up dead, Cavanaugh begins to investigate. His brother, Father Jack Bennis, becomes involved as well when his parishioner at Our Lady Help of Christians, the jury forewoman at Tamika's trial, is brutally murdered after Mass and Bennis notices a psychopathic member of his old Special Forces unit, Earle Nelson, lingering at the crime scene.

As it turns out, William George Fuller, a shadowy billionaire businessman, had hired Nelson as an assassin in order to intimidate the honest Judge Abbruzza into recusing himself from a case involving a low-level drug dealer who was related to the leader of a prominent Mexican drug cartel. Wanting to impress his Mexican criminal associates with his power, Fuller had promised to remove Abbruzza from the case and replace him with a judge who was under Fuller's control. Rather than simply kill Abbruzza, Fuller- a manipulative psychopath- orchestrated the whole Tamika Washington cover story in order to confuse the police. However, with Abbruzza unmoved, Fuller ordered his assassination. Nelson disguises himself as a woman, sets off some bombs as a diversion and shoots Abbruzza in front of his Oakland Avenue home. Believing Abbruzza dead, due to fake news reports planted by Cavanaugh, Fuller meets with his Mexican associates who brutally murder him when they find out the truth (Abbruzza had worn a bulletproof vest and survived). Nelson, however, disguises himself as a nun and tries to assassinate his old commander, Bennis, while he was celebrating Mass at Our Lady Help of Christians. He does manage to hit Bennis, but is killed by a retired cop in the congregation. Bennis' fate is left unresolved.

Staten Island content abounds. The OLHC parishioner who was murdered was a teacher at I.S. 7. Another murder victim was killed on the SIRR. Tottenville is described as a place that aliens would have a hard time finding. The murders are at first contracted by a middle man in Tompkinsville. The Staten Island judiciary and district attorney's office is described as corrupt and incompetent. Earle Nelson worked part time at the Hilton and was hiding out in an abandoned maritime museum on Bay Street. After his "assassination" of the judge, he flees to the Forest Avenue Starbucks in West Brighton. Father Bennis notes that Staten Island used to be a peaceful place and that although some people blame the Verrazano Bridge for what it became, he believes that people in general have just lost all sense of morality. And finally, the author acknowledges retired Judge Charles A. Kuffner Jr. for his help and advice in writing the book.

57. Hopkins, George R. *Unholy Retribution*. CreateSpace, 2015. 294pp.
  While recovering in the hospital from the wounds he received in *Random Acts of Malice,* the severed head of his Moslem roommate is placed in Father Jack Bennis' bed. Although a vindictive detective from the 122nd precinct is desperate to implicate Bennis in that murder and for subsequent killings of Staten Island Moslems, the accusation doesn't quite stick, even though Bennis is tenuously connected with each case. Action ranges from Crooke's Point to Randall Manor and with the help of his half-brother, Detective Tom Cavanaugh, Bennis is exonerated and the true murderer uncovered.

58. Joyce, Eddie. *Small Mercies*. New York: Viking, 2015. 353pp.
  Advertised as the author's "love letter to Staten Island", this novel explores the struggles of the Amendolas, a typical Italian/Irish family from Great Kills, ten years after the death of their youngest son Bobby, a firefighter, on September 11th. When Bobby's widow, Tina, announces that she is finally dating again and plans to invite her new man to her son's upcoming birthday party, a panoply of emotions and memories are stirred up among Bobby's family.

  His father, Michael, a Vietnam veteran and retired firefighter, is focused on continuing his family's tradition of entering the NCAA betting pool at Cody's bar (a transparent stand-in for the famous, real-life pool at Jody's Club Forest). The pool seems to him to be one of the few links he has with his family's happier past and the last remaining method they have for achieving any sort of bond. When he became a firefighter in the 1960s, Michael had defied his immigrant father's wish that he take over the family butcher shop in Dongan Hills. Now, Michael wonders if Bobby would be alive today if he himself had not chosen the dangerous career that his own son would emulate. He would leave the island if he could, but his wife, Gail, won't hear of it. "This is not the place he grew up, not even the place his kids grew up. He and Gail live in the shadow of tragedy, in the overcrowded ruins of a once spacious paradise, surrounded by morons who act like they're constantly auditioning for a reality television program that prizes stupidity, classlessness, and thuggish bravado."

Gail, an Irish-American by blood, but an "Italian by borough" undergoes heartache at what she sees as the breakdown of her family: her youngest son Bobby is dead, and she fears that his widow will marry this new man and move to California with her grandkids, recalling the guilt she felt when she left her own family in Brooklyn to move to Staten Island when she got married; middle son Frankie is a alcoholic ne'er-do-well in his late 30s, whose rage over his brother's death leads him to violently assault an Arab cab driver at the Whitehall ferry terminal and almost assault another Arab in the Mall; and the oldest son Peter, a successful Manhattan lawyer who lives in Westchester, rejects his hometown as the "servants' quarters of the city" and the values he grew up with, although his life seems to return again and again to Staten Island, most notoriously in a workplace affair with a first year associate from his hometown to whom he had once awarded the Bobby Amendola Memorial scholarship when she was a schoolgirl. Now, banished from his family home after the affair became known, he crashes on the couch at a friend's St. George apartment, being awakened each morning by the fog horn of the ferry. A final blow occurs for the Amendolas when a federal investigation shuts down the venerable NCAA pool at Cody's, killing once and for all a treasured family bond. When they all gather together for the birthday party and meet Tina's boyfriend, they find him tolerable, if not eminently likeable, and come to terms with the passage of life.

Staten Island themes, locales and archetypes imbue almost every page of this novel. Irish and Italian-American mixed families hold the St. Patrick's Day parade on Forest Avenue and the Cody's (Jody's) NCAA pool as hallowed community traditions. Tina prefers to take her new boyfriend to Port Richmond's Denino's (described as having the best pizza in the city) rather than go to a fancy Manhattan restaurant. The characters' occupations have the very short range of firefighter, police officer, sanitation worker, Con Edison worker (for men) and nurse, teacher or stay-at-home mother (for women). The Amendola boys went to Farrell, where Bobby was a basketball star. The overdevelopment of the island is a familiar theme ("like some of the builders have personal vendettas against trees..."), as is the strong attachment to the place and the guilt characters feel when they think about leaving. However, despite being a place "with a distaste for newcomers", the island is changing. Michael Amendola is put off by the unfriendly new Russians who moved into the house of long-time Italian neighbors. And Frankie finds himself growing enraged seeing Moslem women wearing hijabs in the Mall.

59. Kelter, Lawrence. *Our Honored Dead.* n.l.: F Street Books, 2012. 256pp.
      In this fourth installment of the Stephanie Chalice mystery series, NYPD detectives Stephanie Chalice and Gus Lido, partners and lovers, begin an investigation of a series of gruesome murders that have a strange Kabbalistic twist. When their beloved retired boss, Nick Sonellio from Staten Island, asks them to run some fingerprints of a suspected burglar, the two seemingly unconnected cases come together when the Jacoby family in Sonellio's neighborhood (near Bancroft Avenue and Edison Street in Grant City) are found murdered.

      A bodybuilding psychotic from Staten Island named Michael Tillerman becomes the focus of the investigation. Chalice and Lido discover that Tillerman has a connection to a local funeral home where a corpse was found roasted in the crematorium. They also tie him to the murder of a woman in the waters under the Verrazano Bridge and to a break-in at a pharmaceutical company near the Outerbridge where thousands of antipsychotic pills were stolen. Tillerman gains possession of the corpses of the family he murdered, by disguising himself as a funeral home worker and tricking the workers at the Medical Examiner's office, located at Seaview Hospital. He then travels into the Greenbelt where he engages in an occult ritual with an unnamed person. A tip from a waitress at a highly-praised Hylan Boulevard diner leads Chalice and Lido to one of Sonellio's friends, Giacomo Babocci, the genial proprietor of a local men's-only cigar bar that caters to Italian-Americans of a certain age.

      The detectives eventually discover the embalmed bodies of Babocci's handicapped son, Tillerman and the Jacoby family behind the wall of the Babocci's basement. Apparently bitter over his son's maiming and literal emasculation in the Gulf War, which came about indirectly while rescuing an Israeli family, Babocci persuaded the unstable Tillerman that he could reunite him with his own murdered family if he murdered the people he told him to. After murdering his own son and Tillerman, Babocci hid the embalmed bodies in a home-like setting, so they could be a family for eternity.

60. Khoudari, Amy S. *Looking in the Shadows; The Life of Alice Austen.* Lincoln, Neb: iUniverse, 2006. 149pp.

   In this fictionalized autobiography of famed Staten Island photographer Alice Austen, the author attempts to explore and explain Austen's inner life and motivations by "looking in the shadows" of her photographs and letters to find the message that Austen was compelled to conceal during her lifetime, namely that of her purported lesbianism. As narrated by an elderly Austen, she tells the story of her life, from her idyllic childhood to her present destitution at Staten Island's Farm Colony in the 1950s.

   Abandoned by her father, Austen and her mother move to Clear Comfort, her grandparents' Rosebank home. Austen recounts her early interest in photography, at that time an unusual pastime for a girl. Austen's growing awareness of her "differentness" is a recurrent theme throughout the book. Eschewing the traditional pursuits of Victorian women, she comes to acknowledge that she prefers the company of ladies to gentlemen, and eventually comes to accept her lesbianism and form a relationship with Gertrude Tate, with whom she spent a great portion of her life. She speculates on the sexual orientation of several of their female friends, most of whom gave into convention and married. In every other respect though, Austen shared the tastes, the mores and prejudices of her class.

   She tells of vacations in the Catskills, a boat trip to Washington D.C. and a visit to the Chicago World's Fair of 1893. She always maintains a proper Anglo-Saxon rectitude in dress and demeanor and expresses concern for the continued dominance of the WASP American establishment. After the death of Austen's mother, Gertrude Tate moves into Clear Comfort, where she and Alice keep a household until the Great Depression forces them to lose the property, to a family of slovenly Italians no less. Adding insult to injury, a chiseling Jew gets all of Austen's possessions at fire sale prices, after which she moves into Staten Island's poor house, the Farm Colony. When a man named Harold Oglesby discovers her photographs and acts to have them published, she uses the proceeds to move into a nicer apartment.

61. Kingsbury, Karen. *Beyond Tuesday Morning.* Grand Rapids, Mich.: Zondervan, 2004. 316pp.

    In the wake of the 9/11 terrorist attack and the events described in *One Tuesday Morning,* Jamie Bryan becomes a volunteer at St. Paul's Chapel in Manhattan, offering a comforting presence to those who come in to pray or talk. Fellow volunteer Aaron Hisel, Jake Bryan's former boss, wants to begin a relationship with Jamie, but she recoils out of attachment to Jake's memory and for the fact that Aaron is not a Christian. In Los Angeles, Eric Michaels is enjoying a vibrant and renewed family life but his brother, police officer Clay Michaels, is single and alone. Following a shootout in which he kills a murderer in self-defense, Clay is put on standard administrative leave during which he chooses to take advantage of detective training in New York City. He and his partner Joe Reynolds travel to New York where they stay in a Staten Island hotel. While traveling to Manhattan on the ferry, Jamie is almost abducted and raped by three men when Clay and Joe rescue her. The attraction between Jamie and Eric is electric and the two start spending more and more time together. Jamie can't fathom seeing another man or leaving Staten Island to be with him, but a note in Jake's Bible that tells her to "choose life" ends her resistance and she and Clay marry and move to California.

62. Kingsbury, Karen. *One Tuesday Morning.* Grand Rapids, Mich.: Zondervan, 2003. 352pp.

    This Christian-themed novel deals with the way three people coped with personal loss from the tragic events of 9/11 and rediscovered their relationship with God. Jake Bryan is a firefighter from Staten Island who is also a strong and committed Christian. His wife Jamie has come to declare herself an atheist after enduring the untimely deaths of her own parents and having to attend myriad funerals for firefighters through the years. They live with their young daughter in the neighborhood of Westerleigh, a place described as "elite" but "quaint," where everyone knows everyone. Jake desperately wants Jamie to come to God, but doesn't push her.

    Jamie's path will eventually cross with Eric Michaels, a successful Los Angeles businessman whose devotion to his work has resulted in neglect of his wife and son. Although a believer at one time, Eric turned his back on God when his daughter was stillborn. Eric is called to New York for a meeting at the South Tower of the World Trade Center on 9/11, the same morning that Jake Bryan is reporting to work at his Manhattan firehouse. As Michaels is evacuating the building after the attack, he briefly crosses paths with Jake Bryan ascending the stairwell to aid victims. Incredibly, the two men are physically identical. Jake Bryan dies in the collapse of the tower but Eric Michaels is rescued from the debris and mistaken for Jake. He has amnesia so he believes Jamie and the doctors when they tell him that he is Jake Bryan. Jamie takes Eric home to Staten Island, where he begins reading Jake's Bible and spiritual journal. The more he reads what he thinks were his own words, the more he rediscovers the faith he rejected when he lost his daughter. His newfound faith also inspires Jamie and when both of them attend church, they respond to the altar call and rededicate their lives to Christ.

Gradually though, Jamie and Jake's colleagues start to notice something off about "Jake's" appearance and mannerisms. His true identity is revealed when Jamie notices a discrepancy in Jake's blood type on some medical documents and she has tests performed. Jamie does some detective work and figures out that her "husband" is actually Eric Michaels, the missing businessman from L.A. Eric regains his memory and is reunited with his family. His experience has made him a better husband and father, while Jamie, although now a widow, has gained the relationship with God that her husband always wanted.

63. Kolff, Cornelius G. *The Haven of Wooden Shoes*. Staten Island, N.Y.: Richmond Borough Publishing & Printing, 1939. 20pp.
    This whimsical story relates the history of the Dutch fairies of Staten Island. On a peninsula in Clifton which was formed from the discarded shells of local fishermen, the fairies would hold their high festivals at the midnight hour. A shanty dweller on the peninsula collected the wooden shoes that Dutch immigrants would throw overboard as they sailed into New York Harbor, and the fairies would use the shoes for boats and sleighs.

64. Kolff, Cornelius G. *Staten Island Fairies*. Staten Island, N.Y.: Richmond Borough Publishing Company, 1939. 48pp.
    Employing the artifice of false documents, the author (one-time President of the S.I. Historical Society) claims to have received this manuscript from the Fairies of Staten Island who, recognizing that encroaching suburban sprawl will soon drive them from the island, wish to preserve their culture and history for the enlightenment and edification of posterity. This quite detailed history of the little people

gives us the exact location of their castle in Greenridge, and includes a map showing where the various groups of fairies live. According to this history, every major ethnic group on Staten Island (Irish, Germans, Poles, et al) has a corresponding group of fairies who share their respective national characteristics. Interspersed with the fairy stories is a great deal of actual Staten Island history.

65. Kuczkir, Mary and Roberta Anderson [Fern Michaels, pseud.]. *Cinders to Satin*. New York: Ballantine Books, 1984. 499pp.

Spunky but impoverished Dublin teenager Callie James is sent by her family to New York during the Irish potato famine to find a better life. After a miserable voyage across the Atlantic, New York Harbor officials discover typhus aboard ship and order the passengers confined at the Quarantine Station in Tompkinsville. Living conditions there are brutal and inequitable treatment of the poor is described, as are the porous quality of the facility's gates (peddlers, friends and family members are allowed to come ago, a foreshadowing perhaps of the spread of disease to the surrounding community, which led to the destruction of the Quarantine by vigilantes in 1858.) Unscrupulous officials falsely claim that Callie has lice in order to shave her hair and sell it to perruquiers. And when a family she befriended aboard ship is told that their child has tuberculosis and must return to Ireland, the desperate, pregnant mother drowns herself and the child in order to ensure that her husband can enter the United States. The victims are buried in a common grave behind the hospital.

Finally released from the Quarantine, she meets up with a cousin in Manhattan, who attempts to turn her out as a prostitute in his brothel. The sex workers, taking pity on the young girl, immediately spirit her away to a charitable institution for fallen women, which turns out to be a brutal sweatshop. Byrch Kenyon, a newspaper editor who had run into Callie in Dublin, meets her again while conducting an investigation of such dubious charities, and rescues her from its clutches. He arranges a position for her with his friends, the Powers family, who live on Staten Island, described as a summer retreat for the city's wealthy. The Powers mansion is located on Todt Hill, anachronistically described as a wealthy enclave. Callie is engaged as governess for the youngest daughter, Mary, who struggles with a growing but secret deafness. Callie is pleased to see how Byrch's investigative exposé has resulted in the reform of the Quarantine Station and the opening of a modern hospital on Staten Island. While Byrch finds himself falling in love with the blossoming Callie, the oldest Powers son, the caddish Rossiter, seduces and impregnates her. Callie is dismissed and consents to a marriage of convenience with an older laborer, whose alcoholism soon consigns them to a shantytown in Manhattan, where a fire kills her husband and son. Byrch Kenyon again rescues Callie and brings her to his home where she becomes his lover and then his wife.

66. Latka, John. *Staten Island Memoirs*. Bloomington, Ind.: AuthorHouse, 2006. 576pp.

   In 2003 the sixty-six-year-old Paris Polanski reminisces over his life in Staten Island in the early 1960s, before the Verrazano Bridge was built. At first thinking to write a straightforward memoir, he instead relates his life story in the form of a fictional tale. A Grant City resident, Polanski studied mythology at "CCNY," where his professor taught about Helen of Troy and the supposed legend that she would be reborn and reunited with her lover Paris. Indeed, she was reborn in the person of the beautiful and privileged Helen Jones of Todt Hill, Staten Island. A pious Catholic child, Helen develops a rebellious streak, smoking marijuana and having premarital sex as a student at Wilson College, an apparent stand-in for Wagner College. Paris has his own experiences with the opposite sex, losing his virginity to an escort in a Clove Lakes high rise. However, all other women are forgotten when he spots Helen sitting at the Corner Steak House in New Dorp in 1961. Lacking the courage to approach her, he has the good fortune to come to her rescue when her car gets stuck in the snow. They develop a relationship and finally declare their love aboard a Staten Island Rapid Transit train. Helen had dreamt of Paris and continues to receive prophetic communications and advice in her dreams from the original Helen of Troy.

   Paris graduates from college with an engineering degree and begins work at Bell Laboratories, while simultaneously receiving a commission as an Ensign in the Naval Reserves. He encourages Helen, a former Ms. Staten Island, to pursue her dream to be a fashion model, which she does successfully. The glamorous life of high fashion exacerbates Helen's drinking problem, which she eventually treats with AA meetings. She and Paris move in together in a Clove Lakes apartment. Paris is called up to serve in Naval Intelligence in Vietnam, where he has many dangerous adventures. On leave back in New York, Paris and Helen get married. Helen is already pregnant and gives birth to a girl they name Helen, while Paris is sent back to Vietnam. After being wounded, Paris returns to Staten Island, while Helen goes to Hollywood to audition for a movie. Helen begins abusing alcohol and marijuana again, which leads to her being sexually assaulted by a predatory director. He does jail time, but is mysteriously murdered after his release, whether by Paris or one of his associates is unknown. Paris and Helen then have a son, whom they name Paris. The story is finally revealed to be untrue. Paris Polanski was a sixty-six-year-old divorcé, an "incurable romantic", who had obsessed his whole life over a girl he had helped out of a snow drift in 1961, but never pursued. The entire book had been an exercise in imagining the kind of life Paris wished he had lived. Now, he finally takes action by going to Wilson College with the intention of finding the girl's identity in the old yearbooks. He doesn't need to go that far, as the girl herself, by the name of Virginia Erickson, is sitting at the front desk of the library. She tells Paris that she had been expecting him as well.

This novel references many Staten Island neighborhoods, restaurants and bars, and describes the leisure activities of young people of the early 1960s, such as riding the bumper cars at South Beach or picnicking at Clove Lakes. Commuting to the city by ferryboat was a necessity. Like many American communities of the time, the 1960s were a time of transition between the traditional morals and mores of the past and the libertine culture of the modern age. Thus, Helen engages in premarital sex, and develops both an alcohol and drug problem. Two characters die of drug overdoses. The Vietnam War creates fissures in the community. There are anti-war protests and violent confrontations. The cultural changes are not attributed to the opening of the Verrazano Bridge, but the pre-bridge era on Staten Island is depicted as somewhat idyllic.

67. Ledbetter, Gladys Manée. *A Wideness in God's Mercy*. New York: Vantage Press, 1965. 445pp.
    Written by the descendant of an old Staten Island Huguenot family, this work of historical fiction traces the fortunes of the Pilou family of Staten Island from the days of the Stamp Act through the Revolution to the fight over Constitutional ratification.

The story begins in 1765, at the time of the Stamp Act and revolves around the Huguenot Pilou family of Bentley Village, Staten Island. The Pilous are made up of Peter and Marie, their children Polly, Suson, Ann, Betsey, William and oldest son James, a student at King's College and a member of the Sons of Liberty. The Pilous are friends and neighbors of Christopher Billopp, the Lord of Bentley Manor and an ardent Tory. Except for James, most of the Pilous share Billopp's Royalist opinions, as they are still grateful to the British crown for providing refuge to their ancestors who fled religious persecution in France. Their sympathies are tested when Billopp announces his intention to persuade General Gage in Manhattan to order his troops to fire upon the crowds protesting the Stamp Act, among which may be James.

With the repeal of the Act, things return to normal. Suson Pilou marries Etienne Latourette, a stable hand at Billopp Manor and begins a family with him. When she dies, Etienne marries her sister Betsey and has more children with her. James meanwhile is courting the beautiful and independent Honorat Pillot. When he delays in marrying her, she marries another man, but more is to be heard from her later. After becoming a lawyer, James marries Hildejonde VerPlank. Although they differ politically, Billopp employs James to represent his business interests in New Hampshire, where he befriends John Sullivan, the future Revolutionary General and raider of Staten Island.

As war clouds gather and the Revolution begins, Peter Pilou starts to share his son's belief in American independence. He even starts to attend subversive meetings at the Christopher House, where he is wounded in a raid by Christopher Billopp, now commander of the Staten Island Native Loyalist militia. Staten Island is occupied by 24,000 British troops, with 1000 being quartered between the Billopp and Pilou properties. Two officers, the Wigger twins, are quartered with the Pilous and strive for the affections of daughter Polly.

Meanwhile, James attends the Continental Congress where he runs into Honorat Laurent (née Pillot) and discovers that their passion for each other has survived their respective marriages. He flees from her arms into the Continental Army where he fights in the Battle of Long Island and wounds Nicholas Wigger, his sister Polly's eventual husband. She cannot forgive James for permanently maiming her dashing Redcoat, so she resolves to destroy her brother. She ends up hung by her own petard as she accidentally falls down the stairs and dies while searching for an incriminating letter of James'.

The adventures of James, and his brother William- also a Continental soldier- are varied and numerous. The characters participate in many famous Revolutionary incidents and cross paths with many noted figures: William fights in the Battle of Princeton and joins the guerrilla band of Francis Marion. While fighting Indians in upstate New York, he finds a woman in an isolated wilderness cabin and marries her. James meets Nathan Hale and participates in the encampments at Morristown and Valley Forge. He fights under Dan Morgan and participates in the raid on Staten Island under the command of his friend John Sullivan. (The Lord Stirling raid on Staten Island is also described).

With the war's end, Christopher Billopp goes into Canadian exile and his property is confiscated. James and Honorat marry, shifting the story to Honorat's son Eliaz, an aspiring lawyer who finds himself in the middle of the rivalry between Aaron Burr and Alexander Hamilton. The books ends with Eliaz finding his true calling in life by becoming a minister and going to live on Staten Island with his family, where he belongs.

Marriages, births and death abound in this story, as do many recognizable Staten Island names: the Billopps, the Seamans, the Latourettes, the Androvettes, the Mersereaus, etc.

68. Loehfelm, Bill. *Bloodroot*. New York: G.P. Putnam's Sons, 2009. 326pp.
Kevin Curran is a history instructor at Richmond College on Staten Island whose area of specialization is the Revolutionary War. On his thirtieth birthday, his brother Danny, a heroin addict, reappears in his life after being out of contact for years. In the course of taking his brother out for a birthday drink, which the men never manage to get, Danny drives to various locations on Staten Island to make several suspicious transactions and finally shoots up heroin while parked on Todt Hill.

Kevin doesn't hear from Danny again for another three years. When he does return, Danny claims that he is drug-free, having literally died and been revived after overdosing. He is dressing expensively and living in an upscale apartment above an Italian restaurant in Park Slope, and making a living installing sound systems for local yuppies. He reveals to Kevin that he also installs surreptitious surveillance cameras in his client's homes so that the Mafia boss, Santoro, can use the footage for leverage and blackmail.

As the brothers are hanging out, Al Bruno, their mutual high school friend and Danny's current associate, comes rushing up to Danny raving about an emergency job they have to perform. Danny insists that Kevin come along, which he does somewhat hesitantly. The men drive to Staten Island, where they dig up two corpses that Bruno had buried in the graveyard of the former Bloodroot children's hospital in Willowbrook. They take the bodies to the closed landfill, which is in the process of being transformed into a park, and burned them. Kevin, the involuntary participant, receives $5,000 from the underboss that Danny and Al Bruno work for, blood money which Kevin keeps.

The Bloodroot Children's Hospital, located in Willowbrook Park, was an institution for disabled children that became notorious for the abuse and mistreatment of its disabled and orphaned charges. The Curran brothers' grandfather, Dr. O'Malley, had been instrumental in its closing in the 1970s. The Dean of Kevin's department, Alvin Whitestone, specializes in the history of Bloodroot and has even started an activist group, Friends of Bloodroot, to agitate for the conversion of the abandoned hospital into a commemorative museum.

The hospital figures large in Kevin's life when he learns that Mafia boss Santoro has the construction contact to build dorms for the Richmond College campus. The only obstacle is Dean Whitestone and the Bloodroot hospital. Danny uses Kevin's faculty access to bug Whitestone's office, in a fishing expedition for incriminating information. Kevin's resistance is undermined when Danny reveals that he had been adopted from Bloodroot at the age of five, and believes that the horrible building should be knocked down and forgotten.

Danny later tells Kevin that he discovered images and videos on Dean Whitestone's computer, of Bloodroot children being sexually molested and physically abused. He claims that Whitestone had been selling these files to perverts all over the world, and resolves to kill Whitestone. Kevin tracks down Danny to the roof of the Bloodroot hospital, which he had set on fire and where he had brought Whitestone at gunpoint. Danny does murder Whitestone (and Al Bruno) and (to Kevin's eyes) jumped off the roof to his death. Kevin barely escapes with his life.

Santoro ends up demolishing the ruins of the hospital and making millions from the dorm building contract. The fire and the murder are blamed on Al Bruno. Danny's body is not found, since he escaped the fire and moved to Las Vegas.

Staten Island locations abound and are sometimes described: Richmond Terrace, Todt Hill, Park Hill, the Red Spot club, the Cargo Cafe, Willowbrook Park, the Fresh Kills landfill (and future park) and the College of Staten Island and the Willowbrook State School (thinly disguised as Richmond College and the Bloodroot Hospital). Staten Island, one character says, was "boring as hell, fourteen miles long and had the gravitational pull of Jupiter."

69. Loehfelm, Bill. *The Devil She Knows*. New York: Sarah Crichton Books; Farrar, Straus and Giroux, 2011. 322pp.

Maureen Coughlin is a twenty-nine-year-old barmaid who lives in a dingy apartment on Staten Island. A Richmond College dropout, she has a cocaine habit and works serving drinks at the Narrows, a bar on Dock Street in Stapleton. On a night she is working, a big fund raiser is being held at the Narrows for Frank Sebastian, a candidate for State Senate from the South Shore. Maureen is told that Sebastian is a friend of the bar owner, Vic, and was given use of the Narrows' private room for free. It is rumored that Sebastian, the owner of a security company, hired people to break into homes on Todt Hill so that the owners would retain his firm.

During the evening, Maureen sneaks a bit too much cocaine and booze, and wakes up after hours in the office of the bar manager, Dennis. When she emerges, she witnesses Dennis performing a sex act on Sebastian, but pretends as if she didn't see anything. Sebastian noticed her however, and confronts her outside the bar, extracting a promise from her to forget about what she saw, which she willingly gives. When she goes to work the next day, the other employees tell her that Dennis is dead after being hit by the train at the end of Dock Street. It is assumed that he passed out on the tracks but Maureen immediately suspects Sebastian. She flees to the Cargo Cafe on Bay Street, which is owned by her upstairs neighbor John, who comforts her and drives her home. When she finds her front door ajar, she tells the whole story to John, who asks his friend, NYPD Detective Nat Waters, to investigate. Her apartment had indeed been ransacked, and she comes to learn that it had been by two men who claimed to be policemen. Sebastian begins making threatening phone calls to Maureen.

Maureen next meets up at the Cargo Cafe with her co-worker Tanya. Tanya reveals that she had dated Dennis, and that he had been in debt to Sebastian. To pay off the loan, he agreed to make sex tapes with Tanya for Sebastian, but then told her that he made other arrangements, which presumably was his sexual submission to Sebastian. However, Sebastian was now demanding the tapes, which were still at Dennis' house. Tanya asked for Maureen's help in retrieving them. When she arrived at the apartment, Sebastian was waiting for her and began to physically threaten her, only escaping when Dennis' brother inadvertently showed up. Maureen decided to hide out with her mother, Amber, on Bovanizer Street. Sebastian finds out and shows up at the house with his wife, since they both had been long time friends with Amber, and even knew Maureen as a girl. Sebastian is a pillar of St. Stephen's church and even set up an outreach program between the church and a battered women's shelter. Maureen then flees her mother's home to stay with John and his girlfriend.

Det. Waters tells Maureen that Dennis had been strangled before being place on the railroad tracks. He also tells Maureen that Tanya was found dead in the Arthur Kill. Waters eventually reveals that he had once served under Sebastian, an ex-cop, in Brooklyn. Sebastian was a brutal, violent cop who beat and raped the street kids who were his informants. One night Waters, not realizing it was Sebastian, shot him when he noticed him beating up a young female prostitute. The NYPD covered up the real story and Sebastian retired with honors. Maureen decides to take the initiative and demands the truth about Sebastian from the Narrows' owner, Vic, at gunpoint. He admits that Sebastian, along with the Russian mob, owns most of the Narrows. He tells her that Sebastian could currently be found at a certain NJ motel. She drives there and spies Sebastian inside a room overseeing the filming of a torture porn video. She calls Det. Waters and tells him where Sebastian can be found. She is noticed leaving, is followed, rammed and kidnapped by Sebastian and his henchman. They bring her back to Staten Island, near the Outerbridge Crossing, "a forgotten corner of a forgotten borough." When they open the trunk in which she was thrown, she kills Sebastian's accomplice and wounds Sebastian himself. Their struggle takes them to the tracks of the old Atlantic train station where Maureen kills Sebastian with a broken bottle. Det. Waters shows up just in time to pull Maureen from the tracks before the train passes. She in turn gives him CPR when he has a heart attack. Maureen turns her life around, and moves back home with her mother, who is now dating Det. Waters.

The books takes place almost entirely on Staten Island, which is depicted as a place rife with official corruption, where it is extremely difficult to know whom to trust. It is a stratified borough, divided between the working/middle class sections and the private streets of South Shore McMansions where the rich wall themselves off from the rest. There is a subculture of night-life and seedy bars and drugs, of which Maureen is a part, and which is centered along Bay Street, with an outpost at the Black Garter Saloon. The island's past as a resort destination is mentioned, to contrast it with the modern island of overdevelopment and overcrowding, of strip malls, diners, barrooms, and blocks of identical houses. However, there are still unspoiled areas which, in this narrative, serve only to obscure the dark deeds of wicked men. Despite the burgeoning population, the island still retains the incestuous small-town culture of yesteryear, where everyone still knows everyone, and where those relationships are often the basis for criminal conspiracy.

70. Loehfelm, Bill. *Fresh Kills*. New York: G.P. Putnam's Sons, 2008. 326pp.
    John Sanders Jr., a thirty-one-year-old bartender at the Cargo Café on Bay Street, is awakened by Detective Nathaniel Waters (a recurring character in Loehfelm's novels) to be informed that his father, John Sr., has been murdered, execution style, in broad daylight on Richmond Avenue near the Eltingville train station. Due to his estrangement from his alcoholic, abusive father, Sanders remains ostensibly unaffected by the news, but feels like he can't help but get involved in the situation, if only for the sake of his younger sister Julia, a graduate student in Boston, who had attempted to retain some connection to their brutish father after their mother's early death. Both brother and sister exhibit psychological wounds, perhaps stemming from their abusive upbringing: John has issues with violence, alcohol and drugs, and is currently involved in a dead-end affair with his high school sweetheart, Molly, who is currently another man's fiancée; Julia has an eating disorder, is undergoing therapy and has a string of abusive lesbian relationships under her belt. During their preparations for their father's funeral, Sanders begins an investigation of his own, using his sister's

grief to justify his curiosity, but what appears to be developing into a murder mystery veers unexpectedly to become an extended interior process of Sanders finally achieving closure from all the harm that his father had inflicted upon him. When Det. Waters reveals that the murder was merely a case of mistaken identity and that the life of the organized crime figure who ordered the hit was being offered up by his apologetic superiors, Sanders declined, as he had finally found peace.

As in Loehfelm's other works, Staten Island is a grotesque place whose inhabitants are desperate to escape, usually to Manhattan, but are unable. It is described here as "The forgotten Fifth Borough. The Cultural Void. Home of the world-famous ferry, the world's largest garbage dump, and the world's largest collection of identical people." The narrative takes place within actual Staten Island physical locations. The protagonist grew up on Katan Avenue. His father played football for Farrell High School and Wagner College. Other physical settings include Scalia's funeral home, Joyce's Tavern on Richmond Avenue, the Crossroads Tavern (formerly the Choir Loft) in Stapleton, the Golden Dove diner, Clove Lakes Park, and a thinly disguised New Dorp High School. The Mall and the Fresh Kills landfill are described brutally, although it is noted that "the Dump" has become hallowed ground due to its role as resting place for 9/11 victims. Familiar cultural touchstones are referenced, such as Staten Island Italians' style of dress, the St. Patrick's Day parade, and the teenage hangout at the South Beach parking lot. A ferry ride is the occasion for poignant reflection on 9/11 and loss by Sanders and Molly.

71. Longfellow, Ki. *The Girl in the Next Room A Sam Russo Mystery; Case 3.* Port Orchard, Wash: EIO Books, 2013. 283pp.
    When his transvestite prostitute neighbor, Holly, is found in Tompkinsville Park badly beaten and stuffed in a duffel bag, private detective Sam Russo sets out to find the perpetrator in 1940s Staten Island. He starts his investigation at the Green Garter strip club on Hannah Street, where Holly sometimes performed singing torch songs. The owner reveals that he saw Holly get into a Bentley Lagonda on the night she disappeared. When Holly- who has been put up in the Manhattan penthouse of Russo's lover, Mrs. Willingford- finally revives, she reveals that she and two other prostitutes were taken to a big mansion in the middle of Staten Island, located deep in the woods, down a long drive with a monogrammed gate, where they stripped for and sexually serviced a group of masked party-goers, a job at the end of

which two of the prostitutes were murdered on film by order of the "Master." Holly managed to escape into the woods but was caught and beaten, only waking up in the Staten Island Public Health Service hospital.

Russo traces the Lagonda to a rich wastrel in Mrs. Willingford's own building, who is murdered before Russo could get any answers out of him. An attempt on Holly's life is also made, which leads Russo to enlist the help of the Irish mafia on Staten Island, the head of which, Mickey Cates, was passionately in love with one of the murdered prostitutes. Russo goes to the Stapleton library to research the great homes on Staten Island that match Holly's description and narrows his search down to a Todt Hill estate, where the caretaker admitted burying the bodies, beating Holly and leaving her for dead in Tompkinsville Park because he wouldn't have a transvestite buried with real women. Mickey Cates arrives and adds the caretaker's body to the mass graveyard. Mrs. Willingford has someone stake out the estate and notify her when the next party begins. She and Russo, Mickey Cates and his crew meet up behind Sea View Hospital and make their way up Blood Root Valley through the woods to the estate where they bust up the depraved murder cult, and rescue the next set of prostitutes who were to be sacrificed. Most of the cult's members were wealthy occupants of Mrs. Willingford's building, and their servants, with the club's Master being a snarky, gay, popular gossip columnist. Mickey Cates and his crew then execute vengeance on the members of the murder club.

Russo notes that Staten Island's undeveloped remoteness led to it being a refuge for the rich and for organized crime, and as a dumping ground for the city's problems, such as unwanted children like Russo's own mother and for garbage at the newly opened Fresh Kills landfill.

72. Longfellow, Ki. *Good Dog, Bad Dog. A Sam Russo Mystery; Case 2.* Port Orchard, Wash: Eio Books, 2013. 237pp.
    Still occupying his low-rent apartment at the corner of Bay Street and Victory Boulevard, private detective Sam Russo is again enlisted by his friend, police detective Lino Morelli, to help solve the case of a corpse- that of a seven-foot-tall giant wearing an Elizabethan ruff- that washed up near the Stapleton docks. Believed to have been carried by the currents from Manhattan, Russo heads to the city with his dog Jane, where his investigation leads him to interactions with Cole Porter,

Jimmy Stewart and the Broadway casts of *Kiss Me Kate*, *Harvey* and *Arsenic and Old Lace*.

73. Longfellow, Ki. *Shadow Roll; A Sam Russo Mystery; Case 1*. Port Orchard, Wash: Eio Books, 2013.

Sam Russo, a graduate of the Staten Island Home for Children, and a veteran of America's last cavalry unit in the Pacific Theatre in WWII, was inspired to become a private detective after watching *The Maltese Falcon* at the Paramount Theater on Bay Street. In addition to being an aficionado of all the fictional hard-boiled detectives of literature and film, Russo's other passion is horses and horse-racing. Now, in 1948, he occupies a fourth-floor walk-up above a Rexall at the corner of Bay Street and Victory Blvd, overlooking Tompkinsville Park. His only cases so far have involved following cheating spouses and going undercover at a Stapleton brewery to catch a beer pilferer, but he gets to investigate a murder when police detective Lino Morelli, Russo's friend and fellow orphan from the Staten Island Home for Children, asks for his assistance with a case at their alma mater that involved a pregnant fourteen-year-old girl being thrown from the roof after being given an amateur-Caesarian. Russo recounts that the Dickensian institution, located on the outskirts of Stapleton, was built on land that the "Vanderbilts stole from the natives." Russo's snooping quickly gets to the bottom of the case and forces the husband of the institution's mentally disturbed matron to admit that he killed the girl, and other pregnant girls, and buried them on the property's "Good Riddance Acre" in order to comply with what he believed were God's commands. His complicit wife was arrested as well, but not before proudly telling Russo that his own mother was one of the girls murdered. From the notoriety he received from the case, Russo is hired to travel upstate and solve the mystery of three dead jockeys at the Saratoga Springs (NY) Race Course, in the course of which he picks up two friends that will become reoccurring characters in the series' subsequent books: a dog, Jane, and Mrs. Willingford, a wealthy lover and patron.

74. Lynch, Lee. "Dumb Bunny" in *Best Lesbian Romance 2012*. Edited by Radclyffe. San Francisco, Cal.: Cleis, 2011. 195pp. pgs 139-155.

In this short story of middle-aged lesbian love, Frenchy is hired by the owner of the Apple Cart grocery chain, her former employer, to train his daughter Bunny to be a cashier at his store in New Dorp. At fifty-three-years-old, Bunny had spent her adult life taking care of her

father, and had never worked at a real job before. Although she is
nervous and somewhat incompetent, Bunny at least learns enough to
keep her errors to a minimum. Throughout the training process, the
women begin a close friendship, and they begin spending time together
at Bunny's waterfront high-rise apartment and at a nearby park, where
they share an intimate but platonic experience watching the sunset
together. In addition to her blossoming relationship with Bunny,
Frenchy starts liking Staten Island more and more, as the people were
so different than "real New Yorkers." Bunny confides in Frenchy that
she has an anxiety disorder she's keeping under control with pills.
Whether it is because of that or Staten Island parochialism, she also
admits that she's only been off the island twelve times in her life.
Frenchy contemplates inviting the endearing Bunny on vacation with
her to Florida, even before Bunny admits that she is gay. When she
hears that, Frenchy begins thinking of marrying her. Bunny further
reveals that her father is grooming her to take over the presidency of
the business soon, and hoped that Frenchy would become vice
president.

75. MacKellar, William. *Alfie and Me and the Ghost of Peter Stuyvesant.*
Illustrated by David K. Stone. New York: Dodd, Mead & Company,
1974. 150pp.
    In this novel for young people, Billy Carpenter lives on Staten
Island but commutes to school in Manhattan every day via the Staten
Island Ferry. One day aboard the ferryboat *Mary Murray* he meets the
ghost of Peter Stuyvesant, who can't stop bemoaning the fact that New
York City never named a bridge after him. The depressed specter of
New Netherland's last Governor General explains that he is forced to
linger on earth to atone for his crimes against Indians and Quakers, but
since Manhattan has changed so much since he was alive, he prefers to
haunt the Staten Island Ferry. When Billy tells this story to his best
friend Alfie Slootmaker, who is something of a loveable hustler, they
both resolve to try to meet Stuyvesant again. When they manage to
encounter him aboard the ferry, he gives them a map to a buried chest
of Dutch guilders, which he had hidden from the English when they
took over the colony. The treasure turns out to be in the middle of
Times Square, but Billy and Alfie concoct a cover story that temporarily
allows them to dig up the street unmolested by the authorities. The
police eventually catch on and arrest them at the moment they find the
treasure. *The Staten Island Advance* picks up the story and major publicity
ensues. Peter Stuyvesant becomes a folk hero to the city's youth, which

leads to headaches for the mayor because he has no bridges he can name for Stuyvesant. Billy eventually comes up with an idea, which is to name the new ferryboat "Peter Stuyvesant", a solution which allows the ghost to finally rest in peace.

A good portion of this book takes place on the ferry, and details some of the sights and characters one would see there. There are a number of Staten Island references, to the 120th Precinct, the *Advance*, and an interesting description of how the Verrazano Bridge was changing the island's neighborhood architecture. Billy's parents are depicted as protesting against construction of a new highway, which may be a reference to the Richmond Parkway, which was an environmental cause célèbre in the early 1970s.

76. Marino, Kelly. *Into the Hourglass*. CreateSpace, 2012. 263pp.

Frances White, a Tottenville High School graduate, is a nineteen-year-old genius who is finishing up her last week of college when the director of hematology at Staten Island Hospital calls her up to tell her that a recent blood donation of hers revealed that her blood type is the Holy Grail of blood, with the potential to heal all diseases. When Frances confronts her mother and father, a Cornell physics professor and a volunteer at Staten Island Hospital respectively, they admit that she was adopted. After being knocked unconscious from a fall, Frances wakes up in 17th century Salem, Massachusetts with Mike Bartels, an emergency room doctor at Staten Island Hospital. He and another woman, Abigail, explain that they and Frances are immortals who, for thousands of years, have been on the run from a terrifying enemy, Yorvick, who is intent on wiping out their kind. Mike and Frances had been called back in time in order to ensure the safe birth of Abigail's baby. In the process of rescuing some girls from the Salem witch trials, the trio confronts Yorvick and manage to kill him with the fortuitous assistance of a black widow spider. Frances and Mike are returned to the 21st century, where they pursue their destiny as soul mates.

Staten Island roads are described as "pothole-scarred" and "construction-clogged" but when Frances is sent back in time, she yearns to return to her hometown, no matter how frustrating its traffic. Mike also muses about how he'd miss Ralph's Ices and Denino's restaurant, reputed to have the best pizza in New York City.

77. McMahon, Judi. *Someone to Watch Over Me.* Xlibris, 2004. 417pp.

In this "novelized memoir," former *Advance* reporter Judi McMahon relates, through her alter ego Annie Rosenberg, her life growing up in an emotionally abusive Jewish family in Brooklyn in the 1930s and 40s, her numerous love affairs, her marriage, her search for spiritual self-awareness in an upstate ashram and her successful career as a writer. Using a windfall from a divorce settlement, she buys a house on Todt Hill Road for herself and her adopted Russian daughter, and finds work writing for the *Advance*. The conservative populace of Staten Island is described as "culturally bereft," "not exactly great intellects" and "mental midgets." The island was "...riddled with fat-necked men who like to beep the horns on their cars and consider intellectual reading a copy of the New York Post" while the women had "way-out hair-do's and sculptured nails- some look more like claws..." and prefer to read the National Enquirer. Nevertheless, Todt Hill is described as a tony neighborhood (although mafia-infested) and the island is described as a safe place to raise her daughter (who attends P.S. 29). The *Advance* is described as somewhat lowbrow and beholden to the good opinion of mob-connected local businessmen. The book's Staten Island content is limited, but would be of interest for its vicious depictions of Advance personnel as backstabbing hacks threatened by the protagonist's talent. The pseudonymous targets of these portrayals might be recognizable to people familiar with the newspaper staff in the 1980s.

78. Mercaldo, David, Ph.D. *Ferry.* Fairfax, Va: Xulon Press, 2002. 196pp.

This story relates the life and experiences of Angelo Marullo, the shoe shine man on the Staten Island Ferry. An immigrant from Sicily, he took a job shining shoes when he couldn't find work as a tailor. What started out as a temporary job turned into a permanent career. This book tells the story of Marullo's life over the next few decades, and the relationships he establishes with people he encounters on the Ferry boat, some of the most prominent being a blind man, a Mt. Loretto nun, an African-American Korean War veteran, an aspiring dancer, and a teacher who gives Angelo the gift of literacy.

79. Mercaldo, David, Ph.D. *Seamstress.* n.l.: Crown Oak Press, 2006. 188pp.

While gathered at the Staten Island wake of one of their circle of long-time friends, a group of elderly ladies- centered on Santina Fortunato- reminisce about their lives, which embodied the Italian-American experience in New York and Staten Island specifically. The "girls" had begun their friendship in the early part of the 20th century as seamstresses in the clothing manufacturing business of the Neuremberg brothers, a pair of cheap, neurotic, cowardly, dishonest sexual perverts whose attempts to cheat or seduce the girls had to be resisted. The book consists of the usual personal stories that make up any life: marriage, babies, relationships, deaths, et al. In the case of these women, second-generation Italian-Americans, the stories also include the particular aspects of life as the children of immigrants in the early 20th century. Their parents straddled two worlds while being determined to make their children into Americans. A hallmark of life for these people was ethnic self-segregation in a melting pot city. This contrasted with the later generations, who started to marry non-Italians and move out of the city. While many of the stories of births and deaths and marriages are common to all people, so many of the stories in this volume seem so distinctive that one can surmise that they must have some foundation in actual Staten Island events the author heard from older people. As for the island itself, Santina went to Port Richmond High School and was married in St. Mary's church in Rosebank. Other characters lived on the island as well. Santina noted that the island changed with the construction of the Verrazano Bridge. It was now noisy and crowded and she felt that the newcomers came to take, not to give. Santina's neighborhood on Van Duzer Street "changed" as well, into a dangerous, predominantly minority area. Nevertheless, Santina and her friends refused to leave the island, as they still considered it different from the rest of the city; it was still more quiet and bucolic.

This book contains the same religious subtext as the author's other book (*Ferry*). Considering the protagonist's identity as an older Italian-American woman, her character's Catholicism couldn't be realistically ignored, but it is derided as shallow and inferior as compared with the faith of minor Protestant characters.

80. Mila, Paul J. *Fireworks.* Bloomington, Ind.: AuthorHouse, 2008. 270pp.
    Although no description of Staten Island is included in this book, its plot revolves around a plan by Islamic terrorists to blow up the Verrazano Bridge while the Queen Mary 2 is passing underneath. Stationed on both sides of the Narrows, the terrorists on the Staten Island side kill an interfering policeman, but the plot is foiled when one character recognizes that the "string of pearls" referred to in an intercepted communiqué describes the bridge, allowing the military to

jam the terrorists' detonation devices in the nick of time. Humorously, despite all the shooting having occurred on Staten Island, the media refers to it as the "Battle of Brooklyn."

81. Millman, John. *Christmas Eve and Other Stories.* Brooklyn, N.Y.: Pageant-Poseidon, Ltd., 1972. 90pp.

    Two of the stories in this collection take place in Staten Island, although the location is only tangential to the plot. While these two stories could also be read as memoir, they are included here because of their context within a collection of fictional stories. In the first, *Dedicated Lady*, the narrator recounts his childhood in the classroom of Ms. Cole at P.S. 5 in Huguenot in 1919. His schoolhouse is described, as is the overt patriotic and Christian ethos of both Ms. Cole and the school curriculum of the time. The second story, *Danton to the Rescue*, recounts the narrator's youthful love affair with silent movies that he viewed at the Great Kills theatre (Greenwald's theatre) in the early 1920s. At time of writing, the theatre was a pizza parlor, but the magic of his early experiences was still fresh. He relates the experience of attending a film there, and describes the orchestra's repertoire, his favorite film idols, the economic cost of going to the movies, and some amusing accounts of seeing his favorite movies.

82. Mills, W(eymar) Jay. *Through the Gates of Old Romance.* Philadelphia: J.B. Lippincott Company, 1903. 281pp.

    Two of the stories in this short story collection about Old New York deal with Staten Island. *A True Picture of the Last Days of Aaron Burr* is an imagining of the final days of Vice President Aaron Burr, who died at the Richmond Inn in Port Richmond 1836. The story is uneventful and simply mentions several of the people who visited Burr on his deathbed. *The Ghosts of an Old Staten Island Manor* deals with a legend surrounding the Bentley Manor, known today as the Conference House. Its owner, Christopher Billop, was an ill-tempered man who was obliged to host a ball for the British officers during the Revolution. Billop's unhappy wife recognized in one of the officers, Harry Fairleigh, a former suitor. When they began to dance the minuet, Billop intervened and crossed swords with Fairleigh. Mrs. Billop promised him a dance another time, but Fairleigh was killed at the Battle of Monmouth. The legend says that two ghostly figures can still be seen dancing together in the garden on the same date every year.

83. Modern, Tom. *Richmondtown.* Baltimore: PublishAmerica, 2003. 161pp.

Roy Hart, a thirty-eight-year-old Manhattan assistant, moves to Richmondtown both to avoid professional burnout and to investigate several Bigfoot sightings that had been reported in the area. He immediately begins witnessing paranormal manifestations such as ghosts, UFOs and a winged cat in New Dorp. He befriends a group of people who are as interested in these things as he is, and they agree to investigate the phenomena. Events in Richmondtown quickly become ever more strange and disturbing. Black-robed cultists in LaTourette Park and mysterious vandals become more aggressive. The group stumbles upon a Bigfoot in the woods. The kindly old man whom Roy had befriended admits to being a ghost and the ghosts Roy had observed and even conversed with are revealed to be demons. Richmondtown's water supply becomes contaminated with a chemical unknown to science, which starts turning much of the population into zombies. Shadowy government paramilitary forces occupy and quarantine the village. The group of friends plans an escape as they begin to be killed one by one, by the UFOs, the government agents and the cultists. The government agents start executing the infected residents of Richmondtown, in an attempt to suppress the true story of the village's strange goings-on. They leave the uninfected residents alone, as they are dying off naturally from the contaminated water. The two hundred or so remaining healthy residents begin fighting the government agents in a guerilla war which leaves much of the village destroyed. The fighting culminates in a battle royale pitting the residents of Richmondtown, the Bigfoots, and Roy's 19th century ancestor, the captain of the Flying Dutchman, against the government forces, the UFOs, the cultists and the zombies. With the help of a secret weapon invented by his ghostly friend, Roy turns the tide in favor of the people of Richmondtown. The battle is won, but the authorities attempt a cover-up.

84. Morris, Mitzi. *Poetic Justice.* New York: Colloquial Media, 2012. 319pp.

This murder mystery set in the world of Manhattan literati revolves around the mysterious death of literary agent Sheba Miller and the even more inexplicable fact that she was found dead in unfashionable Staten Island. Editor Jay Alfred and his partner Ken White, a physical therapist, are the very model of a modern, urbane, gay couple, who spend their time enjoying good restaurants, antiquing and making catty remarks.

Ken, the more adventurous of the two, insists they travel to Staten Island to see the restaurant where the fortyish Sheba died of an apparent heart attack. They find the location at a St. George bar and purchase Sheba's laptop from the waitress. On the boat ride back to Manhattan, they run into Sheba's business partner, Diane Barnes, who reveals that Sheba liked to ride the ferry in order to write. At Sheba's memorial service, Ken and Jay come across a woman they had met in Staten Island, who turned out to be an old friend of Sheba's from their days at the Slam Bam Poetry Cafe. She tells them that the police were investigating Sheba's death as a murder, which only increases Ken's desire to dig into the case. Meanwhile, another editor arranges an urgent meeting with Jay, choosing the Times Square Olive Garden for anonymity (because none of their peers would ever frequent such an establishment), to reveal that a manuscript of Sheba's was being shopped around for publication. Part memoir, part erotic exposé, the bombshell manuscript denigrated most of the figures in New York's incestuous publishing world, which was condemned as a gay boys network that conspired to suppress women writers. (Jay was portrayed as a drunken and distracted misogynist.)

Ken continues his amateur investigation with the assistance of Staten Islander Shelly Martinelli and her NYPD uncle from Port Richmond. Ken pilfers the computer of Sheba's business partner, Mickey, and finds out that he had tricked several young, female writers into ghost writing what they were told was Mickey's own book. When it is discovered that Mickey had been the agent for a book on historic poisonings, the pieces fall into place. Mickey had poisoned Sheba's cigarettes in order to steal the business from her and had tried to poison the young women who had unwittingly ghostwritten the saucy tell-all memoir. Leni, the naive techie who works for Jay, utilized a stylometric computer program to figure out that Sheba had actually been writing poetry on the Staten Island Ferry, in memory of a lover who had drowned after falling over the side while drunk.

To the downtown cosmopolites who people this tale, Staten Island is contemptible and beyond the pale. When someone from Jersey City asks if Sheba lived in Staten Island, the suggestion is laughably derided with the response "Don't be silly. Nobody lives on Staten Island." When Ken and Jay ride the boat for the first time, they note the ubiquity of Century 21 shopping bags and wonder sarcastically if they'd be allowed to board such an unfashionable vessel. They seem to gain something of an appreciation though, admiring the St. George Library and Staten Island Yankee stadium. Shelly Martinelli defends her hometown, saying that it was really a nice place but jokingly warns Ken not to tell his hipster friends because she doesn't want her rent to go up. Similarly, when Ken dines at Denino's restaurant in Port Richmond with Shelly and her uncle, he declares that it serves the best pizza in New York City and even admits to Jay that it was good enough to make him consider moving to Staten Island.

85. Mowat, Grace Helen. *Broken Barrier; A Romance of Staten Island and the Province of New Brunswick.* Fredericton, N.B.: University Press of New Brunswick, 1951. 182pp.

   When his housekeeper Maggie announces that she is leaving his service in order to marry, Staten Island businessman Stephen Trancher tells her that she must find a replacement and train her before she can quit. Because he likes Maggie so much, Stephen orders her to find a girl from the same area she came from, which Maggie reveals to be "The Provinces," the exact location of which is a mystery to Stephen. So Maggie puts an ad in the newspaper seeking a maid who must be from "the Provinces."

   Lydia Allen has come to New York from New Brunswick, Canada in order to earn enough money to save her family farm, which her ancestors had cultivated for over a century and a half. Although she is a college graduate and had hoped to be a music teacher, she lacked the necessary experience and responds to Maggie's ad out of desperation. She takes the ferry to Staten Island for an interview and is hired, not so much for her skills, but for her humble bearing and her roots in the Maritime Provinces of Canada. In addition to her duties, Maggie explains Stephen Trancher to Lydia. He's an odd, white-haired bachelor nearing 40, whose primary joy in life is coming home from the office and reading. Because both his best friend and a cousin had married inferior women, Trancher has vowed never to marry and doesn't hesitate to dissuade other men from matrimony. Lydia seamlessly takes Maggie's place but Trancher doesn't say a word to her and hardly notices she's there. However, they eventually discover that they have a common love of books, and Stephen begins to lend her volumes from his library and discuss literature with her. He also discovers that she can play the piano, and insists on her accompanying him on the violin. The barrier between master and servant begins to strain, as Lydia starts to draw Stephen out of his isolation.

Meanwhile, Stephen has some painful dealings with Cora Farquhar, the witless, social-climbing widow of his best friend Donald, who Stephen believes died from his strenuous efforts to provide for his flighty, materialistic wife. On his deathbed, Donald entrusted Stephen with sole power over his wife's finances because she had no head for money. Cora bristles at Stephen's conservative stewardship and demands that he sell some of her bonds and invest in a mining speculation that a Mr. Cohen had told her would reap large rewards. Stephen advises against it but because of her incessant pleas, he agrees to do as she wishes.

Back at home, Stephen discovers another interesting fact about Lydia. When he casually mentions George Washington in conversation, Lydia blows up and calls him an "old rebel" who had dispossessed her ancestors. She reveals that she is a descendant of those Loyalists who were expelled from the new United States after the Revolution and who settled in Canada with the help of good King George III, "the most misjudged monarch in all history."

Lydia notices that Stephen Trancher often sits and obsessively stares at a miniature portrait in a crystal-covered case, which contains the painting of a Revolutionary-era ancestor of his, Lydia Trancher. She was considered the black sheep of the family because she had eloped with a British soldier and stolen a silver tankard from her father, which she considered part of her dowry. Stephen has been trying to discover what ever happened to her, but without the name of her husband, he has found nothing. One night Lydia surreptitiously examines the miniature and drops it, breaking the crystal cover. She discovers a message on the back of the picture from Lydia Trancher's father, naming the British officer who stole his daughter: Nathaniel Allen, Lydia Allen's distant ancestor, for whose wife she was named. She decides to not tell Stephen until she leaves his service, and has the crystal replaced without his knowing.

By this time, Stephen is going through a financial ordeal. The mining company in which he had invested Cora Farquhar's money went belly up, thus leaving Cora with a third of her income gone. Stephen resolves to make up her lost income by paying out the interest on the bonds from his own money. To do so, he is forced to take a small apartment in the city and rent out his Staten Island house. Lydia has by this time saved up a thousand dollars and returns to Canada to manage her beloved farm, despite her secret affection for Stephen. In her absence, Stephen realizes how much he misses her and needs her, and writes her a passionate letter to that effect, but does not mail it. His only contact with her is a formal letter requesting that she return to his service, which she rejects in an equally formal manner.

Stephen's fortunes change when his burdensome client Cora Farquhar marries the same speculator, Mr. Cohen, who had encouraged her to invest in the flawed mining scheme. Cohen turns out to be an honest man, and promises to reimburse Stephen for the money he spent maintaining Cora in her accustomed lifestyle. This enables Stephen to move back to his Staten Island home. After this change of fortune, Stephen travels to New Brunswick and tracks Lydia down. He declares his love, proposes marriage, and she immediately accepts. After a quick marriage in Canada, they move back to Staten Island, where Lydia discovers Stephen's unsent love letter, which convinces her of his love. The book ends with Stephen declaring his desire and intention of moving back to New Brunswick with Lydia, where she would run the farm and he would learn to handle the business side of the operation.

Although most of the story takes place on Staten Island, local descriptions are few. On Lydia's first trip on the Staten Island ferry, her impression of her fellow passengers was that they "...appeared confident and secure, each absorbed in a private world, oblivious to her." Staten Island is also represented as being a quiet, almost rural, sanctuary from the noise and crowding of Manhattan, where Lydia can garden and Stephen can relax.

86. Mullin, Michael and John Skewes. *Larry Gets Lost in New York City.* Illustrated by John Skewes. Seattle, Wash.: Sasquatch Books, 2010. 30pp.
      On a trip to New York City with his family, a young boy, Pete, gets separated from his dog Larry. Pete and Larry travel throughout the city searching for each other and finally get reunited at the Empire State Building. This children's book in rhyme is interspersed with fun facts about New York City. After their reunion, the family rides the ferry to Staten Island, presumably to stay in a hotel.

87. Nadelson, Reggie. *Fresh Kills*. New York: Walker and Co., 2006. 343pp.
    In this mystery thriller, Russian-American detective Artie Cohen is spending two weeks with his nephew, fourteen-year-old Billy Farone, who is on leave from a juvenile offenders' institution in Florida where he had been sent for brutally murdering Heshey Shank. Although Artie had unspoken doubts about his nephew's innocence, he and his cop friends moved heaven and earth to have the case tried as one of self defense. Heshey's brother, Stanley, a low-level criminal, doesn't buy it and begins making harassing phone calls when he discovers that Billy is back in New York.

    Meanwhile, Artie's boss, Sonny Lippert, asks for his help with a missing person case in Staten Island, in which the Italian-American husband of a Russian woman disappeared from their Todt Hill mansion after a mysterious break-in. As Artie investigates, he begins noting possible connections between the missing man, Stanley Shank and a case that Sonny is obsessed with, involving a serial killer who mutilates children. As he digs deeper however, he begins connecting Billy's increasingly strange behavior with certain crimes and begins to come to the conclusion that Billy is a psychopath who lured Heshey Shank to an isolated fishing shed and murdered him on a whim. He starts to wonder, involuntarily, whether Billy had something to do with the murdered children, as Billy had at least a tenuous connection with the victims. When the young daughter of Tolya, a criminally-connected friend, disappears, Artie confronts Billy while on a fishing trip to Staten Island, near Fresh Kills. Billy's insane possessiveness is revealed, as he admits kidnapping and killing a baby, merely to scare Tolya's daughter into running away from home, because he felt that she threatened his relationship with Artie. Tolya arrives and reveals that his daughter was found unharmed. It is then implied that Tolya, with Artie's acquiescence, kills Billy in order to spare him a life in prison.

    Although only a few scenes, besides the dramatic denouement, take place in Staten Island, this book is remarkable for its extensive descriptions of the island's history and culture. The author shows great familiarity with Staten Island, although she committed two howlers when she had her characters driving cars onto the ferry in the years after 9/11 (still prohibited as of this writing) and described the Fresh Kills area as a prime fishing spot.

To prepare Artie for the case, Sonny reveals all he knows about the "parallel universe" of Staten Island and its "strange" people, so full of "...rage and religion..." and "...[r]edemption if you got lucky", comparing it to something out of Dostoevsky. He even describes former Borough President Albert Manascalo [sic] as "so powerful that he could make a Jew an honorary Italian." After Sonny and Artie cross the bridge, they stop at LaRocca's in Midland Beach. The island is described as remote and empty, yet plagued by suburban sprawl. After being surprised by the sight of an African American interacting with an Italian, Sonny continues his historical and sociological lesson on Staten Island, noting that Staten Island was the only place north of the Mason-Dixon line to support the South during the Civil War and that the Italians who lived there when the Verrazano Bridge was opened were terrified that the island would be overrun by Black people. They felt, Sonny insists, that the island was a White refuge, primarily for Italians, with Irish people tolerated. Instead, the bridge -which became known as the Guinea Gangplank- brought more Italians, who made a fortune out of real estate and garbage. He describes how builders would illegally tear down forests and get retroactive permission from the zoning board to build houses, on the basis of their "Italian logic" that houses would prevent erosion that would result from the loss of the trees. He describes the layout and family dynamic of Mother-Daughter houses. Sonny goes on to describe the shady history of the Fresh Kills landfill, implying that the Mafia made money at every stage of the process, from the sale of land to the private carting businesses. Sonny sums up Staten Island by saying that it is a place where people settled to "nurture their lives and express rage." Taking place almost two years after 9/11, Artie notes that on Staten Island it felt like it had just happened, what with all the flags and paranoia and streets named after dead firefighters.

One character notes that a lot of Russians were moving to Staten Island, which they said was the new Brooklyn (with New Jersey being the new Staten Island), and paying cash for big fancy houses near the water. While visiting Artie's former partner, Hank Provone, in Tottenville, Artie remembers Sonny's story about Staten Island's racial divisions when he sees a Black man at Hank's party. Hank says that the older generation, with their racist rage, is dying away. He reminisces about his father singing the insensitive song "Latin from Staten Island." Hank also notes how people on Staten Island identify with their neighborhoods, like Rossville or Tottenville, more than with the borough as a whole.

88. Nathan, Robert. *Journey of Tapiola*. Decorations by Georg Salter. New York: Alfred A. Knopf, 1938. 121pp.

Tapiola is a Yorkshire Terrier who belongs to Mrs. Poppel, the wife of a prominent Manhattan publisher. He is timid, vain and desperate to be loved. Having listened to all the literary talk of visiting writers and critics, Tapiola begins to fancy himself a sort of Nietzschean überdog, "without pity or other sentimental considerations." Sensitive about his diminutive size and pampered existence, Tapiola decides that he must go out into the world and impress Mrs. Poppel by embarking on a heroic journey. His friend Dicky (Richard), a canary who aspires to be a professional singer, joins him in his escape from the building. The two heroes are accidentally deposited on a garbage scow which is to be dumped in the waters off of Staten Island. With the help of a rat named Jeremiah, who is an ex-preacher, Tapiola and Richard escape death by clinging to a plank which washes up on Staten Island. In search of food, Tapiola meets a white cat who falls in love with him and tries to keep him with her. Like Odysseus, Tapiola rejects the temptation of this feline Circe and rejoins his friends, who have a highly intelligent conversation about love, among other things. Tapiola comes across an opportunity to be a hero when a belligerent beetle attempts to block a road. He emerges the victor in their battle when the beetle lands on his back and can't move. Still in search of food, Jeremiah comes up with the idea of having Richard stage a concert. Unfortunately, the crows, robins and wrens don't appreciate his singing. Only a lowly schoolmarm hen falls in love with both Richard and his voice. Jeremiah next has a plan to have the intellectual Tapiola give a lecture on literary subjects to a group of "serious minded rabbits." Tapiola attempts to recount the literary anecdotes he had heard from underneath Mrs. Poppel's couch, but the audience is unimpressed. Only a single creature, a female rabbit, appreciates Tapiola's qualities. When two dogs break up the meeting, she runs to Tapiola for protection because she knows he is a hero. In the face of the attacking dogs, Tapiola no longer has any desire to be a hero and flees with his friends. They eventually spy Manhattan, but mistake it for Hollywood, where Richard intends to go to achieve success. The group takes the ferry to 23rd Street, where a detective spots Tapiola and Richard and brings them home, where they both now realize they belong. The rabbit and hen had followed Tapiola and Richard aboard the ferry and declared their love, and go to live with them in bliss. Jeremiah, the religious rat, roams the streets looking for a new congregation.

89. Nielsen, Alfred. *The Summer of the Paymaster.* New York: W.W. Norton, 1990. 379pp.

This *bildungsroman* set completely in Staten Island details the formative experiences of its narrator, Andy "Chun" Hapanowitz, and his friends as they grow up in the 1960s. Having dropped out of college and lived the hippie lifestyle in Oregon, twenty-one-year-old Andy returns to Staten Island to await the homecoming of his estranged childhood blood brother, Jimmy Dietz, a decorated Marine who is coming back from Vietnam to dedicate a Little League field to their mutual friend, Corney Walsh, who had been killed in the war. (Andy is exempt from service due to a glass eye). Andy rents a bungalow on the beach near the Orange House, at the foot of Arbutus Avenue, and gets a job as a pump jockey at the Mobil station next to the Fresh Kills landfill. An encounter with an old friend, who relays a gift from Jimmy, leads Andy to reminisce on their boyhood, when Jimmy and Andy went deep into the woods that covered most of the island's South Shore and made a blood brother pact. Jimmy, godlike in his strength and mastery over everything he put his mind to doing, was the undisputed leader of their group of friends. He was also on the fast track to the priesthood. Their idyllic boyhood was the perfect example of the rural/urban hybrid that Staten Island was before the construction of the Verrazano Bridge: The boys swam off the Vanderbilt pier, hunted rabbits in the deep woods, served Mass at Our Lady Star of the Sea and engaged in and endured surprising violence, including gunplay, with rival groups of boys that could be described as gangs. An encounter with a group of Brooklyn boys camping on the island leads Andy to observe: "This was wilderness to them, just as Brooklyn was the jungle to us."

In the summer of 1961, when the song of the cicadas was heard all over the island, Jimmy had led the boys in building a perfectly concealed cabin in the woods near Mount Loretto, which becomes their clubhouse and sanctuary. One day Jimmy and Andy notice garbage mounds and construction vehicles in their woods. One of the construction workers explains that the "bridge to Brooklyn is going up" and everything is going to change. Everything did change after the Verrazano Bridge was opened in 1964: Andy's family lost their house to eminent domain when the state wanted to build one of the highways; they now lived in a North Shore apartment. "The little church- the chapel- where we had gone for many years was too small now. More and more houses had been built every year. Open fields became developments overnight. Long stretches of woods were leveled in a twinkling. New roads crisscrossed where there had been none." The boys began to change too, along with the island and the country. Girls, alcohol, overdevelopment, the Civil Rights movement and the Vietnam War began to take their toll on what had been an Arcadian time and place. Jimmy's priestly mentor, Father Lusenkas, is a freedom rider and an outspoken pacifist who leads Jimmy into anti-war activism. When Jimmy's father forbids him from going to Alabama with Fr. Lusenkas to protest for African American civil rights, Jimmy begins experiencing internal conflict that leads him away from the priesthood. He drops out of Catholic school and enrolls in public school; he starts dating a girl; he begins hanging with a rougher crowd; Jimmy became something of a neighborhood bully, who specialized in beating up guys from New Jersey who dared come to Staten Island. He volunteers for the Marines where he excels in battle and wins the Silver Star.

When Corney Walsh is killed in Vietnam, his father invites Andy and his friends to drink with him at the Seabreeze Hotel in Midland Beach, after the funeral at St. Margaret Mary's. After getting drunk, Andy is led down to the beach where he is brutally beaten by a group of guys who mistakenly believed that he had fired a shotgun blast of birdshot at them when in fact it had been Jimmy, who was retaliating for a previous fight. Andy is put into a coma and loses an eye.

After his sojourn out West and return to Staten Island, Andy started working at Pete's Mobil Station on Arthur Kill Road, an establishment made successful by the landfill, the Bridge and the Highway. Workers there were motivated by the legend of the Paymaster, an oil company employee who drove around the country undercover, awarding money to gas station employees who provided exemplary customer service. Andy not only steps up his game at work in hope of winning the money, but begins imagining conversations with an omniscient Paymaster who exists on the space/time continuum and gives sage advice about the paths in life that are far more complicated than the paths through the South Shore woods. When the real Paymaster does finally show up at the gas station and is about to award Andy the money, Andy accidentally short-changes him, tries to cover it up and gets fired.

When Jimmy is reported missing in action only days before he was to return, Andy goes to seek out the old cabin, not expecting it to really still exist among the endless vistas of identical houses that looked as if they had been "stamped out by a tool-and-die factory," on streets that were named after the children of contractors. Shockingly, the cabin is still there, in a copse of trees in the midst of an encroaching housing development. Andy begins sleeping there, associating the survival of the cabin with the survival of his missing friend. To him, Staten Island had changed into "...something foreign, something uncomfortable, a new place that gluttonously chewed and swallowed memories," where the "sacred places of boyhood" were all fast disappearing. Every day the construction workers moved closer to the cabin, felling more trees and laying more foundations. Finally, the workers begin using dynamite and warn him that the cabin will be gone the next day, and it is implied that Andy then finds out that Jimmy had been killed.

This book is imbued with Staten Island references and cultural signposts: McKee High School, Moravian Cemetery, the Rossville Fire of 1963, various taverns and churches and cultural mores of 1960s teens. There is an extended description of Al Deppe's, while Andy and Jimmy work at the Saturday morning auction which takes place in an old airplane hangar on Richmond Avenue. The rise and fall of Staten Island as a holiday destination is recounted. It's mentioned that for mobsters, "going to Staten Island" meant that someone was going to be killed. The attitudes and practices of Catholics before and after the days of Vatican II are described. In its wistful longing for a community destroyed by overdevelopment and cultural dispossession, the book notes that "Rico from Brooklyn" had moved out to Staten Island for the woods and was now wondering where all the woods had gone. After seeing graffiti and vandalism in their neighborhood, the book observes that it "...was no longer a town circle. It was a sad and abused place, not a place to be proud of. Many of the people who lived here now had arrived from elsewhere and had no idea of how precious a place it had been. They had no idea what had been destroyed."

90. Nieves-Powell, Linda. *Free Style.* New York: Atria, 2008. 262pp.
     Idalis, this novel's protagonist, takes the ferry every day to her job as an administrative assistant at a Manhattan advertising agency. Living on the North Shore, with a view of Bayonne, the "ugliest view in New York City", the Puerto-Rican Idalis is the mother of a young son, Junito. She and her husband Manny have recently separated, due to her resentment of his Playstation addiction and his lack of help around the house. Now living apart, they are trying to understand their new situation and determine where their relationship is going. At thirty-six-

years-old, Idalis is also trying to figure out what to do with her life. Although Manny declares that he wants to reconcile with Idalis, he also tries to make her jealous by bringing his brother's sexy girlfriend to Junito's soccer game and trying to imply that they were a couple.

One day on the ferry boat Idalis meets Cameron, an African-American man with a Latina fetish, who asks for her phone number. They agree to meet for a walk around Silver Lake. When they run into Idalis' friend there, who inadvertently mentions that Idalis was married, Idalis laments that Staten Island is like a small Midwestern town. Although Cameron is initially taken aback, they have another date at a fancy French restaurant in Dongan Hills. Feeling totally out of her element, Idalis goes to Manny's apartment to reconcile but discovers him with a woman. Wanting to recapture their glory days, Idalis and her friend Selenis (whose husband has a problem with internet porn) squeeze into the outfits from their younger days and go dancing in Manhattan at their old stomping ground, Club 90. They smoke pot and dance and reconnect with the old flames they've been romanticizing through the years. Although they want to relive their youth, reality intervenes, as they realize they have families and husbands back on Staten Island and the men from their past that they were fooling around with didn't measure up to their memories and fantasies. In addition, the illusion is shattered when their husbands follow them to the club and force them to leave.

At work, Idalis is promoted when a half-Latino client insists on having a Latino on the creative team for his product, an incredibly ugly doll, modeled on the client's mother, which was to be marketed to Latina girls. Idalis begins to realize that she is stuck in the past and needs to start taking risks and being honest with herself about where she wants her life to go. She meets Manny at the Barnes and Noble on Richmond Avenue and tells him that she wants a divorce. She also breaks off her relationship with Cameron. And although she initially concealed her feelings, she eventually tells the client at work that his doll is horrible and no one would ever buy it. Idalis is demoted back to the secretarial pool, but quits to become the manager at her Uncle Herman's coffee shop on Staten Island. It was Herman's risk-taking that led the family to Staten Island in 1976, when he decided to open a coffee shop there. Under her management the business achieves success.

91. Nunez, Sigrid. *For Rouenna.* New York: Farrar, Straus and Giroux, 2001. 230pp.

     When the narrator, an author, receives a letter from an old acquaintance, Rouenna Zycinski, with whom she had grown up in the same Staten Island housing project decades earlier, it is with trepidation that she meets with the older woman. Rouenna however, merely wanted to ask for help writing a book about her experiences as an Army nurse during the Vietnam War. The narrator declines, but changes her mind after she learns about Rouenna's subsequent suicide. Both of their families moved from Brooklyn to a still-rural Staten Island in the late 1950s, to live in a housing project that would seem to be in Mariners Harbor. Although the projects then were relatively safe and crime-free, compared to their later reputation, there was still a stigma attached to the people living there. Most of the book relates Rouenna's wartime and post-war experiences, but also includes extended descriptions of the ferry, life in the projects, Staten Island history and culture.

92. Nutt, Frances Tysen. *Three Fields to Cross.* New York: Stephen-Paul Publishers, 1947. 368pp.

     This epic of the American Revolution dramatizes most of the historical touchstones associated with that conflict on Staten Island: the British occupation, the divided loyalties, the peace conference, the Mercer, Sullivan and Stirling raids, the depredations upon the civilian population and the clandestine traffic of spies and goods across the Arthur Kill.

     John Blake is a veteran of the French and Indian War who farms a homestead at Oude Dorp with his Dutch-descended wife Faithfull and their daughters Neltjie, the romantic beauty, and Giletta, the thirteen-year-old tomboy who strains against the boundaries of her gender and roams the woods and fields of her beloved island with her Huguenot friend Jacques. As political tensions with Great Britain rise, John Blake begins to feel the enmity of the local group of Liberty Boys, when he refuses to join their company. The Liberty Boys' agitation against Tories grows to encompass violence, as they start to burn the property of Loyalists. The war breaks out and the British descend upon Staten Island in 1776, with the Commander in Chief, Lord William Howe, making his headquarters in the Rose and Crown tavern. Fence rails and cattle start disappearing into the British camps and all private firearms are confiscated by the British.

Nevertheless, the civilian population, politically conservative by inclination and necessity, began an amicable *modus vivendi* with the occupying army that leads to a genuine sociability. A cockfight is held which is attended by Admiral Sir Richard Howe and General Lord Charles Cornwallis. A young British officer, Lian Thorroby, is quartered with the Blakes and falls in love with Neltjie while conducting a merry war with Giletta, especially over the qualities of their respective horses. A great race is held, in which Giletta's beloved horse Liberty beat Lian's by a nose. Liberty is immediately commandeered by the British, as are all horses not used for farm work, in preparation for the Battle of Long Island. Giletta is embittered, but her family invites many British officers, including Major John André, to the birthday party of Faithfull's Dutch mother, Madame Weyant.

Wartime scarcity begins to tell, however, and tensions rise when the island is left under the command of the brutal Hessian General Knyphausen, while the British campaign against the Colonials. Lian begins losing interest in Neltjie and starts falling in love with the spirited Giletta. When Neltjie finds out that Giletta has been secretly meeting with her friend Jacques, now a rebel scout, she informs Lian in the hope of reclaiming her lover and disqualifying her sister. Lian surprises them at their rendezvous, merely to warn them against their treason, but a troop of British cavalry arrives unannounced and kill Jacques. Giletta is taken for trial before Lord Howe, where she only escapes with her life when Lian agrees to wed her then and there as a pledge for her loyalty. The marriage ceremony performed, Giletta escapes with Lian's horse and, with the help of the friendly Indian Kooseka, one of the last remnants of his tribe, flees across the Kill to Elizabeth, taking refuge in the home of the patriotic prostitute who had been sheltering Jacques.

In the meantime, Mark Jackson, the one-time Liberty Boy turned Tory, makes false accusations against John Blake which send him to one of the infamous British prison ships anchored off Brooklyn, where he meets a reformed pirate who reveals that his crew had buried gold on Blake's property many years before. Unfortunately, while in his cups at a tavern some years earlier, the pirate had also revealed that information to unscrupulous Manhattan dandy Riban Verney and been forced to hand over his treasure map to him. Verney, who had since then been surreptitiously digging around the Blakes' property in search of the gold, took his opportunity with John Blake's arrest and had

General Knyphausen transfer the Blake land grant to him. Verney reduced the Blake women to servitude while he searched for the gold. Despite the fact that the pirate had subtly altered the map in order to mislead him, Verney found the buried treasure. After using Neltjie to help him remove the chest from the ground, he moved to shoot her in the back of the head when he himself was killed by the Blakes' loyal slave, Bot. Lian meanwhile has been wounded during Lord Stirling's 1780 raid on the island. Giletta came out of hiding to attend to him in his lonely hut on the top of Todt Hill, but he would have died if not for Kooseka's native medicine. When Lian is wounded a second time, Giletta is captured and Lian court-martialed for harboring a rebel spy. With the help of several peripheral characters, Lian and Giletta escape to New Jersey, where the book ends abruptly with the murder of Lian's orderly by an American spy.

Mrs. Tysen Nutt, descended from a family whose roots on the island go back to 1677, derived much of her material from family documents, producing a work thoroughly imbued with well-known and obscure nuggets of Staten Island history. In addition to the events, people and places mentioned above, the author details the terms of the last sale of the island by the natives to the English in 1670 and implies that small bands of Indians still wandered through collecting the ash, elder and hickory to which their treaty entitled them. The public furor over the trial and hanging of the slave Anthony Neal in Cuckol's Town is described, as well as the widespread and perpetual fears about a slave uprising. The morality of slavery is not considered by the protagonists, but the brutality of the system is laid bare, when Mark Jackson is shown to have beaten and castrated his own enslaved son, and when the Blakes' slave Nance strangled her own baby (fathered by John Blake's brother) rather than see it brought up in slavery. An account is given of a Pinkster Day celebration, held in a field by the bay and attended by slaves and some Whites. The Blakes attend St. Andrew's, where the Rev. Richard Charlton was rector. Many of the old families and significant personages of Staten Island are mentioned, such as Christopher Billop and Benjamin Seaman, John Tysen, the Seguines, Androvettes, LaTourettes, et al.

93. Odets, Clifford. *Clash by Night*. New York: Random House, 1942. 242pp.
    Jerry Wilenski, a dull witted but good-hearted construction worker, lives in a seaside Staten Island house with his unhappy wife Mae, their

new baby and his Polish immigrant father. When he invites a brutish co-worker, Earl Pfeiffer to visit, Mae is at first repelled but then attracted to him. Jerry foolishly insists that Earl rent their spare room, which leads to an affair between Earl and Mae. Jerry eventually discovers the truth and, when confronted, Mae openly admits it and declares that she is leaving Jerry. The distraught Jerry eventually confronts Earl in the movie projection booth where he works in order to tell him that he really wasn't mad at him and wouldn't hurt him. However, Earl attacks Jerry with a wrench which provokes Jerry into murdering Earl. Apart from the setting, there is no significant Staten Island content, besides a passing mention of Rosebank and St. George. This play premiered on Broadway in 1941, starring Tallulah Bankhead and Lee J. Cobb, and ran for forty-nine performances. It was adapted to film in 1952 (RKO Radio Pictures), starring Barbara Stanwyck, Paul Douglas and Marilyn Monroe, but the setting was inexplicably changed to California. The story was also later adapted for CBS television in 1957.

94. O'Neill, Joseph. *Netherland*. New York: Pantheon Books, 2008. 256pp.
     Dutch narrator Hans van den Broek, finding himself alone in New York after his English wife- unnerved by the 9/11 attacks- fled back to London with their young son, rediscovers his boyhood pastime and gets involved with the cricket team that plays at Walker Park in Staten Island. It is there that he meets and befriends Chuck Ramkisson, a Trinidadian umpire who enlists Hans in his quixotic dream to evangelize Americans in the game of cricket by way of opening a cricket arena at Floyd Bennett field. Although the scenes in Staten Island are minimal in this paean to the immigrant metropolis and story of a man's quest for relevance and struggle to keep his family, Walker Park is described in some detail, down to its flora and arboreal border, and Hans' membership in his cricket team plays an integral part of the novel. The park's long and rich history with cricket is related, but it is described as far inferior to a standard cricket field, although its leafy environs make it far superior to the city's other venues, located under or beside highways. The amenities of the clubhouse and quirks of the field are described in detail as well. His team even planted daffodil bulbs in order to "strengthen our claim on the park, a claim which in spite of its longevity we regarded, I believe correctly, as always under threat from unfriendly forces." Chuck, who also has his fingers in less than legal endeavors, is eventually murdered by unknown persons.

95. Petersen, David. *Never Say Never.* New York: iUniverse, 2004. 213pp.

In 1971, 8th grader Andy Hanson, from Ridgecrest Avenue in Eltingville, and his friends spend their time doing what many boys their age do: camping out in the backyard, causing mischief, talking about sex and going fishing. Andy's life takes a dramatic turn when he makes the impulsive decision to stick up for Jeffrey Fleming, a perpetually bullied gay student at their Bernstein Junior High School. Andy's own friends mock him for his actions and the school's most sadistic bully, Eugene, vows to commit horrific violence against the boys. When Jeffrey and Andy humiliate Eugene in a school dodgeball game, he is even further enraged. Despite the social pressure to ostracize Jeffrey, Andy agrees to be his friend. However, their friendship isn't long-lived, as Jeffrey goes missing and is found murdered near the Armstrong Avenue storm sewer.

A pederastic serial killer was at work on Staten Island, leaving victims in Lemon Creek and the Rossville boat graveyard. The police believe the case is solved after the math teacher at Bernstein Junior High passes away and pictures of most of the victims are found in his apartment. But it becomes apparent that an accomplice is on the loose, as Jeffrey's murder didn't follow the killer's usual m.o. and had occurred after the math teacher had died. Eugene runs into Andy in a deserted part of their school and admits that he hunted down Jeffrey and killed him in a homophobic rage, which he followed up by going home and killing his own mother. He tells Andy that he had been the math teacher's catamite until the teacher tired of him. He then served the teacher by bringing him other boys as sexual victims who would be killed when the teacher grew bored with them. Believing that Andy may have witnessed him kill Jeffrey, Eugene tries to murder him, but is stopped by a policeman. Andy goes to Jeffrey's wake and, courageously, admits to everyone that he was Jeffrey's friend.

This book describes the many wooded lots and wild areas that were once so common on Staten Island. The boys play in one that was created when city planners forced Amboy Road to run straighter, and created Old Amboy Road. At one point, Eugene talks about how his father worked on the Liquid Natural Gas tanks in Rossville but the community voted to close them down for fear of the danger.

96. Petrosini, Dan. *Complicit Witness*. CreateSpace, 2013. 224pp.

This novel of mafia types from the 1970s focuses on a couple of friends from the area around Arlene Street and Dawson Circle. Vinny goes straight but Tommy gets involved in his Uncle Lou's operation of loan sharking, gambling and other criminal enterprises. A Russian mobster, Yuri Popov, who has an office above a gym in a strip mall near the Staten Island Mall, forms a partnership with Uncle Lou, running illegal cigarettes and fixing horse races. When Lou gets cancer and dies, Yuri takes over the operation but his dabbling in non-traditional criminal enterprises- specifically those which cheat the city government of its taxes- draws the attention of a politically ambitious DA who vows to bring Yuri down. When Tommy is caught with a van-full of cocaine at the Outerbridge, he agrees to turn informer but gives the feds the slip before trial and starts a new life in Sicily with pilfered money. Various Staten Island street names, locales and restaurants are referenced here, such as Coral Lanes bowling alley, Carmen's restaurant in Annadale and the Jade Garden Chinese restaurant.

97. Pinto, K.T. *Sto's House Presents: Beer with a Mutant Chaser*. Howell, N.J.: Dark House, 2011. 167pp.

The toxic chemicals in the Fresh Kills landfill have caused much of Staten Island's population to develop mutations. Some unfortunates grow extra limbs or eyes or lizard scales, while some gain super powers, like the narrator Diana, a telekinetic who works in the auto center at the Mall. Known colloquially as "Changers," the mutants do their best to keep their powers concealed in a borough "where fitting in is everything." When Diana goes to buy a bean bag couch at the bean bag store in the Mall, she is assaulted by Angel, a Changer with six arms and four eyes, whose lesbian advances Diana had previously rebuffed. Diana is rescued by Chris, aka "Sto", a Changer who has the power to make people feel warm and happy. She is invited to his house, which is a 24/7 hangout for Changers, where they drink alcohol, smoke pot, eat pizza, watch movies and hook up. Most of the book revolves around the Changers rescuing friends from evil mutants and dealing with the various relationship issues most young singles face, with the added difficulty of mutant/mutant and mutant/normal dynamics.

One giant mutant threatens to destroy the Mall if they don't supply clothes that fit him. Another group of plus-sized, physically mutated Changers threaten to eat the Black Garter strip club (now saloon) because they couldn't get hired as performers. One dramatic rescue takes place in the sewer system under Hylan Boulevard and another takes place in an unnamed lighthouse. It's noted that everyone knows each other on the island and nothing is private. The narrator mentioned that the best pizzerias on Staten Island don't deliver. An extensive description of "The Cup" coffee house on Van Duzer St. is included.

98. Powell, Dawn. *The Wicked Pavilion.* Boston: Houghton Mifflin, 1954. 306pp.

The Cafe Julien ties together the multiple threads of this ensemble novel, one of which revolves around the plot by two failed painters, Ben Forrester and Dalzell Sloane, to capitalize on the newfound reputation (and inflated prices) of the artwork of their deceased friend, Marius. Passing off their own paintings as an original Marius or completing some unfinished sketch of his (some of which depicted the old taverns and street markets of Richmond and Tottenville), Ben and Dalzell make out handsomely. However, when Marius' widow from Staten Island comes to a retrospective event at the Cafe Julien bearing two theretofore unknown works by Marius, Ben realizes that something is amiss, as the long-dead Marius couldn't have painted a Staten Island bus line that only started running two years ago or the ruins of an island brewery that only burned down the previous year. Ben and Dalzell go out to Staten Island to investigate. As a place the trio would visit when they wanted to escape from the pressures of Manhattan relationships or financial troubles, it brings back happy memories. In fact, Ben recalls that the trip to Tottenville used to remind them of the one from Paris to St. Germain-en-Laye and indeed, the landscape and domestic architecture is described charmingly: "...as the sleepy little villages slipped by like pictures through an ancient stereoscope, ivy-grown station shanties, old corner taverns with pointed roofs, winding roads with weather-beaten houses whose gardens were already turning green, the meadows and village four corners seeming unchanged through the centuries." However, despite being the scene for many happy jaunts, Ben declares that he hates the island, since "...I only came there when I was dead broke or in trouble, and you know how you blame a place for that." They take the train to Tottenville, the "end of the world," to a ramshackle farmhouse where they discover a living Marius, who had taken advantage of his mistaken death to escape creditors, ex-wives, lovers and child support. He had considered hiding out in Rio but figured that Tottenville was even further from civilization.

99. Randisi, Robert. *The Disappearance of Penny.* New York: Charter, 1980. 234pp.

Henry (Hank) Po is a special investigator for the New York State Racing Club. He is sent to the horse track at Staten Island Downs to investigate the disappearance of Penny Hopkins, the beautiful daughter of renowned owner and trainer, Benjamin Hopkins. Penny was last seen alive by her father's hated rival, Paul Lassiter, with whom it was rumored she was having an affair. In the course of his investigation, Po begins his own affair with both a beautiful female jockey and Paul Lassiter's wife, while becoming entangled in the problems of two jockeys, one of whom ends up dead and the other missing. In the meantime, Penny's body is discovered buried near Staten Island Downs. Po eventually connects the death of the one jockey to mafia race-fixing and captures the culprit by running him down with a horse. He then located the missing jockey, a bisexual gun-fanatic, who admits to having a hand in Penny's death. It is revealed that, after getting the idea from an old movie, Penny decided that she could reconcile her father and Paul Lassiter, whose mutual enmity was causing her terrible grief, by committing suicide. In exchange for sex, the bisexual jockey lent her his gun and buried her after she committed suicide.

Staten Island references are mainly geographical, with references to place names and landmarks, such as Todt Hill and the Verrazano Bridge, but is it mentioned that Staten Island Downs was built in the Clove Lakes area in order to develop the island.

100. Reigada, Flora. *The Face Behind the Veil.* Bloomington, Ind.: AuthorHouse, 2004. 613pp.

Probably close to four hundred pages of this episodic, Christian-themed, multi-generational epic take place on Staten Island, but even when the various characters leave for other locales, they are continually drawn back home.

The patriarch of the Kahn family, Abraham, flees German anti-Semitism in the early part of the twentieth century and settles on Staten Island where he changes his name to Albert, converts to Protestantism, joins the Brighton Heights Reformed church, and buys a group of row houses (now landmarked) on the southern part of Westervelt Avenue, known as Horton's Row, where he resides with his extended family and assorted tenants. In 1925 Albert's son Jacob and his wife Estelle have a daughter, Naomi, who is born with a caul over her face, an ancient sign that she would have the gift of prophecy and special supernatural insights, although the culturally Christian Kahns don't put much stock in the legend. However, Naomi would indeed often see and feel the presence of demons and angels, hear comforting divine messages, and even experienced a vision of God. Mr. Jesse, the old, African-American custodian at the St. George Theater where her father worked as a projectionist, was a devout Christian who spoke to Naomi about Jesus and prophesied that God had a special purpose for her life, but as Naomi grew older she dismissed the supernatural experiences of her childhood as juvenile fantasies.

Naomi moves to Fort Hill with her family, in a house located across from the ruins of Daniel Tompkins' mansion and on top of a Hessian cemetery. During World War II she begins dating an English sailor, Cedric, who is a devout Christian and wants to marry her, but his ship is torpedoed by the Nazis and he is presumed lost at sea. The Kahns then move into a house on Vanderbilt Avenue, across from the U.S. Public Health Service hospital. When Naomi begins working as a switchboard operator at Halloran Hospital, she meets and marries a wounded Marine, Rick, who turns out to be a violent alcoholic with PTSD. After divorcing him, her old beau Cedric returns to Staten Island, alive but insane from the horrors he experienced after his ship was sunk. When he hears about Naomi's marriage, he attacks her and is forcibly committed to an insane asylum and deported. The next damaged man Naomi gets involved with is Walt, a married ne'er-do-well she meets at Tompkinsville Pool. After impregnating her, he joins the Merchant Marine, but returns to her, divorces his wife and marries Naomi. They have a daughter Rebecca and move into one of the apartments on Horton's Row. They are continually arguing, mostly about Walt's inability to find work, which he attributes to his debilitating migraine headaches. A move to Boston doesn't work out so they come back and live on Grymes Hill, where they can see the Verrazano Bridge being constructed. Although overdevelopment was apparent even by the late 1950s, the island still existed in a state of splendid isolation, but Naomi couldn't help but notice the rising number of minorities and the increase in crime in their old neighborhoods of Stapleton and St. George, while sensing that the new bridge would only exacerbate the problems. In particular, Naomi notes how the Italians who used to live in the area around the Jersey Street Sanitation garage were leaving and being replaced by African-Americans and Hispanics.

Naomi finally leaves the hapless and abusive Walt and moves to Miami with Rebecca after the deaths of her grandfather Albert and her father Jacob, but eventually returns to an apartment on Horton's Row. Rebecca, who has inherited her mother's gift of supernatural perception, attends Curtis High School and begins hanging out with Puerto Rican girls who drink, smoke pot and drop acid. However, she starts dating the girls' cousin, the handsome, born-again Christian Mike Perez. They get married, move to Virginia and start a family, with Rebecca eventually having a born-again experience and devoting herself to God. Naomi remarries as well and moves to Queens. Her husband Hank is mentally unbalanced but generally kind, and it was his influence that convinced Rebecca's daughter Teresa to convert to Catholicism as a young woman. From a hundred different threads of plot, too obviously autobiographical to be truly coherent in a novelistic way, characters live and die and only some of them come to Christ in the end. However, after the death of her husband, Naomi moves back to Staten Island where she eventually buys and restores her father's house in Stapleton. One day she is surprised to see her old sweetheart Cedric, now aged, show up at her door. Still deranged, he tries to murder Naomi, but before he can strike she cries out to Christ as her Messiah and is saved, spiritually and physically, by divine intervention.

In addition to the above, characters here go sledding at Silver Lake during the Depression, and eat at the Woolworth's lunch counter near Stapleton Park, where mothers would leave their babies in their carriages on the sidewalk while they went shopping. The Decoration Day parade in 1941 is described as a major local event, proceeding down Victory Boulevard to Stapleton Park. Naomi sees Frank Sinatra perform at a club on Forest Avenue. Mention is made of the transformation of Halloran Hospital into the Willowbrook State School. St. George Theatre is described as hosting Mae West, Jimmy Durante and Ted Lewis, among other acts. The author maintains a website, www.simemories.com, in which many of her biographical details can be seen to have been the basis of her characters and story.

101. Rendelstein, Jill Ellen. *Staten Doll.* (Master's thesis). Washington D.C.: American University, 2000. 98pp.
It is 1987 on Staten Island, the age of big hair and "mint" guys with white Trans Ams, herringbone chains, Drakar Noir cologne and Cavaricci pants. Jackie is a fourteen-year-year old girl who lives in a newly constructed townhouse development on Arthur Kill Road, next

to the Fresh Kills Landfill. Tall and gawky, she is beginning her freshman year at Tottenville High School and dealing with more than the usual share of adolescent angst and insecurities. She pines to get a boyfriend and finally get kissed, as her best friend Michelle seems to have little problem doing.

For no apparent reason, Jackie is bullied and even beaten by a clique of older and more popular girls. Some neighborhood boys even pelt her and Michelle with eggs and pour urine on them. One night Jackie and Michelle put on their most provocative clothes and hitch a ride with a couple of boys in a Trans Am, who take them down to Wolfe's Pond. Michelle goes off with the more handsome boy and engages in some inadvertent outercourse, while Jackie converses uncomfortably with the other boy. When Michelle asks Jackie's help cleaning herself up, the boys drive off and leave the girls behind. They hitch another ride to the UA bowling alley in Travis and meet up with some friends. While there, Jackie catches the eye of a "mint" boy named Marc from Bayonne. Even though they hit it off and he admits he likes her, Michelle swoops in and is making out with him before he leaves. After stewing over the incident, Jackie calls up Marc and demands an explanation. She wins him back by her assertiveness, which leads to a visit from Marc in which they engage in some heavy petting while her parents are out. Before his second visit to Staten Island with two of his friends, Jackie brags to her neighborhood antagonists that her boyfriend and his posse are going to beat them up. When they arrive, the neighborhood boys are waiting for them with their older brothers and they beat up Marc and his friends. Marc is convinced that Jackie set him up and refuses to speak to her. She gets a friend to drive her and Michelle to Bayonne to try to win Marc back. She is determined to sleep with him if that's what it will take. When she is let into his house, he is cool towards her but takes her into the bathroom and coerces her into giving him sexual relief of a manual nature. That seems to make things right and then she is basically dismissed. As she leaves, she is wondering if one of Marc's friends likes her.

Jackie's father is a native Staten Islander and tells her about the days when the island was quiet and friendly. In Jackie's day though, she views the people of Staten Island as rude, ignorant, selfish, aggressive and close minded. Granted, most of them are not from Staten Island, since the island was undergoing a massive population influx in the late 1980s with accompanying overdevelopment and change. Trees were being torn down and new houses constructed, that would be occupied by new people. The landfill was a metaphor for Staten Island, since it was not only getting literal garbage dumped on it by the rest of the city, but it was getting people dumped on it by the other boroughs. A transplant herself, Jackie viewed the North Shore of the island as a place of run-down houses and businesses, while the South Shore was clean and new but had to bear the albatross of the dump.

102.   Reynolds, D(ewey) B. *Master of Plagues*. CreateSpace.com, 2011. 257pp.

When a group of his NYU classmates play a horrifying prank on him, nerdy Stuart Dufflemeyer from 695 Barlow Avenue, in the mixed Italian/Jewish neighborhood of Arden Heights, recites some incantations over a talisman an old rabbi had given him and is granted the power to control animals and the elements of nature. He summons armies of rats, bees, sharks and other creatures to physically plague the classmates who pranked him, while righting other wrongs in the world. He finally meets and loses his virginity to a beautiful Jewish virgin (whom he later marries), while convincing his tormentors to apologize for their prank and learn to treat others as they would be treated. Besides the protagonist's very specific Staten Island address, there is no other Staten Island content.

103.   Robertson, Eleanor Marie (J.D. Robb, pseud.). "Missing in Death" in *Ritual in Death and Missing in Death*. London: Piatkus, 2013. 292pp. pgs 137-281.

In this installment of the futuristic *In Death* series, set in the 2050s aboard the ferry *Hillary Rodham Clinton*, a female tourist goes missing after she enters an out-of-order bathroom and sees a man standing above a murdered woman. Lieutenant Eve Dallas and partner Delia Peabody begin to investigate, when the missing woman suddenly reappears but without any recollection of what happened. Dallas' investigation leads her into a maze of corporate espionage, sci-fi weaponry and assassins to discover why the victim had been killed on the ferry and how her murderer spirited away the corpse.

104.   Rozan, S(hira) J(udith). *Absent Friends*. New York: Delacorte Press, 2004. 367pp.

This novel centers around a group of Staten Island friends who have to deal with the loss of one of their circle on 9/11 and the subsequent revelation that he may not have lived up to his heroic public image. When legendary firefighter James McCaffery died at the

World Trade Center on 9/11, a memorial fund in his name was set up with his childhood friend and former lover, Marian Gallagher, as its administrator. When reporter Harry Randall is assigned to write a hagiographic story on McCaffery, he instead uncovers some facts that suggest the martyred firefighter had illegal dealings with Eddie Spano, a mafia-connected developer from the old neighborhood. For propriety's sake, Marian had rejected Spano's donation to the memorial fund, but Randall's story threatens to discredit the entire endeavor. When Randall jumps to his death off the Verrazano Bridge, his colleague and lover, Laura Stone, takes up his baton and vows to not only pursue the truth about McCaffery but prove that Randall was murdered.

The basis of the allegation against McCaffery involves his role in providing for the widow of a murdered friend, Mark Keegan, who was imprisoned for the 1979 killing of Jack Molloy, the son of the local Irish mobster. Although he was found to have acted in self-defense, and only received a short sentence for weapons possession, Keegan was killed in a jailhouse brawl. When Phil Constantine, the lawyer for Keegan's widow, Sally, refused to sue, McCaffery claimed to have brought a lawsuit against New York State and won a sizeable monthly stipend for Sally, that was disbursed to her through Constantine. However, Harry Randall discovered that no lawsuit had ever been filed against the state, so the question was how McCaffery was able to provide so generously for Sally Keegan and her son out of his firefighter's salary, and why. As the circle of friends from "Pleasant Hills" included members of both the Spano and Molloy crime families, an illegal connection was assumed. As Laura Stone travels back and forth to Staten Island on the ferry to interview people, a story emerges.

The head of the Molloy crime family had asked McCaffery to tell his son Jack, a wild and violent criminal, that the police were about to bust him and that he should tone down his activities. McCaffery confided this to Mark Keegan, who took it upon himself to warn Jack. The paranoid Jack Malloy assumed that Mark had some involvement with the police and confronted him with a gun while they were hanging out with Jimmie McCaffery and his other brother, Tom Molloy (who later dismantled his father's criminal empire and went straight.) Laura Stone's working theory is that Jimmy McCaffery killed Jack Molloy but Mark Keegan took the blame to save his friend's firefighting career. An ex-policeman tells Laura Stone that he suspects that the Spanos planted the story about Jack's arrest so as to create dissension in their rivals' ranks. When Mark Keegan's son, Kevin, hears about this theory, he goes to confront Eddie Spano at one of his ugly Staten Island townhouse developments and gets killed when he attacks him.

Laura Stone later discovers papers that Jimmie McCaffery had left behind, revealing that it was Tom Molloy who not only invented the story about the imminent police bust, but who killed his brother in self-defense when Jack shot at Mark Keegan. Mark Keegan took the blame to protect both Jimmie McCaffery's career and Tom Molloy's relationship with his parents. Laura also comes to realize that Harry Randall really did kill himself from guilt over destroying the reputation of a desperately needed hero in the city's darkest hour. Although the Staten Island neighborhood where the characters grew up is given the fictional name of "Pleasant Hills", the fact that the local church is St. Ann's might mark it as a thinly disguised Dongan Hills. In flashbacks to the 1970s, characters eat at Montezuma's restaurant in St. George and meet at Flanagan's Bar. One character describes Tottenville in 1980 as a "mini-Appalachia...where rusting cars were lawn ornaments and chickens shared the yards with scruffy dogs."

105. Sampson, John. *O, Call Back Yesterday.* Castleton, Vt.: Thornfield Press, 1989. 197pp.
    Ted Bradbury is an American accountant who is a good friend of British politician and wealthy industrialist Geoffrey Farrington. On a trade mission to the U.S., Farrington causes a diplomatic incident with some impolitic remarks and then disappears after withdrawing a large sum of money and visiting the Soviet embassy with copies of top secret documents in his possession. Both the British government and the FBI suspect Farrington of espionage. Bradbury locates Farrington at the Bayview estate in Staten Island, the home of the wealthy Henry and Nellie Van Twiller. Mr. Van Twiller had run into Farrington at South Ferry and so impressed him with tales of Staten Island history that Farrington decided to visit the island that day. Van Twiller showed him around and invited him back to his home, where Farrington had a sort of nervous breakdown. The doctors advised rest, so he had been staying there ever since.

Farrington justified his actions to Bradbury as perfectly innocent, explaining that he was using his time at Bayview to write the biography of Cola di Rienzi that he had been planning to do since he was a student in Italy. A frustrated humanist, Farrington had been forced to marry for money and go into his father-in-law's business. During one of their forays into New Dorp, Farrington and Bradbury rescue a girl, Jackie Singleton, from a violent suitor. She becomes his secretary at the bungalow on the Bayview estate where Farrington is staying, and falls in love with him. Farrington's shrewish wife locates him and initiates divorce proceedings. That pleased Farrington since, during his convalescence, his friends manage to track down and bring his old flame, Lisa, to Staten Island. The couple comes close to ending their respective marriages and rekindling their relationship, but Lisa demurs. Farrington eventually steals Bradbury's rich, virginal Spanish girlfriend and plans to marry her, but that relationship too fails. The scorned woman retaliates by informing the FBI of Farrington's whereabouts. He and Bradbury are arrested for espionage, but Farrington's highly placed connections pull some strings and get them released. Farrington finally realizes that Jackie Singleton is the woman for him and they set sail for England aboard the QE2 intending to get married.

As with other of his books, Sampson's Staten Island is a place of mystery, enchantment and senseless violence. The lake at Bayview is the source of an Indian legend that anyone who swims in it has his wishes come true. Staten Island settings populate the book: Orbach Lake, the Vanderbilt mausoleum, New Dorp, Snug Harbor, St. Andrew's, the Moravian church, the Lane Theatre, and more. Farrington attends a public meeting being held to discuss the fact that land which was intended to become a park was now going to be made into a military installation. The local politicians are described as acquiescent, and the public as passive, until Farrington fires them up with his Parliamentary eloquence. He even makes favorable reference to the Secession movement. When a heckler objected that they didn't need "no foreigner" telling them what to do, the man was beaten by the crowd. Farrington concluded by urging Staten Islanders to stand up to outsiders, stop being pushed around and to take charge of their own affairs.

106. Sampson, John. *Up at Lighthouse Hill*. Hinesburg, Vt.: Thornfield Press, 1999. 203pp.
      In the years after the Vietnam War, young Frank Paradino of Staten Island rents an apartment at Quiberon House, a Lighthouse Hill home which is reputed to have been built by the pirate Black Dick, and which has been in old John Pettigrew's family since the Revolution. As Pettigrew is aging and in poor health, the tenants of Quiberon House

are concerned about the disposition of the property after his death, especially since rents on Staten Island have soared in recent years. Pettigrew has a son, Sebastian, whom no one has ever seen but who is known to have been a wild and violent young man who hasn't been heard from since he was compelled to join the army. The tenants are eager to discover Sebastian's whereabouts, in order to alert him to his father's failing health and determine his intentions for Quiberon House. One night a mysterious stranger named Mr. Memphis arrives and threatens John Pettigrew's life, which sends him into a rapid decline and quick death.

Frank Paradino works as a waiter in a St. George restaurant, where he regularly serves the wealthy financier Daniel Prescott Connor, his beautiful daughter Cynthia, her fiancé Jorge Dablado, and her friend Maud Sealy. They frequently visit Staten Island in order to see Mrs. Connor, Cynthia's mother, who is estranged from Mr. Connor. One night, Frank breaks up an attempted mugging of Cynthia and Jorge and captures the assailant, for which he receives a $5000 reward from Mr. Connor and a growing acquaintance with Cynthia. Frank is then summoned to the Howard Ave. home of Cynthia's mother, who encourages him to date her daughter, as she believes that Cynthia's needs a strong hand, which the tough, working-class Paradino can provide. His relationship with Cynthia develops into a romance, but he begins a friendship with Maud Sealy as well, and takes her to see Staten Island and meet his friends at Quiberon House. They visit the Tibetan Museum, Richmondtown and St. Andrew's church.

Frank and Cynthia's relationship is flourishing, but Cynthia angrily dumps him when pictures of their romantic weekend in Atlantic City are splashed all over the newspapers. When Frank goes to confront Cynthia at her apartment, he catches her in a compromising situation with a business associate of her father's, whom Mr. Connor had encouraged her to sleep with in order to gain some advantageous information. Frank and the businessman fight over Cynthia and Frank gets arrested. The news of the altercation is kept out of the newspapers due to the influence of Mrs. Connor and Congressman Jimmy Puckering, a former student of Stella Atkins, a retired Wagner College professor and a resident of Quiberon House. Because he had taken his boss' car to go to Cynthia's apartment, Frank loses his job at the restaurant.

Tom Bramhall, a resident of Quiberon House, bought a local newspaper, the Weekly Mercury, and employed his son Charles as editor. Thanks to the encouragement of Stella Atkins, Frank has been furthering his education, and is invited to do some reporting for the Mercury, where he flourishes as a journalist. As a favor to Stella and Frank, Congressman Puckering investigated Sebastian Pettigrew and determined that he had been involved in drug smuggling, but was now dead. Therefore, Quiberon House would be put up for auction by the city.

Before that can happen however, a party of English people arrive claiming ownership of the property. Lady Rockhampton and her son Viscount Peter Kingsbury explain that their ancestor, Lord Rockhampton (Admiral Lord Howe's second-in-command during the American Revolution), built Quiberon House in 1776 as a fortified dwelling for his commander. After the war the property was left in the care of a Lt. Pettigrew, whose Patriot family ensured the house against confiscation. Admiral Howe died and left the property to Rockhampton, who leased it to Pettigrew. The transaction was then forgotten by both families until now, when the Rockhamptons re-discovered their ownership of Quiberon House and have come to reclaim it. The people of Lighthouse Hill become inflamed by the rumor that the British are plotting to fortify Quiberon House with the aim of retaking Richmondtown and perhaps all of Staten Island. The English are hissed by a mob of people after services at St. Andrew's, anti-British placards are hung all over the area and a public meeting is held, in which all manner of hysterical xenophobia is given vent. When Sebastian Pettigrew is discovered alive, but on death row in a Tennessee prison, the opponents of the British find him a useful pawn.

Sebastian had faked his own death and continued his life of crime, culminating in the murder of his wife. The people of Staten Island rally behind him and hire a lawyer to have him freed and declared the lawful owner of Quiberon House. The English concede, as they do not have the money to fight for the house in court. However, when Lady Rockhampton's daughter Ramona, who has been mute and catatonic since the death of her husband Fred on their wedding day, suddenly begins to speak when she mistakes Frank Paradino for her late husband, Viscount Kingsbury decides to fight for what is rightfully his.

In the meantime, the Weekly Mercury runs a story about Mr. Connor that does substantial harm to his business. He nevertheless offers Viscount Kingsbury a position in his London office. The English decide to return home and invite Frank to come with them for a visit. While there, Ramona makes a complete recovery and Viscount Kingsbury and Cynthia Connor begin a romantic relationship. Frank returns home with the intention of marrying Maud Sealy.

He comes back to find Richmondtown preparing to welcome home Sebastian Pettigrew. In fact, a committee of citizens had gone down to Tennessee to escort him home, but all of them abandoned him as they saw what a violent drunkard he was. When Sebastian and his friend Mr. Memphis finally make it back to Quiberon House, he brandishes a gun and orders all the residents to leave within five minutes. With the help of Viscount Kingsbury, the residents of Quiberon House fight off Pettigrew and Memphis, kick them out, barricade the doors and defend the house from their attack, which includes burning part of it down with Molotov cocktails. The people of Quiberon House successfully beat back the onslaught and Pettigrew and Memphis are never heard from again.

107. Sholl, Anna McClure [Geoffrey Corson, pseud.]. *Blue Blood and Red.* New York: Henry Holt, 1915. 395pp.

In this novel of cross-class and interfaith romance, fourteen-year-old orphan Neal Carmichael lives in his aristocratic Staten Island family's hilltop mansion which overlooks the bay, a homestead which a seafaring ancestor had established in the eighteenth century. The household was headed by Neal's grandfather, Alexander Carmichael, and populated by various eccentric aunts and uncles. Neal attended the private Bradford Academy, whose students were disdained by the working-class boys who lived at the bottom of the hill and attended P.S. 49. Nevertheless, Neal- a passionate baseball player- worshipped one of those public school boys: James "Chick" McCoy, the star pitcher of the Irish Terriers. When Chick was injured in a game, Neal fought for his chance to replace Chick on the mound and proved a worthy understudy. The boys return to the McCoy household to celebrate, where Neal meets several people who would play a role in the later life: Dr. Murphy, Father Carew (the Catholic priest), and Chick's sister Patricia. Neal was charmed by these Irish, working-class people, with whom he identified. Patricia, on the other hand, was an aspiring aristocrat and became smitten with Neal. When Neal decided to invite

Chick and Patricia to a party he was hosting, the intermingling of classes stirred up a great deal of consternation in both the McCoy and Carmichael families. And while the boys of Neal's acquaintance immediately took to Chick, Patricia was snubbed by the girls, especially by the twelve-year-old Ada Fleming, who saw Patricia as a rival for Neal's affections. Nevertheless, Neal and the McCoys bonded, until one day Alexander Carmichael summoned Neal and ordered him to quit the baseball team and cut off all contact with Chick and Patricia. Neal's dissolute uncle Jack, who was known for his affairs with lower class women, had gotten one into trouble and been exiled to Venice. The family patriarch was trying to avoid a similar problem with the egalitarian Neal.

The children went their separate ways, with Neal attending Oxford and Patricia obtaining a master's degree and becoming a nurse who works with the poor in the tenements of the lower East Side. Upon Neal's return to the United States, he is informed by his cousin Peter that the family fortunes are low and the deed for Carmichael house is held by Dr. Murphy. Despite the Carmichaels' financial need, Neal rejects a job in the stock market and becomes a reporter for the Courier, covering the immigrant-filled tenements of the East Side, where he eventually reunites with Patricia. Still carrying a torch for Neal, she has consistently rejected the proposals of Dr. Murphy's son Thomas, a successful wrecking-yard owner. Neal and Patricia's activities are initially limited to their charitable and progressive endeavors, but when Neal's cousin Polly eloped with a penniless man and become pregnant, Patricia assists in the childbirth, which killed both mother and child.

Neal is also reunited with the seductive and scheming Ada Fleming, his great love, and proposes marriage. Noticing his infatuation with Patricia, when Ada reads about a charitable census of Staten Island that Neal and Patricia are working on, she breaks off their engagement and sails to England where she eventually becomes engaged to Wentworth, an English nabob. While conducting their Staten Island census, Neal proposes to Patricia, fulfilling her lifelong dream. The Carmichaels, devastated by the death of Polly, reluctantly accept Patricia and the couple begins a lackluster preparation for a wedding. Trouble becomes apparent when Neal, although gradually losing his faith, violently declares that any children they might have must be raised in his family's Anglican religion and not Patricia's Catholicism. Patricia reluctantly accedes, but breaks off the engagement when she recognizes that Neal is still in love with Ada.

Neal, realizing the same thing, sails to London and marries Ada. As a wedding present, the wealthy Ada lifts the Carmichaels' mortgage and rescues the family from impoverishment, but her purse strings prove to be chains as she asserts her control over the entire family, occupying the late Polly's bedroom, renovating the entire house in her own style and running around with a series of young paramours, while openly declaring that she won't bear Neal's children. Their relationship becomes estranged, as Neal becomes a stock broker in the hope of breaking free of Ada's gilded cage.

Patricia meanwhile has given in to family pressure and accepted Tom Murphy's proposal, advising him that she will be a good wife but never love him. Her path intersects with Neal again when he agrees to give some Carmichael land to Jim and Lil, a reformed thief and prostitute couple whom Patricia had been helping. Neal kisses Patricia, who declares that they must never see each other again. A short time later they both by chance happen to take shelter from a storm in the same deserted farmhouse, where they give into their desires and make love. Guilt-stricken Patricia finds out that she's pregnant and runs away to Jim and Lil's cottage to give birth, leaving a letter with her family explaining that she's on a nursing assignment. When her father, captaining his tugboat up the Arthur Kill, discovers her sitting on a dock with a baby, he realizes the truth and flees from her in horror. With her secret exposed, Patricia has her baby- named Neal- baptized by Father Carew and flees to the mountains of Tennessee to help an old doctor care for the hill folk.

Ada meanwhile has run away with her old lover Wentworth, and had Neal served with divorce papers. When Neal finds out what has happened to Patricia, he resolves to find her and bring her back as his wife. Neal's friend, an Anglican priest, advises him to "...go to her altar, if she will not kneel at yours." Neal does track her down in the mountains and the book ends with the implication that Neal will become Catholic and thus somehow be able to marry Patricia in the near future, (a strange plot device, noted by some reviewers of the time, considering Catholic belief in the indissolubility of marriage).

Most of the story takes place on Staten Island, with several scenes taking place on the ferry, whose leisurely sociability would seem very familiar to a modern reader. Other island landmarks are thinly disguised: Patricia has an old sailor uncle who lives at "Mariner's Rest," an institution for retired seamen; although the McCoys' Catholic church- St. Margaret's- could not be discerned in any historical place of worship, the Carmichaels' St. Anne's Episcopal seems- by way of geographic description- to clearly be St. Andrew's. The Proceedings of the Staten Island Institute of Arts and Sciences (Vol VI. Part II. Feb.-May 1916) notes that the mill where Patricia and Neal kissed, and the farmhouse where they made love, were well-known buildings in the Richmondtown area and that several other pseudonymous place names and landmarks would be recognizable to readers.

108.   Smith, F(rancis) Hopkinson. *Tom Grogan*. New York: Houghton Mifflin, 1896. 247pp.

In this didactic, anti-labor union novel, Mary Grogan, universally known as "Tom," is an Irish-American stevedore foreman who is supervising the unloading of supplies for the construction of a seawall at the Lighthouse Depot in St. George. Mary's husband, Tom, had been injured on a job site seven years earlier, in an act of labor union sabotage, and was confined to a state institution because of his injuries or, some said, because of mental illness. Mary had taken over both Tom's position and his name and had earned her place at the head of the crew through her indomitable will and mastery of the trade. Her independent existence, as a woman in charge of a business, and as a non-union employer, draws the enmity of the local labor union and her business rival Dan McGaw.

McGaw repeatedly tries to ruin Grogan, in every possible, underhanded way. He first badmouths her to her employer, Babcock, and tries to shame him for hiring a woman, an unheard-of phenomenon. When that fails, he appeals to the powerful local Union, which goes through back channels to try and suborn Tom's workers and even tries to enlist the support of the local Catholic priest, all of whom reject the Union's enticements. The sons of the Union men even beat Tom's crippled son, Patsy, a tactic to which their fathers regularly resort against recalcitrant non-Union workers. Tom meanwhile, wins a contract to haul coal to the German brewery but chooses to give it up when the tenement wives tell her that the Union will call a strike and boycott of the brewery if it gives the contract to Tom, resulting in misery for their families. When the village Board of Trustees calls for bids on a road building project, Tom and McGaw vie for the contract, with Tom's low bid winning the job at the last minute. McGaw's son sets fire to Tom's barn and McGaw himself tries to kill Tom with a hammer in order to ensure that she not sign the valuable contract, but she survives and stumbles into the Village Hall on the verge of death, signing the paper at the 11th hour. McGaw next challenges the legality of Tom's signature, not only for being that of her husband but, it is revealed, for being that of a dead man, as Tom Grogan had actually died seven years earlier. Mary explains that she had maintained the fiction of his hospitalization and continued to sign his name to documents, as she wanted to honor his memory and also because she feared the reaction of employers who, although satisfied with Mary's work, might object to employing a woman who lacked the spiritual cover of a living (albeit absent) husband. The honest Judge Bowker finds for Tom when he discerns that no fraud was intended and all parties were aware of Tom's identity. McGaw later drowns and his son is sent to prison for the arson, but his family is saved from ruin when Tom employs his youngest son in her business.

Although the anti-union attitude is most obvious, with unions and their members being described as dishonest, violent, lazy and corrupt, its anti-Irishness is less overt but obvious. Its protagonist is indeed Irish, but so are every wicked union member and profiteering politician on the Village Board of Trustees, the only two honest members of which are the Anglo-Saxon and Scot. The intricacies of awarding labor contracts are described intimately.

Although Staten Island is the vague background for this story, with only a few place names being mentioned, some of the small details, such as the German brewery and the character descriptions of the members of the Board of Trustees, give the feeling that they were written by someone familiar with the place. Arthur Bartlett Maurice's *New York in Fiction* (Ira J. Friedman, Inc. 1899) reveals that Smith was inspired to write *Tom Grogan* by his own experiences as a contractor for the Lighthouse Depot on Staten Island. It was there that he met the real life "Tom Grogan," a stevedore named Mrs. Bridget Morgan. That book contains photographs of the home and barn of Mrs. Morgan, as well as the sea wall that played a part in the novel. Maurice intimates that the episodes in the book were based on actual events, going so far as to identify the saloon where Dan McGaw laid his plots and the specific room over the Stapleton Post Office where Judge Bowker ruled in favor of Tom.

109. Smith, Martin Cruz. *Gorky Park*. New York: Random House, 1981. 365pp.

When three mysterious corpses are discovered in Moscow's Gorky Park, Soviet police detective Arkady Renko's investigation leads him into a murky labyrinth of high politics and shady business dealings involving millions of dollars of sable martens, valued for their fur. Renko's investigation eventually takes him to New York where, in cooperation with the FBI, the sables are revealed to be hidden on Staten Island, in a salvage yard on the Arthur Kill, an area described as consisting of "... all woods and swamps, a couple of refineries, a few local people who mind their own business and no cops." Although only the final confrontation and shootout take place on Staten Island, some passages bear noting. Taking a car ferry over to the island, an American notes that the deck of the ferry is one of the favorite suicide spots in New York City. Upon first sight of St. George, an FBI agent says that it's "...a part of New York City, no matter what people say." And Arkady Renko muses that "St. George was practically a Russian village. The streets were deeply rutted in snow and the traffic was almost stationary. The cars were old and rusted, the people drably dressed in hoods and boots. The houses were small, with real chimneys and real smoke. There was a statue with snowy epaulets. But the shops had fresh meat and poultry and seafood."

110. Smith, Patricia, ed. *Staten Island Noir*. New York: Akashic Books, 2012. 252pp.

The *Noir* series of short story collections by Akashic books feature noir fiction set in many of the world's great cities, with volumes for the other four boroughs of New York having been previously published. In *Snake Hill* by Bill Loehfelm, the younger incarnations of his characters from *Bloodroot* accidentally hit an old man while driving down Snake Hill after a night of partying. They find the man alive but suffering and suffocate him to death. *Sister-in-Law* by Louisa Ermelino tells of a protective sister who has her prospective sister-in-law murdered and encased in her Florence Street wall when the woman casually mentioned moving away from Staten Island after their marriage. *In When They Are Done with Us* by Patricia Smith, the narrator has to deal with a violently abusive sixteen-year-old-son. Inspired by the real life case of Leisa Jones, who murdered her family and committed suicide in

2010, the narrator does the same to herself and her dangerous son. In *A User's Guide to Keeping Your Kills Fresh* by Ted Anthony, an inept hit man is stymied by the closing of the Fresh Kills landfill when he finds that his dumping ground is now off limits. In *Dark Was the Night, Cold Was the Ground* by Shay Youngblood, an African American widow gets involved with a group of Italian American women in South Beach who fantasize about killing their husbands. In *Mistakes* by Michael Penncavage, a spilled drink at a bachelor party ends in justifiable manslaughter on the Staten Island ferry. *Abating a Nuisance* by Bruce DeSilva dramatizes the burning of the Quarantine in 1858. In *Paying the Tab* by Michael Largo, a Four Corners bar owner has a deadly run-in with the ghost of bank robber Willie Sutton. *Assistant Professor Lodge* by Bonnie Kirshenbaum tells the story of a Wagner College professor who watches a colleague murder his wife. In *...spy verse spy...* by Todd Craig, a hit man deals with betrayal and a bad cop on the mean streets of Park Hill. *Before it Hardens* by Eddie Joyce describes the thoughts and emotions of an Annadale teen who believed that he had impregnated his girlfriend. *The Fly-Ass Puerto Rican Girl from the Stapleton Projects* by Linda Nieves Powell tells the story of how an interracial relationship between a Puerto Rican girl from Stapleton and a Rosebank Italian boy led to the girl's abduction and murder thirty years ago. In *Teenage Wasteland* by Ashley Dawson, a teenage punk rocker becomes an environmental justice crusader after surreptitiously observing illegal dumping at the Fresh Kills Landfill. In *Lighthouse* by S.J. Rozan, a junkie with voices in his head tries to rob the Tibetan Museum but falls to his death when he tries to kill his hallucination of a Buddhist nun.

111. Spellman, Francis Cardinal. *The Foundling*. New York: Charles Scribner's Sons, 1951. 304pp.

In this pious tribute to New York's Catholic charitable institutions for orphans, and to the clergy who ran them, Paul Taggart, a maimed veteran of the Great War, discovers an abandoned baby in the Christmas crèche at St. Patrick's cathedral and takes it to the New York Foundling Hospital for care. Having fallen in love with the baby boy, Taggart and his new wife want to adopt him, but the nuns who run the hospital forbid it because of the Taggarts' Protestantism. Nevertheless, the couple maintains contact with the boy (christened Peter Lane) and mentor him through his youth as he grows up at "Mount Mary", the bucolic orphan farm on Staten Island, a transparent stand-in for Mount Loretto. As one of the nuns describes it: "It's beautiful out there...Most New Yorkers don't know Staten Island. Only a short- and exciting- ferry ride from Manhattan, and then real country!" Peter grows up at the Mount, learning farming and music in addition to the standard curriculum. When he graduates, Peter stays on to work for the institution as assistant caretaker, while attempting to complete the unfinished symphony of a beloved nun who had died. Although he spends most of his life at the Mount on Staten Island, detailed description is lacking, but the priests and nuns who administer the place are portrayed as loving and nurturing towards their charges, among whom number the handicapped and racial minorities, who are treated with equality and respect. The adult Peter goes on to find true love and fight in World War II.

112. Spiers, A(ugustus) M(ansfield). *Nell of Narragansett Bay.* Boston: The Stratford Co., 1925. 294pp.

When, in 1899, horticulture Professor Jack Fox Mansfield hears about the extraordinary prices being obtained for prize carnations, he decides to quit his position and go into the floral business. Reading about some greenhouses for sale on Staten Island, he decides to relocate there, especially considering his family's distant roots on the island (he knows that certain ancestors were buried at St. Andrew's in Cuchelstown and an old family legend tells of a treasure buried on a nearby Lakes Island). Mansfield makes his way to New York and takes the ferry to Staten Island, the "beautiful 'Isle of the Sea' as poets and writers fondly call it..." To him it appeared "a huge fairyland with toy villages dotting the landscape... [with] an abundance of trees and shrubs between the houses..." He is directed to take the streetcar to its last stop at Richmond and to walk up the hill past St. Andrew's. He does so and meets Mr. Depew, an old man with a long memory.

Depew reveals that Cuchelstown is now called Richmond and the St. Andrew's church Jack had just passed was the burial place of his ancestors. He talks about the history of the Fox Estate, where the greenhouses are located, which was once one of the biggest estates of Staten Island but which began to be sold off in the 1750s. The marshes on the estate were used by the Americans during the Revolution and Depew mentions Lakes Island, which is actually a peninsula on the Kill where the last Squire of the Fox Estate met with George Washington. It was that Squire's daughter who eloped to New England with a Hessian officer named Mansfield and who, Jack realizes, were his direct ancestors. Jack buys the greenhouses but the land itself is held by a real estate company, albeit with an uncertain title since the rightful heir

(Jack of course) has never come forward. In a conversation with the County Clerk, Joseph Simonson, it is recommended that Jack buy up the property at once, because land values had already risen to $1000 an acre since Staten Island had been "swallowed up" by New York City, and were bound to increase even more. Jack resolves to conceal his full identity, make his greenhouses a successful business and then buy up his family's ancestral estate.

He does make a success of Evergreen Nurseries, and falls in love with Nellie Ray, the sixteen-year-old daughter of the Fox Estate's caretaker, a girl known for her beauty, virtue and talent at floral arrangements. He impresses her with rides on his sixty-eight-foot motor yacht which he re-named for her: the *Nell of Narragansett Bay*. They agree to marry, with her father's fervent approval. However, Nellie is insulted when Jack breeds a prize-winning carnation but, because he feels that such a flower needed the patronage of a prominent society lady with public name recognition, christens it the "Mrs. Ernest Flagg" after the wife of the renowned Staten Island architect. Nellie is determined to make Jack jealous by going for automobile rides with Clarence Long, a vulgar and pushful schoolmate. On the same day that Jack finds out that a twister destroyed all his greenhouses, he overhears Clarence bragging in the nearby roadhouse about how much Nellie favors him, so the two get in a fistfight from which Jack emerges the victor. He goes to sleep off the fight in a rowboat but wakes up adrift, financially ruined, romantically spurned and marooned on the New Jersey shore without any oars.

A tugboat captain rescues Jack and suggests a business partnership in which Jack would harvest the salt grass that grew wild on the islands and marshes of the western shore of Staten Island and sell it for packaging material. Jack signs contracts with the United Fruit Company and the Atlantic Terra Cotta Company and sets to work, hiring dozens of washed-up denizens of Bowery flop houses and giving them a new lease on life. He grows a beard and further disguises himself by feigning a gruff voice, determined to come back to Nellie when he had built up a salt hay empire and let her decide between him or Clarence. Nevertheless, he watches Nellie surreptitiously, and sees her riding in the *Nell of Narragansett Bay* with a school chum named Fred, Clarence Long and his ostensible sweetheart, Rose, the roadhouse keeper's daughter. One night Jack had to rescue Nell from the water where she had jumped to escape Clarence's advances. Fred recognized Jack and brought him to Nellie when she wouldn't recover from her illness. When Nellie recovers simply by Jack's return, she repents of her girlish machinations and they reconcile. The book ends with many happy occurrences: a serendipitous discovery of a letter reveals the location of the Squire's treasure, under a slab in the estate's rose arbor. Jack expanded his salt hay empire up and down the East Coast which resulted in his owning a million dollar corporation. He further increased his wealth by patenting a process of turning salt hay into paper pulp. Jack also grows another prize-winning breed of carnation which he names "America." Jack's identity as the heir of the estate is revealed and he purchases his rightful inheritance. And finally, Jack and Nellie marry. In addition to the people mentioned above, Jack socializes with Deckers, Crocherons, Vreelands and Mersereaus.

113.   Spollen, Anne. *The Shape of Water.* Woodbury, Minn.: Flux, 2008. 305pp.
        In this work of juvenile fiction, fifteen-year-old Magdalena Sorrin learns to deal with her mother's death, her father's remarriage and her own social isolation and awkwardness. Maggie and her father live in a bungalow on the beach near Raritan Bay. Her mentally unbalanced mother had fallen into the ocean and died a year earlier and Magdalena responded to this and other traumatic events in her life by starting major fires in the woods and creating a family of anthropomorphic fish who converse with her in her mind. In addition to her mother's death, Magdalena has to deal with her best friend being transferred to Our Lady Queen of Peace after being caught making out with a boy. Her father begins dating and eventually marries a widow with a drug-addicted and disturbed son. Her father sells their home and buys a cookie-cutter house near the Mall for the blended family. When a girl from school invited Magdalena to her St. George home, Magdalena is comforted by its proximity to the water and by the girl's older, idiosyncratic home, but the budding friendship is ruined when the girl tries to initiate a sexual relationship. When her stepbrother-to-be tries to commit suicide, Magdalena's Aunt Hannah gets her to realize that everyone is doing the best they can and that she has to learn how to forgive. This epiphany produces a sea change in Magdalena, who banishes the fish from her mind and learns to get on with life.

        Descriptions of Staten Island architectural geography are detailed. Magdalena describes her beachfront neighborhood as unbalanced, with bungalows abutting modern homes, bait shops next to family residences, some houses on top of one another with some separated by fields. A four lane Boulevard (most likely Hylan) separated her "older, beachier" neighborhood from the newer, symmetrical houses "above the boulevard" where the streets were as predictable as the homes and the people who inhabited them. The house near the Mall that Magdalena is forced to move into is "plain, gray and shaped like a toaster, the kind of house a child might fashion out of discarded boxes", exactly like all the other houses in their development. While walking along the beach in her old neighborhood, Magdalena meets a college professor who is photographing all the bungalows for an exhibit before they're knocked down and replaced with the prevalent indistinguishable designs.

114. St. Jean, Catherine Avery. *Caleb Takes a Ride on the Staten Island Ferry.* Illustrated by Paul J. Frahm. CreateSpace, 2011. 24pp.

In this picture book for children, a young boy named Caleb is excited about taking a ride on the ferryboat *American Legion*, which is captained by his grandfather. Caleb gets to ride in the pilot's house with his grandfather, who points out the sites in the harbor and even lets him steer the boat. It is a special day, not only because Caleb gets to ride with his grandfather, but because the QE2 is leaving New York on its last voyage. This is a re-telling of *A Staten Island Ferry Tale*, re-written for younger readers.

115. St. Jean, Catherine Avery. *A Staten Island Ferry Tale.* Illustrated by Paul J. Frahm. Xlibris, 2003. 32pp.

In this children's book, a boy named Paul takes a ride in the Pilot house of the ferry with Captain Nick, who served in the Navy with Paul's dad. Paul will get to see the QE2, his favorite ship, sail out of New York Harbor to England. We learn all about the various workers on the ferry and how the boat works. Captain Nick shows Paul how to signal other vessels and how to navigate through the harbor. Near the Statue of Liberty they meet up with the QE2 and salute her with the ship's whistle.

116. Stone, Robert. *Outerbridge Reach.* New York: Houghton Mifflin, 1992. 409pp.

Owen Browne, graduate of the Naval Academy and veteran of the Vietnam War, is the top salesman and copywriter for the Altan shipbuilding company, whose repair yard is located in New Brighton where he, an experienced sailor, stores his own boat. Browne takes his vessel for a sail down the Arthur Kill, whose islands and sights are described. At the place on the charts known as Outerbridge Reach, he passes his father-in-law's salvage yard and boat graveyard, where he pulls in to explore some of the rotting hulks. When Matty Hylan, the owner of Altan's parent company, goes into hiding after news of his financial mismanagement and imminent bankruptcy become public knowledge, Browne travels to corporate headquarters to appraise the racing yacht that Hylan was to have sailed in an upcoming around-the-world race. The powers-that-be at the Hylan Corporation, eager to salvage the company's reputation and obtain some good publicity, don't have to work too hard to convince the middle-aged Browne to take Hylan's place in the race. He begins sleeping at the Staten Island shipyard, outfitting the boat and taking its measure on the water. At one point he takes a walk along a somewhat geographically imaginative North Shore, past decaying housing projects, a veterans' hospital and cemetery and the old Bethlehem Steel shipyard, where he had reported to the first and only ship of his naval career. Before Browne begins his voyage, a hostile documentary filmmaker goes to Tottenville to interview a couple of Altan shipyard workers who wanted to voice their criticism of Browne. The wife of one is described as speaking the "...pure and uncorrupted Brooklyn poissard, a diction almost extinct in its home borough."

117.   Telford, Robert S. *Between Two Wars*. Bloomington, Ind.: Trafford, 2012. 213pp.
        Although only 40 pages or so of this novel have anything to do with Staten Island, the specificity of the details leads one to think that they must bear some relation to the author's family history, especially since it was promoted as being based on "true events." The protagonist, a journalist turned WWI soldier, relocates to Staten Island and builds a house at 97 Nelson Avenue. He gave patriotic speeches at P.S. 8 and it is noted that Tottenville was the only high school on the island at the time. The family attended church at the Rev. Minert's Moravian church located on a dirt road off of Cleveland Avenue. Moving to Staten Island resulted in few visits from friends.

118.   Temple, W(illard) H(enry). "The Eighth-Grade Picnic; A Staten Island Story," in *Picnic Adventures*. Edited by Elizabeth L. Gilman. New York: Farrar and Rinehart, 1940. 192pp. pgs 90-107.
        In this collection of stories about picnics, *The Eighth-Grade Picnic* deals with the rivalry between two Tottenville boys over a girl. The two are reconciled when the girl refuses both of their invitations to the

graduation picnic at the beach. When the boys see the girl sloppily eating a hot dog at the picnic, their infatuation with her is destroyed and the two maliciously ruin the picnic by tossing all the sandwiches into the ocean.

119.   Wallis, Geraldine [Hope Campbell, pseud.]. *No More Trains to Tottenville*. New York: McCall Publishing Company, 1971. 170pp.

In this novel about generational misunderstanding, sixteen-year-old Jane Andrews lives on the Upper West Side of Manhattan with her parents. Because of their difficult relationship, she is always threatening to run away. Her pot-smoking brother Dick has already run away, first to a liberal college and then to California where he's become a beach bum. Jane's father, Brook, a failed entrepreneur, sometimes disappears for days at a time in pursuit of one scheme or another. One day, Jane's exasperated and unappreciated mother, Wanda, just disappears, leaving behind a letter announcing that she's gone to India to live in an ashram. Jane is forced to take over her household duties and reflect on her mother's mysterious absence.

One day, on a whim, she decides to take the ferry to Staten Island and the train to Tottenville, the southernmost point of the Island, and of New York State. She describes the town as somewhat desolate. Jane wanders into a seedy bar whose jukebox only plays WWII-era music. She meets a young man who she calls Scorpio, because of his interest in astrology. She gets drunk and tells him about her mother. He walks her back to the train, where the avuncular conductor makes sure she gets back to the Ferry without incident. Intrigued by Scorpio, Jane later returns to the bar in Tottenville to find him and have him read her mother's horoscope to find out when and if she might return. He takes her to the Tibetan Museum and to the Richmondtown Restoration, where they sneak into one of the historical houses to spend the night. They begin to kiss, but Jane stops things before they go any further. However, she does love Scorpio and wants to stay with him in Staten Island, where she'll have her own personal Tibet and guru. However, he puts her back on the train.

When Jane arrives home, she realizes that her father was frantic with worry and had the police looking for her. Brother Dick comes home at the same moment. Their father yells at both of them and storms out. He does not return that night. Jane and Dick get drunk and hold a mock wake for their parents. They look through their old photo albums and come to realize that their parents were young once too, and are actually real people like themselves. The next day they face the fact that they're going to have to figure out a way to make it on their own. Dick gets a job at a garage, while Jane does the grocery shopping and cooks the meals. They start squabbling however, and realize that they can't take care of themselves. Their previously lenient father comes home after a few days with a new job and firmly lays down the rules that Dick must continue working and Jane must continue cooking and cleaning. Jane sees what her mother had to endure. She meets up with Scorpio one last time and finally blurts out her real name and address, but they never meet again. Jane has come to the realization that there is no generation gap, except the one between the living and the dead. She sees her parents as people who once wanted the same things as she does and begins to see them in a new light. Her mother returns as unexpectedly as she left, and a new family dynamic of respect and obedience emerges.

120. Weisgard, Leonard. *Suki, the Siamese Pussy*. New York: Thomas Nelson and Sons, 1937. 32pp.
      Pampered pussy cat Suki wants to take a boat to Paris, like his owners, so he takes the train down to the southern tip of Manhattan and chooses the Staten Island Ferry as the appropriate vessel for his transatlantic trip. After failing to catch a fish, getting wet and being chased by a dog, he falls asleep in the captain's coat. After sleeping through the disembarkation and return trip, he finds his owners waiting for him with open arms at Whitehall and goes home.

121. Weiss, Ed. *Peter Pigeon of Snug Harbor*. Staten Island, N.Y.: Rocky Hollow Press, 2008. 89pp.
      In this humorous and whimsical tale, Captain Hardtack, one of the salty old residents of Snug Harbor when it was still a home for "aged, decrepit and worn out sailors", rescues a sick baby pigeon from imminent trampling. The Captain nurses the pigeon back to health with love and South Sea grog, and names him Peter Pigeon. He adopts the bird, and teaches him everything he knows, which amounts to seamanship and the English language. On Peter's third birthday, it is announced to the Snugs that they will be relocated to Sea Level, North Carolina. When the Snug Harbor administrator, Ms. Martinette, insists on shipping Peter down to North Carolina in a crate and requires him to live in a cage, Captain Hardtack realizes that a young bird should be having adventures out in the world, and not live cooped up with a

bunch of old sailors. So he sadly bids Peter farewell and arranges for him to remain in Snug Harbor. As Peter escorts the Snugs' airport bus down to St. George, he notices the Staten Island Ferry and decides to take a ride. Captain Hardtack's lessons enable him to actually steer the Ferry across the harbor with the skill of an experienced sailor, earning him a salute from the Ferry's captain. Upon his return to Snug Harbor, which has been converted into an arts center, Peter meets an eccentric, starving artist named Maria Maria (sic), who becomes his roommate and friend. She is determined to win a cash prize in an art contest sponsored by the *Staten Island Advance* and works obsessively on the painting she plans to enter. On the night before the deadline, as she prepares to apply the finishing touches, Peter falls in a bucket of paint and accidentally tracks pigeon prints all over her painting. She yells at him but soon realizes that his little footprints are just what the painting needed, so she has him make more. They then win the contest and become successful local artists.

122. Westlake, Donald. *The Fugitive Pigeon*. New York: Random House, 1965. 172pp.

Only one chapter of this humorous mafia novel take place on Staten Island, but it contains some interesting descriptions. Low-level mob flunky Charlie Poole is mistakenly ordered rubbed out by higher-ups, but Poole manages to slip through the fingers of the hit men sent to kill him. He decides to appeal directly to the organization's boss, a "Farmer" Agricola who lives on an actual farm in Staten Island. Poole takes the ferry to the island and finds Agricola's Annadale address in the local phone book. He takes the bus to the intersection of Arthur Kill Road and Richmond Avenue and walks down Drumgoole Road, a desolate, crater-marred road built by the Army during the Second World War and neglected ever since. He turned right onto Huguenot Avenue, described as containing a few seedy houses amidst fields, woods and farms, and found Agricola's farm down a dirt road. He sneaks into the house and finds Agricola dead, leading to a complex series of chases and revelations.

The island is described as an "odd" place, which is distinctive for its underdevelopment and rural character. The narrator notes that the old time comedians who made fun of Canarsie and New Jersey as unfashionably *outré* places, ignored Staten Island out of sympathy for the Islanders, "...or maybe it was because Staten Island is so improbable, in concept and appearance, that even a comedian couldn't think of anything to say about it." Poole also observes that "all of Staten Island, even the most expensive parts like Princess Bay, has a faintly grubby look, as though everyone had given up years ago in the attempt to keep the place looking bright and cheerful...The Island, from end to end, has the same feeling as the ferries that service it."

123.   Wheat, Carolyn. *Fresh Kills*. New York: A Berkley Prime Crime, published by the Berkley Publishing Group, 1995. 236pp.

     Cass Jameson is a Brooklyn lawyer who is asked by her friend Marla Hennessy, another lawyer, to represent a client in a routine adoption case. Jameson's client is a young woman, Amber, who has promised to give her baby to Josh and Ellie Greenspan, a Brooklyn couple represented by Hennessy. Jameson and Hennesy go to visit Amber in Staten Island, where she lives in a home for unwed mothers, run by Dr. Chris Scanlon, a famous pro-life activist. Amber explains that the baby was conceived through rape, but she couldn't abort it, especially since a previous child of hers had died within a week of birth, some five years before. After Amber gives birth and relinquishes her baby to the Greenspans, she changes her mind and has Hennessy go to court to get her baby back. The court rules in favor of Amber, since a binding agreement was not yet signed.

     In the course of the case, it is revealed that Josh Greenspan is actually the baby's biological father. It is also revealed that Amber had married a rich punk named Scott Wylie, from the Latourette Park area, a week before the baby's birth. Shortly after the court case, Amber disappears and is found murdered in the Fresh Kills swamp. Jameson begins to investigate the true story about Amber, Doc Scanlon and the baby. She discovers that on the night she disappeared, Amber and Scott met the Greenspans at the Staten Island Mall with the intent to sell the baby to them for $10,000. However, Amber double-crossed everyone by running off with the money and the baby. An eyewitness, the manager of Friendly's, spotted Amber getting into a car, which Jameson tracked down to a pizza parlor owner in Tottenville, a place described as "stuck in a time warp." The owner, Jerry Califana, claims to be Amber's ex-husband. He also claims that their baby, who Amber said had died, was actually given to Dr. Scanlon, who sold it to a childless couple. Califana had an appointment with Amber that night at the Greenbelt Native Plant Center, with the agreement to give her $20,000 in exchange for information about their baby's whereabouts, but she never showed. Amber had also met with a Kyle and Donna

Cheney at Friendly's that night. Originally, Jameson suspected that
Amber was trying to con money out of them as well, under the
pretense of selling them her baby, but she eventually deduces that the
Cheneys' daughter was actually Amber's first child, and that the
Cheneys were paying Amber hush money so she would let them keep
the child. Jameson concludes that Kyle killed Amber, who was a threat
to his family, and took her newborn. She tracks down the baby to the
home of Dr. Scanlon's ex-wife, Betsy, who is also Kyle Cheney's sister.
When Jameson manages to get possession of the baby, she is chased
into the William T. Davis wildlife refuge by Kyle Cheney, who
threatens to kill her. She uses her lawyerly persuasion to get him to
surrender to the police, and the baby is given back to the Greenspans.

In addition to the locations mentioned above, this novel contains
numerous Staten Island references, from the Willowbrook State School
to Heartland Village to Westerleigh.

124. Whitehead, Jeffrey. *The Scorpion's Weather*. Baltimore: PublishAmerica,
      2004. 257pp.
      An old man on his deathbed encounters a supernatural visitor who
      prompts him to tell his life story, growing up on Staten Island during
      the Depression and fighting in World War II. A difficult family life and
      his brother's involvement with the local mafia play a prominent part in
      the story, but there is no local description beyond the name of the
      story's setting.

125. Whitney, Phyllis A(yama). *Ever After*. Boston: Houghton Mifflin, 1948.
      279pp.
      This novel for older girls limns a young woman's attempt to
      achieve both professional success and happiness in marriage. Margaret
      Elizabeth "Marel" Gordon comes to New York City from Chicago to
      be a professional illustrator and luckily lands a job as a secretary in a
      highly regarded studio, where she resourcefully finds opportunities to
      practice her art. She meets aspiring writer Chris Mallory, who takes her
      to Staten Island to visit the airfields, as he's doing research on a book
      involving the ferry and airplanes. As the island was much like
      countryside, Marel couldn't believe that it was really part of New York
      City. After their visit to the airfields, which were located 9 miles from
      the ferry, next to a "highway," which seems to describe the airports in
      the New Springville area, Chris and Marel ate dinner that night at a
      restaurant that, as described, seems to indicate the Lake Club (present-

day Stone House) in Clove Lakes Park. When Marel doesn't hear from Chris, she begins to jealously imagine that he is ignoring her in favor of an aviatrix he knows on Staten Island and, when she finds out that he is going there, intercepts him on the ferry, where he proposes to her. The rest of the book deals with the troubles that the couple have to deal with: trying to find lodging in a city experiencing a post-war housing shortage; the problem of an artist and a writer trying to hone their respective crafts in the same tiny apartment; the interference of Chris' mother in their marriage; and the conflicting pressures that young women of the time felt between work and family life. The lessons imparted might seem retrograde to a modern reader but were probably thought of as progressive at the time. The Staten Island content is minimal but significant enough for the author's daughter to consider it as one of her mother's "Staten Island books" (The Phyllis Whitney Papers, The College of Staten Island Library Archives).

126.   Whitney, Phyllis A(yame). *The Island of Dark Woods*. Illustrated by Al Fiorentino. Philadelphia: Westminster Press, 1951. 190pp.

The Kane sisters- thirteen-year-old Laurel (Laurie) and her fourteen-year-old sister Celia- are taking a train from Chicago to New York to spend the summer with their aunt Serena in Staten Island. Serena has bought a house on Victory Boulevard across from Clove Lakes Park and has decided to open up a bookshop in an outbuilding on her property. The ramshackle old house next door is occupied by crotchety Mr. Bennett and his grandson Norman and is reputed to be haunted. Aunt Serena tells the girls all about Staten Island history and the ghost story of the Bennett house: ninety years earlier, when Victory Boulevard was known as Richmond Turnpike, an unknown woman was traveling on a stagecoach with her baby daughter Serena when she fell ill and was taken in by the Bennett family, where she died. The Bennett family adopted the baby, who is revealed to be an ancestor of the Kane family, but legend says that the woman is still sometimes seen entering a ghostly stagecoach and then reappearing in the room where she died.

With the help of Aunt Serena's friend, local author Katherine Parsons, the girls, along with friends Norman Bennett and Russ Sperry, begin to investigate the mystery, which takes them to the Staten Island Museum and the Staten Island History Museum at Richmondtown. In an old issue of the Richmond Gazette, Norman discovers an article stating that the woman died muttering the name Alma. Mr. Bennett has in his possession a book that the mystery woman owned and gives it to Laurie, who discovers a letter sealed inside the binding, which reveals that the woman, Amelia, was fleeing from a husband, Clyde, who had allied himself with someone historically disreputable. Having been informed by Katherine Parsons about Mexican Emperor Santa Anna's exile on Staten Island, Laurie speculates that Amelia was muttering the word "Alamo" and that her husband Clyde had formed an association with Santa Anna, the conqueror of that famous Texan fort. Further examination of the history books showed a Clyde Dibney who was arrested for trying to help Santa Anna regain power in Mexico. They track down an old woman named Dibney in Tottenville, who turns out to be Clyde's niece, and the aunt of Katherine Parsons, thereby solving the mystery and revealing a whole web of new familial relationships.

Staten Island history, from the Dutch colonial days to the Revolution to Daniel Tompkins' creation of Richmond Turnpike are explained. The children attend a dance at Westerleigh Park. Several of the buildings in Richmondtown are described and Aunt Serena explains how she is involved with a group that is trying to preserve the village as a historical destination. The girls take a ferry ride and ride their bikes up Victory Boulevard and Todt Hill. Mr. Bennett remarks about how he would prefer not to be reminded that Staten Island is part of New York City and Katherine Parsons, a proud native islander, refers to her own father as an "off-islander." Pride in beautiful Staten Island and its rich history are palpable and the children even stage a play recreating the death of Amelia Dibney in order to raise money for Richmondtown. (This novel was re-issued in 1967 under the title of *Mystery of the Strange Traveler*)

127. Whitney, Phyllis A(yame). *The Quicksilver Pool.* New York: Ace Books, 1955. 319pp.

In this Civil War romance, Lora Blair lived with her doctor father in a border state during the Civil War, tending to the wounded of both sides of the conflict. After nursing Union soldier Wade Tyler of Staten Island back to health they marry, despite their both harboring emotions for dead lovers: Wade for his late wife Virginia, drowned in a Staten Island pond, and Lora for her fiancé Martin, killed in the war. Wade brings Lora home to his family's Dogwood Lane mansion, which is inhabited by his young son Jemmy and his autocratic mother Amanda. Amanda Tyler's ideas about sumptuary, social and Sabbath propriety comes into conflict with Lora's. Wade, who confines himself to the study in hope of writing a novel and who, in any case, is just as cowed by his mother as anyone, does not defend his wife from his mother's attacks. Finally, Lora decides to stand up to Amanda by buying Jemmy a puppy, a thought which horrifies her mother-in-law and sends her into confinement for three months with a feigned illness. Lora barges into the sickroom at last and uses her nursing experience to give Amanda a forcible but rejuvenating massage, which somewhat ameliorates her mother-in-law's cantankerousness.

Meanwhile, Morgan Channing- the sister of Wade's late wife- gets Wade involved with the Knights of the Golden Circle, a secret society of Copperheads who are plotting to fight the draft and end the war with a negotiated peace. Lora had been warned to avoid Morgan because of her lifelong desire for Wade and because of her generally conniving and dishonest character. In fact, Wade had intended to marry Morgan until she attacked his mother with a curling iron for trying to forbid their relationship (Morgan and Virginia were the daughters of Amanda Tyler's servant.) When he had seen Morgan's true nature, he ran into the arms of sweet, comforting Virginia and married her instead. Morgan had consoled herself with a Southern planter who holidayed on Staten Island (a popular resort destination for Southerners) and who left her vast holdings in the South, including slaves, when he died. Morgan uses her ownership of her servant Rebecca's mother and sister to maintain control over the girl, in spite of abuse and mistreatment. It is Lora who takes the girl under her wing and advises her that Morgan has no more legal control over her mother and sister since Lincoln's Emancipation Proclamation.

Wade continues to meet with the Copperheads but becomes disillusioned after their plans become violent and anti-Negro. He leaves their organization and begins meeting with prominent journalists, especially Sidney Howard Gay, who encourage him to eschew novel-writing, for which he has no talent, and focus on writing articles dealing with current events, and advocating for Union victory, the only way to really end the war. When the draft riots of 1863 break out in Manhattan, the spirit of rebellion spreads to Brooklyn and Staten Island. Small mobs start forming up and mindlessly attacking Negroes and people of property, The island's African-American population flee to the woods and to New Jersey. Despite her Copperhead affiliation and the fact that she turned Rebecca out of her house in fear, the frenzied mob attacks and loots Morgan Channing's home. The mob turns its attention to the Tyler mansion, where Rebecca has taken refuge, but Wade, Mrs. Tyler and some neighboring men defend the house by force of arms, shooting and wounding some of the rioters.

The characters amuse themselves by going sleighing at Silver Lake, and attend a ball at the Pavilion Hotel. Mrs. Tyler is revealed to have been part of the Underground Railroad, which used her house as a station.

128. Whitney, Phyllis A(yame). *Secret of the Emerald Star.* Illustrated by Alex Stein. Philadelphia: Westminster Press, 1964. 233pp.
      Thirteen-year-old Robin Ward has just moved from Chicago to Staten Island with her family, where they reside in a big house on a kind of cul-de-sac off of Jersey Street called Catalpa Court, which one could hardly believe was part of New York City. Robin's father has taken a job as the curator of biology for the local museum. In one of the older houses off Catalpa Court lives Mrs. Agnes Devery, a member of one of Staten Island's old families. Mrs. Devery lost her husband in the First World War and her son to Castro's revolutionaries. Her deceased son's wife, a Cuban woman, and their strange daughter Stella fled from Cuba and live with Mrs. Devery. Robin attempts to befriend Stella and discovers that Stella is blind and that she and her mother have a strained relationship with Mrs. Devery, who bosses Stella around and hinders her independence by coddling her. Mrs. Devery refuses to drive Stella and her mother to Mass at St. Peter's, presumably because they are Catholic. She also confiscates Stella's emerald and diamond pin, which she had received from her Cuban grandmother, and which Mrs. Devery believes to be too valuable for a young girl to wear.

      Robin and Stella take up sculpting, which Stella- by making busts and then destroying them, uses as a cathartic means of getting out her frustrations with her grandmother and with a mysterious purported relation, Mr. Lemon, who has moved into Mrs. Devery's house. The children later discover that Mr. Lemon is playing on Mrs. Devery's family and political sympathies to get her to fund a gun-running operation to the Cuban opposition. Mrs. Devery experiences several changes throughout the book. First, when Robin's mother lends her a book about blindness, she learns how to relate to her granddaughter in a way that encourages her independence and eases some of the everyday problems she has to face. Second, her anti-Semitic prejudices are softened when Ira Hornfeld, a Jewish sculptor on Catalpa Court, asks to borrow a portrait of her as a young woman for an exhibit at the museum of Staten Island that will feature artists from "former days." Third, she begins to assert herself with Mr. Lemon, who is exposed as a fraud, but not before he locks Robin and Stella in the basement and absconds with Mrs. Devery's jewelry, including- apparently- the pin that she had confiscated from Stella. As it turns out, Stella had secretly taken back her pin and hidden it inside a bust of herself that Robin had sculpted.

A funny commentary on Staten Island insularity is put in the mouth of Mrs. Ward who, by way of dismissing the notion that Mrs. Devery would get involved in sending guns to Cuba, notes that Mrs. Devery is "...patriotic all right, but her country is old Staten Island. She considers everything else foreign, I'm sure." In an afterword, the author- who had lived on Fort Hill Circle- reveals that Catalpa Court was based on the type of old Staten Island neighborhood where she was then residing. The diversity of such a place was why she included a Jew, a Catholic and a Protestant as her main characters. The vivid descriptions of life as a blind child was informed by the author's research which involved visiting a special school for blind children in Manhattan.

129. Whitney, Phyllis A(yame). *Step to the Music.* New York: Thomas Y. Crowell, 1953. 256pp.
      This novel for young people dramatizes the divided loyalties of two Staten Island families during the Civil War. Seventeen-year-old Abbie Garrett lives with her parents on Bard Avenue. As the news of the fall of Fort Sumter comes trickling in, Abbie learns that her Southern mother, who had been visiting family in Charleston, is bringing her niece Lorena Emory back to Staten Island for an extended visit. Lorena turns out to be an ardent and outspoken Southern nationalist, who doesn't miss any opportunity to offend her hosts and their friends with her fanatical secessionist opinions. The Garretts' neighbors, the McIntyres, are also returning to Staten Island after having lived in the South for years for Mr. McIntyre's business. Abbie's childhood playmates, the McIntyre boys, have differing views of the conflict, in opposition to their father's strong Unionism. The serious and courteous Douglas not only has a slight Southern accent but also decided Southern sympathies; the impudent Stuart leans more towards diplomacy and pacifism.

Abbie's father enlists with Dr. Samuel McKenzie Elliott's 79th New York Highlanders and is wounded at the Battle of Bull Run. His Southern wife's loyalties were so torn that she did not even show up at his regiment's parade to see him off. Lorena's father Benton has also enlisted, but for the Confederacy. She continues to inflame local feeling when she wears a South Carolina palmetto cockade to a charity ball at the Pavilion Hotel, held to benefit the families of local Union troops. When she hears the mistaken rumor that Union troops had burned Charleston she flies into violent hysterics and has to be physically restrained from desecrating an American flag. In the meantime, she has been working her charms on Douglas, whose loyalties were already resting on a knife's edge, and he decides to go South and fight for the Confederacy. He declares that he will marry Lorena after the war, to the great disappointment of Abbie, whose more reserved demeanor went unnoticed by him.

One day a Union soldier from New Dorp who was home on leave tells the family that he had news of Douglas. Douglas had encountered the wounded soldier in a swamp, and upon finding out that he was also from Staten Island, risked his own life to bring the man back to the Union lines. Douglas was discovered and shot, but whether he was alive or dead the man from New Dorp did not know. Stuart, now working in Horace Greeley's *Tribune* office as a newspaperman, used his connections to find out that Douglas was indeed alive in a Union prison- although missing a leg- and managed to secure his brother's parole to his family. At first rude and surly, Douglas manages to reconcile with Abby and his intended, Lorena, who has also softened towards the Yankees, even volunteering to make bandages for the United States Sanitary Commission. Mrs. Garrett, Abbie and Lorena are in Manhattan when the draft riots break out, and on the ferry ride home hear that mobs are waiting at the terminal to attack African Americans, Republicans and the upper classes. The women encounter a free colored woman of their acquaintance on the boat and managed to smuggle her in disguise past the mob at the ferry terminal back to their Bard Avenue home. The Bard Avenue families barricade themselves in their homes and do their best to hide familiar Africans Americans. Although the mob actions on Staten Island amounted to no more than rowdyism on the whole, they did steal the rifles from Tompkins Lyceum and attack the African American enclave on McKeon Street (present-day Tompkins Street) in Stapleton. At one point Abby and Stuart confront a mob, after which they kiss and Stuart announces that he's enlisting in the Union Army to help defend freedom. As the war is ending, Douglas and Lorena marry and move to Charleston and Stuart returns from the Army and prepares to marry Abby.

In addition to the Staten Island places and people mentioned above, the characters attend services at the Unitarian church in New Brighton, where George William Curtis was in the habit of reading sermons that had been preached elsewhere, in this case reading something of Henry Ward Beecher's. The Richmond County Gazette was the source of news, and Mrs. Garrett had had her portrait painted by Jasper Cropsey in her youth. The uniforms of one-time Staten Island resident Giuseppe Garibaldi's red-shirt army had become an inspiration for female fashion. The characters go ice skating at Silver Lake and picnicking at Britton's Pond, now Clove Lake.

130. Wilder, Elyzabeth Gregory. *Fresh Kills*. London: Methuen Publishing Limited, 2004. 63pp.

Eddie and Marie are a married, Staten Island couple with a six-year-old son. Money is tight, but they have a loving relationship. However, Eddie has been conducting an erotic online correspondence with a sixteen-year-old boy named Arnold, and meets up with him in an abandoned parking lot at the Fresh Kills landfill. Eddie is too nervous to get physical with the boy and resists Arnold's sexual advances. He regrets meeting up with Arnold and tries to sever the relationship, but Arnold threatens to expose Eddie. At their next Fresh Kills rendezvous, Eddie mentions that he'll soon be taking his son camping. Arnold's own father never spends time with him, so he demands that Eddie take him along, but Eddie refuses. To get his way, Arnold later shows up at Eddie's house and tells Marie that Eddie is going to take him camping. Their cover story is that Arnold and Eddie know each other through the Big Brother/Little Brother program. They go back to their spot at the dump and agree that Arnold will get out of Eddie's life if he takes him camping. They then have their first sexual encounter, but get caught in the act by the police. Marie's brother Nick, who is a cop, bails Eddie out of jail and calls in a lot of favors to have the police drop the charges. Arnold is told to stay away from Eddie, but shows up at his house on the morning of the camping trip. Eddie becomes exasperated with Arnold's continued attempt to insinuate himself into his family and an argument ensues. Arnold reveals the truth about their relationship to Marie, who tells Eddie to leave the house and promises that she'll never let him see their son again. When Eddie calls up Arnold's father, Arnold slits his own throat.

131. Wylly,   Phillips.   *Staten   Island.*   College   Station,   Tex.: Virtualbookworm.com Publishing Inc., 2006. 652pp.

Hugh Allan Crawford is an eighteen-year-old stoker aboard a British warship during WWI. While in His Majesty's Service, the physically impressive Crawford was recruited and trained to box. When the fleet visits New York on a goodwill tour, several of the ships docked at Staten Island hold a series of boxing matches on the pier. Crawford's ultimate victory wins shore leave for his entire ship, during which his mates treat him to a romp at "Mother's" brothel in Stapleton, where he falls in love with that evening's girl, Mary Catherine, and vows to come back and see her some day. After returning to Britain, Crawford kills a Royal Marine in self defense and flees the country for fear of the consequences. He works his way across the Atlantic under an assumed name, and ends up back in Staten Island, where he ekes out a living as a day laborer on a construction site. He befriends an Italian immigrant, Franco Tucci, whom Crawford recruits to become a bouncer with him at a bar, Angelo's, across the street from Mary Catherine's brothel.

In the meantime, a WWI veteran named Walter Sinchak comes home from the war and plans to make money by sending his younger brother Stanley and a couple of thugs to rough up some prostitutes and convince the brothels where they work to pay him protection money. After running into trouble in the more sophisticated Manhattan brothels, they target the Staten Island brothel where Mary Catherine works, because of its perceived lack of security. Crawford and Tucci are alerted during the attack and rush in to observe the prostitutes being sexually assaulted. They kill two of the thugs, while Mary Catherine bites off Stanley Sinchak's penis during his first sexual encounter. He is sentenced to prison but vows revenge on the woman who unmanned him. Crawford marries Mary Catherine and accepts her young daughter Kathleen as his own. She later reveals that Crawford was her first and only "client" so therefore Kathleen was his own natural daughter. Tucci becomes Crawford's loyal partner in all of their future endeavors, from money lending to "protection" to bootlegging after Prohibition. In time, they become feared and powerful men on Staten Island. Walter Sinchak prospered in the 1920s as well; he opened a brothel and speakeasy in New Jersey, and was unknowingly getting his liquor supplied by Crawford, through a middleman. When Stanley Sinchak was released from prison, he began working for his brother, and went with this middleman one night to pick up a liquor shipment from Crawford at the end of Seguine Avenue on Staten Island. Of all nights, Mary Catherine decided to ride along with her husband and Franco Tucci. When Stanley Sinchak recognized her, he tried to kill her. In the ensuing gunfight, Tucci ended up dead and Sinchak ended up in prison again. Crawford looked after Tucci's family as his own and moved everyone to a compound in Arrochar, where he operated a growing criminal empire.

The novel then focuses on a young drummer named Charles "Chuck" Stacey, from Joliet, Illionois, who becomes a successful Big Band leader during the Depression. While performing at a New Year's Eve Ball at the Prince's Bay Yacht Club, he becomes acquainted with Kathleen Crawford, who is now a teenager and dreams of becoming a singer. She is good enough to garner a job offer from Stacey, and convinces her father to let her accept. Hugh Crawford uses his money, influence, blackmail and violent intimidation to achieve national prominence and success for his daughter and Chuck Stacey's band. Stacey and Kathleen fall in love but their romance is halted by Hugh's disapproval. Kathleen eventually leaves the band to become a movie star. Meanwhile, Stanley Sinchak is paroled early due to a mob contact he befriended in prison and is sent to work in the family's Las Vegas hotel, which is actually owned by Hugh Crawford. When Hugh and Mary Catherine visit the city, Stanley Sinchak is given the job of driving them into the desert for some sightseeing. When he sees who his passengers are, he plans to kill them, but Hugh recognizes Sinchak and kills him first.

The book ends with Hugh Crawford "going straight" and Chuck Stacey and Kathleen Crawford marrying and having a son, who is christened at the Grymes Hill estate Hugh has bought them for a wedding present. As he looks out over the Harbor, he reminisces about the first time he came to Staten Island.

132. Yockey, Ross. *Diva Gate; A Novel in Three Acts.* (Master's thesis). Charlotte, N.Car.: Queens University of Charlotte, 2003. 271pp.

Most of this novel focuses on the relationship between aspiring opera singer Mara Weber and her worshipful husband, Adin, a television reporter who gave up his career for the sake of his wife's ambition to sing on the stage at the Metropolitan Opera. After a number of years living in his wife's shadow, Adin returns to work and is assigned to cover the story of the Willowbrook State School that had originally been exposed by the Staten Island Advance. When he arrives at Willowbrook, an angry demonstration is taking place for the purpose of demanding the reinstatement of a Dr. Fred Evans and a social worker, Jane Small, stand-ins for the real-life Dr. Mike Wilkins and Elizabeth Lee. Adin interviews the mother of a toddler who is a Willowbrook patient, and who expresses her fear that her daughter would eventually be transferred to Building 5, where the treatment of patients is horrific. The protesters try to enter the administration building to speak to the director of the school, but when they are denied entry they go to the Building 6, where the dismissed Dr. Evans lets everyone in. Although the scene takes up only a small portion of the manuscript, it is vivid and reflects the horrors that were uncovered in Geraldo Rivera's famous exposé. As opposed to the history though, the events in this work take place in 1976 and Building 6 is described as having well-kept private rooms for wealthy patients, one of whom was the brother of Mara Weber's employer, a famous opera singer/impresario who refuses to help Adin publicize the conditions at Willowbrook for fear that it could hurt her career.

133. Zindel, Paul. *Amulets Against the Dragon Forces.* New York: Dramatists Play Services, 1989. 80pp.
      In this dramatic adaptation of Zindel's 1977 novel *Confessions of a Teenage Baboon*, which takes place in 1955, Mrs. Helen Boyd, a practical nurse who pilfers from her patients, moves with her son Chris into the Prince's Bay home of Floyd Dipardi to care for his mother in her dying days. Floyd, a drunken and abusive shipyard worker, lives with a teenage boy-toy named Harold. Floyd, in fact, is infamous in the neighborhood for his predilection for young men and for hosting wild pool parties with young hustlers. Actually, in the Boyds' peripatetic existence, Chris too prostituted himself to older men. Floyd finds out that Chris serviced the Borough Hall night watchman in the clock tower. Chris reminds Floyd of himself as a young man and comes on to the boy. Harold and Chris make plans to run away to Chris' father in Florida, just as Mrs. Boyd is about to close on a Staten Island house and give her son a more stable life. In the climax, Chris reveals that he had met Floyd before when he was picked up hitchhiking on Richmond Terrace. The inebriated Floyd took him to the shipyard where he fell asleep holding Chris' hand. Chris declares that he wants to

learn to love whoever he loves and not be ashamed and angry like the repressed Floyd.

There are various references to Staten Island places, such as the Victory movie theatre and the Empire Theatre, the Mayfair bar and Carmen's restaurant. Chris had attended P.S. 8, McKee High School and New Dorp High School, where a teacher was almost driven to suicide by the students' disrespectful behavior. Chris was working on a model of the Hormann mansion on Grymes Hill. And in an interesting observation, Harold notes that the boy prostitutes on Hyatt Street were cheaper than the ones on Stuyvesant Place, but they were lower class and even the cops "make them do stuff."

134.   Zindel, Paul. *Attack of the Killer Fishsticks*. New York: A Bantam Skylark Book, 1993. 117pp.

In this book for young readers, a group of eleven-year-olds at New Springville Elementary School form the Wacky Facts Lunch Bunch club for the purpose of exchanging strange trivia, jokes and just having all-around fun. They befriend a nerdy boy named Max and help get him elected as class representative in the face of opposition from bullies. The locale is unnamed but unmistakable enough, if geographically jumbled: New Springville sounds more like Travis, and the children walk home from school through Bulls Head to the neighborhood around Main Street and Yettman Place. Max's visit to his mother's grave in Moravian Cemetery is observed by the bullies, who use the fact to try and unnerve Max during the school debates.

This book series eventually comprised three more installments detailing the adventures of the Wacky Facts Lunch Bunch at a zoo, at a Halloween party, and at a talent show, but none contained any significant Staten Island content.

135.   Zindel, Paul. *Confessions of a Teenage Baboon*. New York: Harper and Row, 1977. 154pp.

Mrs. Helen Boyd, a practical nurse who pilfers from her patients, moves with her son Chris into the home of Lloyd Dipardi in order to care for his mother, Carmelita, in her dying days. Lloyd is a drunken and abusive shipyard worker who lives with a teenage boy named Harold. Floyd in fact is infamous in the neighborhood for the nude pool parties he hosts with the teenage boys who are always hanging around his house, drinking and listening to loud music. Chris, whose father left the family and subsequently died, clings to his father's coat as a sacred relic. Despite his alcoholism and abusive nature, Lloyd recognizes the lack of a father figure in Chris' life and tries to mentor him but Chris resists any advice from the brutal man. One of Lloyd's teenage circle reveals that when he was three years old, Carmelita caught Lloyd playing doctor with a female cousin and punished him by taking him to the oven and threatening to burn off his genitals. The teen believes that it was that experience that drives Lloyd to want to prove his manhood by surrounding himself with teens.

When Helen walks in on another loud party that Lloyd is hosting in the house where his mother is dying, she quits the assignment and takes Chris back to live in the Ritz Hotel in Tompkinsville. While riding the 103 bus down Hylan Boulevard, she tells Chris that she intentionally left his father's coat behind. Chris immediately goes back to Lloyd's house, where Carmelita had just passed away. Helen arrives shortly after with police, who beat up Lloyd for his presumed improprieties with teens, causing Chris to come to his defense. The police throw Chris out of the house, but he sneaks in and overhears them demanding a payoff in exchange for a reduced sentence from an amenable judge. Lloyd grabs a hidden gun and kills himself. Chris wanders away and realizes that he had forgotten to take his father's coat, but finds that he doesn't need it anymore. Chris begins to understand that his experience has changed him and caused him to grow up and is thankful to Lloyd for his hurtful advice because otherwise Chris might have ended up like him.

There are passing references to various Staten Island schools, bars and neighborhoods. Harold and Chris go to the South Beach amusement park to go on the rides. Lloyd drives his car into the water off the pier of the Great Kills marina for the insurance money. This book was adapted as a play in 1989 and renamed *Amulets Against the Dragon Forces*.

136.   Zindel, Paul. *The Girl Who Wanted a Boy*. New York: Harper and Row, 1981. 148pp.
       Fifteen-year-old Sibella Cametta, an awkward, science-minded Port Richmond High School sophomore who fixes cars for pocket money and dreams of owning a Mobil gas station, confides to her diary about how she desperately wants a boyfriend. She "discovers" him in the sports section of the Advance when she reads an article about the

midget raceway in Mariners Harbor and sees a picture of one of its workers with whom she immediately falls in love. She goes to the racetrack to find him, and when she does, introduces herself by way of offering him a set of tools as a gift, which disconcerts him and sends him running. She follows the young man, nineteen-year-old Dan Douglas- a graduate of McKee Vo-Tech- to the "Drop Inn" bar on Innis Street, where she declares how much she worships him, an admission which makes him definitively reject her.

Sibella's older sister Maureen, who is cohabitating with a man, takes Sibella to a male strip club in St. George in order to awaken her sister's sexuality. In fact, Sibella's single mother and Maureen both are incredibly concerned that Sibella is more interested in science than sex, although Sibella declares that she just wants to be liked first. The family even hires a boy to take her out, for the planned purpose of kissing and fondling her, but she sees through the ruse. Dan Douglas is everything to her, so she tracks him down to a ramshackle house next to the racetrack, where he reveals that he is depressed, alienated, unemployable, estranged from his family in Travis and dreams of nothing more than owning, living in and dying in a Dodge Surfer van. Although they spend a little time together, Dan cannot understand why Sibella thinks so highly of him. She is driven to depression when she later spies him at the Drop Inn getting physical with another woman.

Finally, Sibella takes the ferry to Manhattan to get advice from her father, who tells her to not to give her heart away too quickly, but not to be afraid to be a little crazy in pursuit of love. Sibella returns to Staten Island and buys Dan the van of his dreams. She presents it to him on Innis Street on Christmas Eve, but he reacts with fury and insults her. He later comes to her home on Treadwell Avenue to apologize and tells her that he's moving to Florida and would like to take the van. Sibella is happy that he at least would realize his dream, and they spend the night together in the back of the van. When Dan departs, Sibella walks to the middle of the Bayonne Bridge and contemplates suicide, but convinces herself to have hope and endure.

137. Zindel, Paul. *Harry and Hortense at Hormone High*. New York: Harper and Row, 1984. 151pp.
      Although the narrator, Harry Hortense, makes a pretense of disguising his high school's real name out of a fear of repercussions from the Board of Education, its proximity to the Bayonne Bridge and

its location on the thinly camouflaged Vinnis Street (Innis Street) reveals it as Port Richmond High School. Harry and his girlfriend Hortense McCoy are theatre critics for the school newspaper whose lives are changed when they meet Jason Rohr, a transfer student who starts hanging up fliers advertising himself as a reincarnation of the ancient Greek hero, Icarus, and who is in possession of a divine revelation that will change the world. As journalists, Jason thinks that Harry and Hortense can help promulgate his message, so as an introduction to his ethos, he takes them to the Staten Island Brighton Museum to see its collection of Grecian artifacts and statuary. However, when Harry and Hortense sneak a peek into the school's student records, they discover that Jason's father murdered his mother and then committed suicide when Jason was a child.

When his erratic behavior gets him sent to a teenage sanitarium on the grounds of the former Tuberculosis hospital, "Sea Vista," on "Manor Hill Road", across from the street from the old poorhouse, the teens visit Jason's aunt, with whom he lives, who reveals that Jason is building a set of "wings" in the garage, out of an old hang glider, feathers and a lawn mower engine. His aunt also relays the request, from Jason, that they smuggle a car jack to him in the hospital, to be used for his escape. They do so, and he further weaves his spell over them, especially Hortense, by telling Harry and Hortense that they are the reincarnations of Euripides and the Delphic oracle, respectively. However, Hortense tells Jason that they know the truth about his past and writes him a letter urging him to get psychiatric help. He does escape and hides out in a construction shack near Glen Street near where the new highway was being built. When the teens learn that dynamite turns up missing from the site, they fear the worst.

Indeed, Jason takes over the high school's PA system and tells the students to gather in the auditorium, where he rants and raves insanely. He threatens to blow up the school and does blow up part of it, but not before flying off the roof with his homemade wings. His machine manages to fly through the air over the Kill Van Kull, but heavy winds blow his contraption into the cables of the Bayonne Bridge, causing him to crash into the water and die. Harry and Hortense reason that since every hero story involves a boon dearly won at the price of the hero's death, they would be Jason's "boon" and spread his message that everyone, even the kids at Hormone High, can be a hero.

138. Zindel, Paul. *I Never Loved Your Mind*. New York: Harper and Row, 1970. 181pp.

Dewey Daniels is a high school dropout who gets a job at Richmond Valley Hospital which, judging by the description of its location, seems to be a stand-in for St. Vincent's Hospital. He becomes interested in a co-worker, Yvette Goethals, a standoffish eighteen-year-old dropout who pilfers hospital supplies. When he asks her out on a date, she dispassionately agrees, but tells him that she prefers a pound bag of vegetable seeds rather than flowers. They meet at the corner of Forest Avenue and Clove Road near Clove Lakes Park where, Dewey notes, a lot of muggings and rapes take place. Rather than go to the movies, Yvette asks for the $5 Dewey would have spent but is amenable to getting some beers at the Bridge Café near the Bayonne Bridge (where Dewey notes is the place where they have a lot of knife fights and the neighborhood is known for burning mattresses in the gutter, stripped cars and interracial molestation). Yvette also asks for the money he would spend on bus fare and they hitch a ride to the bar. She even cops free drinks from a man by flirting with him and pretending that Dewey is her brother. When she reveals that she shares a house with the three members of the band (The Electric Lovin' Stallions) and a platonic bed with the drummer, Dewey storms out. Yvette chases him down and they walk over the Bayonne Bridge, where she points out the homes of all the hypocritical and corrupt people that she knows as well as the blocks and blocks of ugly houses that used to be woods where she'd play as a child. She reveals how she used to get so mad at the corruption and overdevelopment that she would climb the arch of the bridge. Although terrified at the thought of it, Dewey climbs to the top of the arch with her, where Yvette shares her bleak thoughts and the teens kiss.

Yvette agrees to another date, but Dewey shows up early at her ramshackle Van Pelt Avenue house where he discovers that Yvette likes to do cleaning in the nude. Such unorthodox housecleaning methods lead to a night of physical intimacy, but their relationship ends when Yvette and the band members are evicted for keeping two horses in the house. In a convoluted bit of reasoning, Yvette blames Dewey since she believes that if she hadn't spent the night with him, she would have woken up early and prevented the landlord from discovering the horses. She won't reveal where she is now living, but Dewey and a coworker, George, follow her to a hippie commune called "Love Land" near Arthur Kill Road. Dewey and George give a ride to one of the commune's residents, who invites them to a party there. Dewey confronts Yvette, who declares that sex for her is as inconsequential as a burp, and tells him that she and the band members are moving to New Mexico. When pressed, however, she does admits that the real reason she doesn't want to be with him is that she does feel something for him, which doesn't fit in with her countercultural ideals. Dewey can't understand why Yvette is discarding him when she had told him that she loved him. She yells to him as she drives off with the Electric Lovin' Stallions that she "never loved your mind." Nevertheless, his time with Yvette changed Dewey's life, so he quits his job at the hospital and vows to do something "phantasmagorically different" with his life.

The book contains an interesting description of how the peace and love ideals of the counterculture didn't live up to their ideals when the commune explodes into violence after the "Squatters," who live in the yard, steal the corn flakes of the "Dwellers" who live in the house.

139.   Zindel, Paul. *My Darling, My Hamburger*. New York: Harper and Row, 1969. 168pp.
This novel is perhaps Zindel's most frank treatment of the subject of teenage sex. High School seniors Maggie and Liz both have boyfriends but have two completely different experiences. When Dennis begins kissing shy Maggie on a date, she takes her teacher's advice about what to do when a boy gets physical, and suggests that they get a hamburger. In any case, while she likes the equally diffident Dennis, she is not bowled over. On the other hand, Liz is madly in love with Sean, and while she initially resists his advances, the lack of trust and respect she receives from her family pushes her over the edge. When she finds herself pregnant, she wants to get an abortion, but Sean declares that he will marry her. However, after speaking with his repulsive father, Sean changes his mind and gives Liz the money for the abortion. Maggie and Rod- a boy who had once tried to rape Liz at a dance- take Liz to get an abortion in New Jersey. When they get back to Staten Island, Liz begins bleeding, and Maggie, despite Liz's explicit instructions, run to Liz's parents for help, revealing all. Liz breaks off her friendship with Maggie and can't graduate with her class. At the graduation ceremony, Maggie wishes Dennis platonic good will and a vague promise to get together in the future.

Despite the locale remaining unnamed, and the protagonists attending the fictitious Ben Franklin High School, there are numerous references to Staten Island place names, such as Port Richmond High School, Victory Boulevard, Howard Avenue, the Goethals Bridge, Travis and Hylan Boulevard.

140.　Zindel, Paul. *Pardon Me, You're Stepping on my Eyeball.* New York: Harper and Row, 1976. 262pp.

Fifteen-year-olds Louis "Marsh" Mellow and Edna Shinglebox attend Curtis Lee High School on Staten Island. They come together when their eccentricities and problems get them thrown into the same group therapy class at school. Edna's mother is extremely concerned that her socially awkward daughter has never had a date, while Marsh is obsessed with a father he claims has been committed to a California insane asylum by corrupt politicians. He takes Edna out to a college party near Wagner College and then brings her to his ramshackle house at 619 Richmond Avenue (present day Port Richmond Avenue) to read her his father's letters, which she quickly realizes had been written by Marsh himself. Disturbed by his lying and paranoia, Edna tells Marsh off, but returns to his house when he's out and asks his alcoholic mother about her husband's real whereabouts. Mrs. Mellow reveals that Marsh's father is in an urn under Marsh's bed, as he had stumbled drunk out of a Hollywood bar and been killed by a bus over a year ago, as Marsh looked on.

Edna visits a palmist at the intersection of Willowbrook Road and Richmond Avenue (Port Richmond Avenue) who gives her some good advice about how to get Marsh to accept his father's death. When Edna attends a wild party at the architecturally radical, all-glass house of an Emerson Hill friend, Marsh shows up with another girl just to make Edna jealous. After a group of hard-partying cultists show up, the party devolves into drinking, drug taking, nudity, fighting and eventually, a full-blown house fire. Marsh and Edna come together again and Edna agrees to go with Marsh to rescue his father in California. They make it as far as Washington D.C., where they crash their car. Edna notices Marsh's father's urn and dumps it into the river, without any opposition from Marsh. They flee into Arlington Cemetery, where they use JFK's eternal flame to light up a very special firework that Marsh's father had given him. Edna insists that before setting it off they should write what they hate the most on the firework. Edna writes that she hates not being able to tell Marsh she wants to touch him. Finally coming to grips with his father's death, Marsh writes that he hates that his father is dead.

141. Zindel, Paul. *The Pigman*. New York: Harper and Row, 1968, 182pp.
Dedicated to the "boys and girls of Stapleton", *The Pigman* details the relationship between high school sophomores John Conlan and Lorraine Jensen and Angelo Pignati, an old man they grow to love, after initially trying to scam. John and Lorraine were making prank calls when they called Mr. Pignati claiming to be charity workers. When he readily agreed to give them money, they arranged to come to his house at 190 Howard Avenue the next day. His house was run-down in comparison to the other homes in the neighborhood. He invited them in and showed them his room full of prized pig figurines. The teens took an immediate liking to him and agreed to meet him at the zoo the next day where they helped him feed his best friend, a baboon named Bobo. John and Lorraine began visiting him frequently, drinking wine and eating well and generally having a fun, unstructured good time with a loving man. Although Pignati claims that his wife is visiting his sister in California, John discovers evidence that she has recently passed away. On one occasion the three are playing roller skate tag in his house when Pignati has a heart attack. While he is in the hospital, John and Lorraine throws a party in his house that gets out of hand and results in damage to Pignati's collection of pigs. The teens attempt to reconcile with Pignati by going to the zoo with him, but when he discovers that Bobo has died, Pignati collapses and dies.

Both John and Lorraine wait for the bus at Victory Blvd. and Eddy St., a stone's throw away from the Pigman's house, in what is described as a socioeconomically mixed neighborhood. Drinking at Masterson's tomb (a stand-in for the Vanderbilt Mausoleum) in Moravian cemetery is described as a popular teenage activity. Some other Staten Island streets are named in passing and other recognizable institutions are thinly disguised (i.e. St. Ambrose Hospital for St. Vincent's and Baron Park Zoo for Barrett Park Zoo).

142. Zindel, Paul. *The Pigman's Legacy*. New York: Harper and Row, 1980. 183pp.
In this sequel to *The Pigman*, John and Lorraine are now sixteen-years-old and admit that their friendship with Angelo Pignati and his subsequent death caused them to lose their childhood innocence and

grow up. While walking through his old neighborhood, past the "old villas" that used to house "the elite of Staten Island," they notice someone in the window of the Pigman's vacant house at 190 Howard Avenue. They investigate in order to ensure that's it's not the Pigman's ghost, and discover a cantankerous and paranoid old man squatting there, who's convinced that John and Lorraine are either from the IRS or are there to rob him. They purchase some fudge for him at the drugstore on Clove Road and Victory Boulevard to gain his trust. He claims that his name is Gus and asks the teens for help in retrieving something of his from the St. George townhouse of his former employer, the Colonel, a famous designer of subway systems who had been knighted by the king of Sweden. Gus has a yellow Studebaker which he lets John drive down to 107 Stuyvesant Place. The house is abandoned and boarded up but Gus instigates the teens to break in. John and Lorraine find the trunk that Gus is looking for and, while rifling through it, discover that "Gus" was in fact Colonel Parker Grenville, the famous subway designer. He owned the house where his trunk was stored, but lost it because of unpaid taxes.

When the Colonel doubles over with stomach pain and is taken to Richmond Hospital for treatment, John and Lorraine enlist the help of Dolly Racinski, the lunchroom custodian at their high school. The former assistant dietician at Hill View Hospital when it was a tuberculosis sanatorium, she was demoted to sweeper when a miracle cure for TB was invented. Now, she designs a special diet to help the Colonel's stomach problems, which she reveals to be diverticulitis. All four go to Atlantic City to celebrate his renewed health and the sale of silver coins that the Colonel had stored in his trunk. John loses a small fortune that the Colonel had won, but it is quickly forgiven. When his illness flares up again, he is taken to Staten Island Hospital where he marries Dolly before he dies. John and Lorraine declare their love for each other.

Besides the several street names already mentioned, Hyatt St. in St. George is described as having "a couple of wild bars" where "...Coast Guard guys and shipyard workers get drunk and beat each other up so you can read it about it the next day in the *Staten Island Advance*." The area of Stuyvesant Place where the Colonel's townhouse is located is described as "the only section of Staten Island that looked sophisticated" but where the houses also look dirty and all have wrought iron bars on the lower floor windows because of all the crooks in St. George. It is noted that the favorite sport of Staten Island kids is breaking and entering with their second favorite sport is beating up kids from New Jersey. While strolling along Howard Avenue, John and Lorraine note the house where opera singer Eileen Farrell once lived and a haunted house where English witch Sybil Leek hosted a TV program. Lorraine recalls walking past the St. George home of Staten Island author Phyllis Whitney, who also gave a speech at her high school.

143.   Zindel, Paul. *Rats*. New York: Hyperion, 1999. 203pp.

Fifteen-year-old Sarah Macafee and her ten-year-old brother Michael live with their father in a housing development abutting the Fresh Kills Landfill. Mr. Macafee, who remembers when the dump was full of tidal pools with fish, crabs and muskrats, is the person in charge of the dump and dreams of one day turning it into a park by covering all the mounds of garbage with asphalt. Sarah blames the dump for her mother's death at the hands of a drunk driver on Richmond Avenue, since the city widened roads and disregarded safety features in its haste to build the dump.

Without warning, hordes of rats begin appearing in toilets, Jacuzzis, pools and in the dump itself, attacking and even killing people. The rats begin swarming all over the shoreline and begin spreading to Bayonne and the rest of New York City. It is discovered that by capping off the garbage mounds with asphalt and not giving the methane gas any means of escape, the rats were forced to the surface. Michael's tame pet rat, Surfer, hears the call of the wild and joins his brethren. Michael uses a tracking device to trace him to the Willowbrook Pond drainage pipe which leads to an underground labyrinth of tunnels. Sarah follows Michael and encounters the rat emperor, who is momentarily distracted by Sarah's laptop computer, allowing her and Michael to escape. Sarah uses a remotely controlled spark to ignite the methane gas in the tunnel and incinerate many of the rats, making reference to the 1973 explosion at Liquid Natural Gas tanks on Staten Island. Travis and New Springville are evacuated because the National Guard is ready to firebomb the dump. Finally, the children discover that the rats are made docile by the flashing lights and electronic sounds of video games.

Biographies

Abbruzzi, Patrick

A retired police officer, the author based his stories on real-life events from the 1960s through the 1980s.
(Author bio from book)

Adinolfi, JoAnn (1965-)

Born into an Italian-American family on Staten Island, the author is a graduate of the Fashion Institute of Technology and the Art Academy of Munich. The author and illustrator of *Tina's Diner*, she has illustrated over twenty-five books for children.
(http://www.joannadinolfi.com/)

Ambrose, Dominic

Currently an independent writer and photographer, the author has worked overseas for the United States Information Service and as a college instructor and high school foreign language teacher in New York City.
(https://www.linkedin.com/pub/dominic-ambrose/1a/b37/21a)

Amessé, Susan

The author grew up in Staten Island and still resides there. When not writing, she likes to pursue her creativity in dance, travel, gardening, decorating and planning special events.
(http://www.scholastic.com/teachers/contributor/susan-amesse)

Anderson, Roberta [Fern Michaels, pseud.]. (August 22, 1942-)

The author co-wrote many historical and contemporary romances with Mary Kuczkir under the joint pseudonym Fern Michaels. Mrs. Anderson hasn't published anything since 1989 when Mrs. Kuczkir obtained the legal right to use their pseudonym on her own works.
(*Contemporary Authors Online*, New York: Gale Group, 2005, accessed 5 May 2015)

Anthony, Ted

A longtime journalist, Anthony is currently the Director of Asia-Pacific News for the Associated Press.
(Author bio from book)

Baker, Etta Anthony (December 8, 1866-?)

Born in Cincinnati, the author resided at 97 St. Mark's Place, a now-landmarked home. In addition to the works annotated here, she was known for writing the *Fairmount* series of books for girls and The *Youngsters of Centerville*, a book for boys. Mrs. Baker was well known for her community involvement, being involved with the Bible Class for Young Men in the Dutch Reformed Church, the United Boys Brigade, as well as being noted for her "particular friendship for the Curtis High School boys." She was president of the Chicago Women of New York, president of Fideles, secretary of Priors, and was for four years president of the Women's Club of Staten Island.

(William T. Davis and Charles W. Leng. *Staten Island and its People*. New York: Lewis Historical Publishing Co., 1929)

Bergal, Gilles, see Gallerne, Gilbert

Bettinger, Keith

The author is a highly-decorated, retired police officer from the Suffolk County, NY police department. He has been writing for law enforcement publications for twenty-five years and has received eighteen awards for his articles, stories, poems and books. He is an active member of the Public Safety Writers Association, an organization largely composed of authors also involved in public safety.

(http://www.examiner.com/article/spotlight-las-vegas-mystery-writer-keith-bettinger-is-former-police-officer)

Bowles, Jane (February 22, 1917-May 4, 1973)

The wife of writer and composer Paul Bowles, she and her husband honeymooned on Staten Island and rented a house at 1116 Woodrow Road in Prince's Bay for a short time, where they entertained a number of cultural figures, including Leonard Bernstein. Their house was the model for the ramshackle Staten Island farmhouse in *Two Serious Ladies*.

(Christopher Sawyer Lauçanno. An Invisible Spectator; a Biography of Paul Bowles. New York: Grove Press, 1989)

Brett, R.

An author, poet and journalist, Brett lives with her family along Lake Winnipeg in Manitoba, Canada,

(Author bio from book)

Brown, Tracy (1974-)

Born and raised on Staten Island, Tracy Brown grew up in the Mariners Harbor Houses and was attending McKee High school when she became pregnant at the age of fifteen. Despite a teacher there telling her she'd be on welfare for the rest of her life, she graduated high school and worked several jobs to support her daughter. After receiving encouragement to write a novel, Brown penned her semi-autobiographical *Black* while commuting to work on the Ferry, and immediately found a publisher. She has found material for her subsequent novels in her observations of everyday life on Staten Island and from interviewing Jersey Street neighbors who both used and dealt crack. Her novels, which have been *Essence* bestsellers, continue to inspire with their theme of women triumphing over adversity.

(Staten Island Advance, 11 March 2011,
http://www.silive.com/northshore/index.ssf/2011/03/for_staten_island_author_tracy.html)

Burdge, Anthony

An independent scholar and blogger, Mr. Burdge has contributed essays, articles and reference entries to a number of collections, such as The J.R.R. Tolkien Encyclopedia, The Mythological Dimensions of Doctor Who, and The Mythological Dimensions of Neil Gaiman. With wife and literary collaborator Jessica Burke, they founded Myth Ink Books in 2013 in order to bring to publication "those who've written work that others may find just a bit too weird, eclectic, or profound for print."

(Publisher bio page, http://mythinkbooks.com/about/)

Burke, Jessica

A College of Staten Island English professor, a self-taught herbalist, a writer and publisher, Jessica Burke and husband Anthony Burdge have been collaborating on writing and research projects for over a decade, including the two collections annotated here. A formative experience for her was, as a five year old, discovering an LP recording of J.R.R. Tolkien reading from *The Hobbit*, an event that fired her passion for genres and writers that would become her life's work. Jessica Burke has published on a range of topics from J.R.R. Tolkien to Beowulf to Doctor Who.

(Publisher bio page, http://mythinkbooks.com/about/)

Burleigh, Cecil [Harry Moore, pseud.]. (1859-December 2, 1921)

Under the pseudonym of Harry Moore, both Burleigh and Stephen Angus Douglas Cox wrote six hundred and twelve entries in the *Liberty Boys*

series, with Cox writing the first one hundred and twenty five titles and
Burleigh the next four hundred and eighty seven.
(The Dime Novel Companion: A Source Book By J. Randolph Cox
Greenwood Publishing Group, 2000)

Burtone, Gaetano J.
    The author, who says that he was "blessed" to have grown up on
Staten Island, is an avid sports fan and collector of sports memorabilia who
lives in San Antonio, Texas with his family.
(Author bio from book)

Cameron, Caryn, see Harper, Karen.

Campbell, Hope, see Wallis, Geraldine.

Colia, Frank
    Born and raised in Staten Island, Colia's short stories have been
included in several anthologies of supernatural horror.
(Author bio from book)

Corson, Geoffrey, see Sholl, Anna McClure

Coston, Alicia
    The author of *The Men Who Sleep with my Husband*, in addition to the
work annotated here, Alicia Coston is a songwriter, hip-hop artist, poet and
freelance writer in the Washington D.C. area.
(http://www.smashwords.com/profile/view/AliciaCoston)

Craig, Todd
    A former professor at the College of Staten Island, Craig's creative
output straddles fiction, creative nonfiction and poetry to explore and
depict urban culture.
(Author bio from book)

Daulton, Agnes Warner McClelland (April 29, 1867-June 5, 1944)
    Born in New Philadelphia, Ohio, Daulton was married to author
George Daulton. She published many novels and articles, lectured on child
psychology, insects and literature, and was a noted authority on floriculture.
For a time she and her husband resided at 386 Richmond Terrace (now
demolished).
(The Kingston Daily Freeman, Kingston, NY, June 5, 1944)

Davis, J.T.
The author is a retired professor who resides in San Antonio, Texas with his partner of over thirty years. He has written a sequel to *New York Stories* entitled *San Antonio Stories*.
(Author bio from book)

Dawson, Ashley
A Professor of English at the College of Staten Island and the CUNY Graduate Center, Dawson's works have focused on global migration and postcolonial literature.
(Author bio from book)

DeCandido, Keith R(obert) A(ndreassi). (April 18, 1969-)
A native of the Bronx, the author is a musician, editor and writer of fantasy and science fiction. While he has written fiction in universes of his own creation, he is best known for his prolific work in writing media tie-ins for properties such as Star Trek, Buffy the Vampire Slayer, Doctor Who, Supernatural, Andromeda, Farscape, Leverage, Spider-Man, X-Men, and Sleepy Hollow. In 2009, his work earned him the title of Grandmaster by the International Association of Media Tie-In Writers.
(http://en.wikipedia.org/wiki/Keith_DeCandido)

Dee, Sylvia, see De Sylvia, Josephine

DeSilva, Bruce
A longtime journalist, DeSilva is the author of the trilogy of *Mulligan* detective novels which have won Edgar and Macavity awards. He is married to author and poet Patricia Smith.
(Author bio from book)

DeStefano, Anthony [Anthony John, pseud.].
No information available.

De Sylvia, Josephine [Sylvia Dee, pseud.]. (October 22, 1914-June 12, 1967)
Born in Arkansas, de Sylvia worked as a copywriter before forming a successful song-writing collaboration with Sid Lippman. Their most popular numbers, for which de Sylvia wrote the lyrics, were *Too Young* (popularized by Nat King Cole), *Chickery Chick* and *My Sugar is So Refined*. *Dear Guest and Ghost* was dramatized for television by the Philco Television Playhouse in 1950.
(New York Times, 13 June 1967, pg 83)

Drew, K.

Drew is a Canadian writer whose creativity first manifested itself in cinema, where he produced a number of short films that won awards at international festivals. He lives with his dog Mylo, and pursues his passions of sculpting, travel and painting.
(http://www.dreamspinnerpress.com/store/product_info.php?products_id =4036)

DuBois, Theodora (September 14, 1890-February 1, 1986)

The great-great-great-granddaughter of Cornelius Melyn, Staten Island's third patroon, and a descendant of Roger Willams, the founder of Rhode Island, Theodora Brenton Eliot McCormick was born in Brooklyn. Her father died when she was one-year-old, which led to her mother's second marriage to an overbearing and controlling man, a figure who inspired several such stepfather characters in her books. The family moved to Manhattan and then to Yonkers where Theodora began writing plays, poetry and short stories. In 1917 she married Delafield DuBois, an electrical engineer, and the couple moved to Dongan Hills in Staten Island. Theodora DuBois published numerous stories in magazines through the 1920s but as market demand changed with the Depression, she published her first novel in 1930, a genre she would pursue for another 35 years, writing mysteries, juvenile fiction and historical novels. Her negative depiction of the House Un-American Activities Committee in *Seeing Red* led to a public backlash and to her publisher, Doubleday, not publishing any more McNeill mysteries. The family lived in Connecticut and abroad for over a decade but returned to Staten Island in the early 1950s. DuBois was interviewed by the New York Times in a 1966 article about Staten Island's vanishing old elite. (Theodora DuBois Papers, Archives & Special Collections, Department of the Library, College of Staten Island, CUNY, Staten Island, New York)

Du Bois, William Pène (May 9, 1916-February 5, 1993)

A prolific author and illustrator of children's book, Pène Du Bois was honored with several prestigious awards, including the Newberry Medal for *The Twenty-one Balloons* in 1948 and two Caldecott Honor Awards in the 1950s for *Bear Party* and *Lion*. He was one of the founding editors of the Paris Review in 1953. The author's father, famed artist and critic Guy Pène du Bois, wrote about his own boyhood on Staten Island in his autobiography *Artists Say the Silliest Things* (Duell, Sloane and Pearce, 1940). (*Contemporary Authors Online*, New York: Gale Group, 2003, accessed 13 March 2015)

Earle, Olive L. (1888-1982)

A native of England, Earle moved to Staten Island in 1934 in order to paint murals for the WPA (Works Progress Administration) at the Staten Island Zoo. A painter whose works were exhibited throughout the country, she also wrote and illustrated many nature-oriented books for children.
(The Staten Island Museum,
http://www.statenislandmuseum.org/collections/art-collection/white-footed-mouse)

England, George Allan (February 8, 1877-June 26, 1936)

A prominent science fiction writer in the early twentieth century, England is best known for his novel *Darkness and Dawn*, in which a single man and woman survive a deadly gas that kills the rest of humanity. A passionate Socialist, England ran as a Socialist candidate for Congress in 1908 and for Governor of Maine in 1912.
(*Contemporary Authors Online*, New York: Gale Group, 2003, accessed 13 March 2015)

Ermelino, Louisa

The author summered in Staten Island with her family and the island is the home of her husband's family and "the site of a large part of [their] courtship." She is the reviews director at *Publisher's Weekly* and has authored three novels.
(Author bio from book)

Forgione, Louis (June 21, 1896-July 1968)

A second-generation Italian-American, the author published three well-regarded novels within the space of four years dealing with the Italian-American experience. Despite his literary success, his biographical details are shrouded in mystery, with one source claiming that he was a successful naval engineer in New York and another claiming that he dropped out of the College of the City of New York to work when his father fell ill. The detailed descriptions of shipyard work as well as the manners and mores of the working class in *Reamer Lou* seem to indicate a first-hand familiarity with manual labor in New York's waterfront industries.
(Durante, Francesco, ed. *Italoamericana*. New York: Fordham University Press, 2014. 997pp.)

Friedman, Robin (1968-)

Born in Israel, she came to the United States with her family when she was five, residing in Staten Island, among other places, before settling in

New Jersey. Having desired to be a writer since she was a little girl, she has been an editor, copywriter and journalist in addition to writing five books. (Author website, http://www.robinfriedman.com/about/about.html)

Gallerne, Gilbert [Gilles Bergal, pseud.]. (1954-)
    A French writer, Gallerne has published more than twenty-five books in various genres (crime novels, thrillers, science fiction, horror, fantasy). He won the 2010 prix du Quai des Orfèvres for his novel *Au pays des ombres*. (http://fr.wikipedia.org/wiki/Gilbert_Gallerne)

Gilman, Mildred (1896-January 3, 1994)
    An acquaintance of several members of the Algonquin Round Table, Gilman was a newspaper reporter in New York during the 1920s. She specialized in highly personal accounts of lurid headline crimes, earning a reputation as one of journalism's first "sob sisters", a moniker she used for the title of a novel which was later made into a Hollywood movie (Fox Film Corporation, 1931). She is known to have lived at 148 Hamilton Avenue (present-day Hamden Avenue) in Grant City for a time.
(New York Times, January 6, 1994, pg. D19)

Goldfarb, Aaron (February 10, 1979-)
    Born in Manhattan and raised in Oklahoma City, Goldfarb is best known for his satirical novel *How to Fail: the Self-Hurt Guide*. He is a screenwriter for television and film, and an aficionado of craft beer. (http://aarongoldfarb.com/)

Goldsborough, Robert (Gerald) (October 3, 1937-)
    A journalist and writer, Robert Goldsborough was introduced to the "Nero Wolfe" mysteries of Rex Stout by his mother when he was a teenager. After Stout's death in 1975, Goldsborough wrote a Nero Wolfe novel for his mother out of gratitude, but it took eight years for him to obtain permission from the Stout estate to use his characters and settings in a published work. In addition to nine Nero Wolfe novels, Goldsborough has also published a series of mystery novels featuring a Chicago reporter named Snap Malek, a character of his own creation.
(*Contemporary Authors Online*, New York: Gale Group, 2015, accessed 16 March 2015)

Grayson, Richard (June 4, 1951-)
    A 1975 graduate of Richmond College, Mr. Grayson has been a prolific writer, a political activist and a performance artist. He has run two satiric

campaigns for President, in 1984 and 2012, but has also been a committed activist for gay rights for several decades.
(*Contemporary Authors Online*, New York: Gale Group, 2003, accessed 14 March 2015)

Gross, Andrew (1952-)
A successful business executive in the sports fashion industry, Gross' writing career began when author James Patterson read a manuscript he had submitted and asked him to co-author a book, a partnership that has led to six best-selling novels.
(http://www.andrewgrossbooks.com/index.html)

Harper, Karen [Caryn Cameron, pseud.]. (April 6, 1945-)
The author of numerous works of carefully-researched historical fiction, Karen Harper is perhaps best known for her series of books featuring a young Queen Elizabeth I as an amateur sleuth. A former high school teacher and college instructor in Ohio, Karen Harper was the winner of the Mary Higgins Clark Award in 2006, for *Dark Angel*.
(*Contemporary Authors Online*, New York: Gale Group, 2013, accessed 9 February 2015)

Harrington, Joseph (1903-1980)
A journalist, Harrington wrote three police detective mysteries, with *The Last Known Address* being made into a French/Italian film, *Dernier domicile connu*, directed by Jóse Giovanni in 1970. His papers are preserved at Boston University.
(http://fr.wikipedia.org/wiki/Joseph_Harrington)

Hellstrom, Christopher (January 5, 1973-)
A former staffer for Mayor Rudolph Giuliani, the author is currently the Director of Development for the Greenbelt Conservancy.
(http://hieroglyph.asu.edu/members/hellstrom7/)

Hoff, B.J. (1940-)
A direct descendant of Irish ancestors who came to America before the Revolutionary War, the author states that she has "…a heart for Ireland and the Irish…" and bases her historical novels on the experiences of Irish immigrants to America. A former church music director and music teacher, her deep Christian faith informs her characters and writings, which include poetry and inspirational works as well as fiction.
(Author website, http://www.bjhoff.com/)

Holding, Elisabeth Sanxay (June 8, 1889-February 7, 1955)
    Born in Brooklyn but educated in part at Miss Botsford's School (New Brighton) and at the Staten Island Academy, Holding began her career writing romantic novels during the 1920s but the Depression forced her to turn to the more lucrative genre of hard-boiled detective fiction, where she earned acclaim from both critics and peers. Her novel, *The Blank Wall*, was twice adapted to film.
(Contemporary Authors Online. Detroit: Gale, 2003. *Literature Resource Center,* accessed 29 Dec. 2015)

Hopkins, George R.
A Staten Island resident, the author retired as assistant Principal from Susan Wagner High School. As a Marine, Hopkins had served on active duty during the Cuban Missile Crisis.
(Author website,
http://www.georgerhopkins.com/About_the_Author.html)

John, Anthony, see DeStefano, Anthony

Joyce, Eddie
A Tottenville native who was a basketball star at Tottenville High School in the early 1990s, Joyce went on to graduate from Harvard University and Georgetown University Law Center. A practicing lawyer for ten years, Joyce- now a Brooklyn resident- retired to raise his three daughters and pursue his dream of writing.
(Staten Island Advance interview, March 11, 2015)

Kelter, Lawrence
    A Brooklyn native, Kelter was encouraged in his writing career by Nelson DeMille, who declared that Kelter reminded him of a young Robert Ludlum.
(Author website, http://lawrencekelter.com/BIOFAQ.html)

Khoudari, Amy
    An avid photographer and self-described computer geek, the author and her life partner live in New York City.
(Author bio from book)

Kingsbury, Karen (June 8, 1963-)
    A former Los Angeles journalist, Karen Kingsbury began her writing career in the true crime genre, but transitioned to collections of miracles

and answered prayers. Her first fictional work was rejected by secular publishers for its lack of sex and profanity, which led to her finding a Christian publisher and a new career as a Christian novelist. Dubbed the "Queen of Christian Fiction" by *Time magazine*, her dozens of novels have sold millions of copies. She hosts a nationally syndicated radio show and has written songs that have been recorded by Marie Osmond and country singer Richie McDonald.
(*Contemporary Authors Online*, New York: Gale Group, 2014, accessed 14 March 2015)

Kirshenbaum, Bonnie
    A professor at Columbia University, the author taught at Wagner College two decades ago. Kirshenbaum is the author of two short story collections and six novels.
(Author bio from book)

Kolff, Cornelius G. (September 8, 1860-February 27, 1950)
    Cornelius G. Kolff was one of Staten Island's most vigorous civic promoters and overall valuable citizens, who more than lived up to his nickname of "Staten Island's Most Obedient Servant." He was born in Manhattan to German parents who, when he was seven years old, brought him back to Germany where he lived until he was seventeen. When he returned to the United States he spent six years in the West before settling in Staten Island. A protégé of developer Erastus Wiman, he founded the Kolff and Kaufmann real estate firm in St. George and went on to a fabulously successful real estate career, with over 36 developments on Staten Island, including Woods of Arden, Bement Estates, Emerson Hill (which he named) and Shore Acres (where he made his home at 15 Harbor View Place), in addition to brokering the 1911 sale of the Fox Hill Villa to the Jesuit Order to become Mount Manresa. Kolff played an instrumental role in rehabilitating the Conference House, and was intimately involved with the Staten Island Historical Society, the Institute of Arts and Sciences, Belles Lettres, and other civic organizations. Harboring mixed feelings about the effects of his development on Staten Island, sentiments he expressed in an essay entitled "Vanishing Beauties," Kolff founded a Tree Planting Association on Staten Island and- through his work as a director of the New York City Park Association- played a large role in the development of public parks in the borough. In 1910 Kolff hired a former slave to build a log cabin, dubbed the "Philosopher's Retreat," on Emerson Hill, where Kolff maintained a sort of rustic salon, where the borough's eminent men would gather for fellowship and philosophizing. One of the last steam-

powered ferryboats, completed in 1951, was christened the Cornelius G. Kolff.

Kuczkir, Mary [Fern Michaels, pseud.]. (April 9, 1933-)
The bestselling author of, by her own count, more than one hundred novels, Mary Kuczkir began writing when the youngest of her five children went off to school and her husband ordered her to get a job. Although she collaborated on her early works with Roberta Anderson, in 1989 Mrs. Kuczkir obtained full legal rights to use the pseudonym Fern Michaels on her own works. Born in Pennsylvania and having raised her family in New Jersey, the author currently resides in a three-hundred-year-old South Carolina plantation house that is inhabited by a friendly ghost named Mary Margaret.
(*Contemporary Authors Online*, New York: Gale Group, 2011, accessed 5 May 2015)

Largo, Michael
The author of three novels and four works of nonfiction, Largo won the Bram Stoker Award for *Final Exits: The Illustrated Encyclopedia of How We Die*. He was born on Staten Island and grew up a few blocks away from where Willie Sutton lived.
(Author bio from book)

Latka, John
A retired Engineer, the author lived on Staten Island from 1953 to 1977, with an interval in the U.S. Navy from 1956 to 1960. His novel annotated here was inspired by his memory of a beautiful young woman he once knew.
(Author bio, http://bookstore.authorhouse.com/Products/SKU-000340260/STATEN-ISLAND-MEMOIRS.aspx)

Ledbetter, Gladys Manée (April 3, 1903-June 9, 1987)
The daughter of a Tottenville native, the author was inspired to write the novel annotated here by reading about the 1776 peace conference on Staten Island. A Huguenot descendant herself, and member of the Huguenot Society, she proudly made that obscure group the protagonists of her story.
(Author bio from book)

Loehfelm, Bill (October 5, 1969-)

Born in Brooklyn, Loehfelm grew up in Eltingville and, after graduating college, taught English at Monsignor Farrell High School and at St. Peter's Boys High School. Like his heroine, Maureen Coughlin, Loehfelm moved to New Orleans, where he still resides, pursuing a writing career and playing drums in a rock n' roll cover band.

(*Contemporary Authors Online*, New York: Gale Group, 2014, accessed 23 March 2015)

Longfellow, (Pamela) "Ki" (December 9, 1944-)

Born to an unmarried sixteen-year-old mother in Staten Island, the author bounced around from foster home to a relative's home until her mother briefly regained custody and took her to California to live with another family member. With her mother's marriage to a navy man, Longfellow and family moved frequently, living in New York, California and Hawaii. She had a daughter at age eighteen, acted in *Once a Thief* (1964, starring Alain Delon), worked briefly as a fashion model in New York, wrote for CARE (Cooperative for Assistance and Relief Everywhere) and volunteered with the VISTA organization on a Blackfeet Indian reservation in Montana. Traveling throughout the world, she eventually formed a relationship with the manager of the English folk band, Fairport Convention, and became a British citizen. In the late 1970s she married British musician/author and artistic provocateur Vivian Stanshall. Among other projects, the couple converted a cargo ship into a floating theatre called "The Old Profanity Showboat", where they produced *Stinkfoot, a Comic Opera*, a piece which has seen several revivals. Longfellow began writing novels in the 1980s, but is most famous for a trilogy of novels, inaugurated by the best-selling *The Secret Magdalene* (2005), dealing with the concept of the Divine Feminine.

(http://en.wikipedia.org/wiki/Ki_Longfellow)

Lynch, Lee (1945-)

The author began writing lesbian fiction and non-fiction in the 1960s and has been cited by younger lesbian writers as a major influence and inspiration.

(*Contemporary Authors Online*, New York: Gale Group, 2006, accessed 23 March 2015)

MacKellar, William (February 20, 1914-July 10, 1994)

Born in Scotland, the author came to the United States with his family when he was eleven-years-old. A veteran of the Second World War and a

successful businessman, he authored many books and short stories, one of which (*The Silent Bells*) was adapted to a musical play in 1991.
(*Contemporary Authors Online*, New York: Gale Group, 2002, accessed 9 March 2015)

Mancuso, Christopher
An author, paranormal investigator and accomplished screenwriter, Mancuso co-directed the documentary *Haunted Snug Harbor*.
(Author bio from book)

Marino, Kelly
Born in California, the author now lives with her husband in his hometown of Staten Island, where they have two children.
(Author bio from book)

McMahon, Judi
The author of several self-improvement books, a former *Staten Island Advance* columnist, and a contributor to various beauty magazines, McMahon currently operates a successful direct mail skin care business.
(http://www.rebornangel.com/pages/meetjudi.htm)

Mercaldo, David
In addition to the works annotated here, veteran educator David Mercaldo, Ph.D. has written plays, a children's book, a religious polemic and a defense of U.S. Army Lieutenant Colonel Terry Larkin, who was imprisoned for questioning Barack Obama's eligibility to serve as President.
(http://www.davidmercaldo.com/)

Michaels, Fern, see Kuczkir, Mary and Anderson, Roberta

Mila, Paul J.
The author gave up a corporate career in 2002 to devote his time to scuba diving and underwater photography. His photographs and videos have appeared in National Geographic, among other publications and web sites.
(http://www.paulmila.com/index.html)

Millman, John
The author was a World War II veteran who participated in the invasion of Normandy.
(Author bio from book)

Mills, W(eymer). Jay (1880-May 25, 1938)
An editor for Vogue from 1920-1923, Mills authored or edited several books revolving around colonial and Revolutionary America. He lived in Italy and England for the last fifteen years of his life and passed away in Germany after a lingering illness.
(New York Times, May 26, 1938)

Modern, Tom
Born outside Cleveland, Ohio, the author came to New York City to perform and record his music, but also acted, painted and produced conceptual art as well as trying his hand at writing.
(Author bio from book)

Moore, Harry, see Burleigh, Cecil.

Morris, Mitzi
Raised in the suburbs of Cleveland, Ohio, Morris moved to Manhattan and wrote *Poetic Justice* as a "mash note" to her new hometown. A software engineer, she likes to ride the Staten Island Ferry.
(http://www.criminalelement.com/blogs/2012/10/spying-on-harriet-the-spy-mitzi-morris-middle-grade)

Mowat, Grace Helen (1875-February 1964)
Born into an old Loyalist family in Beech Hill, near Saint Andrews, New Brunswick, the author studied in England and at the Women's Art School of Cooper Union in New York. After teaching in Nova Scotia, she returned to her family's St. Andrews farm to care for her widowed father. An active member of the community, she became interested in traditional skills like spinning, weaving and pottery as a source of income, and founded Charlotte County Cottage Craft in 1915, a business which employed impoverished local women to produce handicrafts in the privacy of their own home, a movement which flourishes to this day.
(New Brunswick Literary Encyclopedia,
http://w3.stu.ca/stu/sites/nble/m/mowat_grace.htm)

Mullin, Michael
Mullin is the author or co-author of several books and book series for young adults and children. He used to work as a writer for the Disney corporation with illustrator and co-author John Skewes.
(http://larrygetslost.com/about.html)

Nadelson, Reggie

Born and raised in Greenwich Village, Nadelson moved to London to write for several British newspapers and produce documentaries for the BBC. She now divides her time between London and New York. (http://www.reggienadelson.com/about/)

Nathan, Robert (January 2, 1894-May 25, 1985)

A successful novelist, poet, screenwriter and playwright, several of Nathan's work's were adapted to film, most notably *The Bishop's Wife* (RKO, 1947) with Cary Grant, Loretta Young, and David Niven.
(*Contemporary Authors Online*, New York: Gale Group, 2003, accessed 24 March 2015)

Nielsen, Alfred

In addition to the novel annotated here, the author has been a lab technician, farm hand, dissector of cadavers, marketing representative for IBM, bartender, educational video tape producer, and teacher of emotionally disturbed adolescents. He lives with his family in Poughkeepsie, New York, where he is a health inspector and part-time college inspector. (Author bio from book)

Nieves-Powell, Linda (1970-)

A filmmaker, novelist and playwright from Staten Island, Nieves-Powell is perhaps best known for her award-winning play, *Yo Soy Latina*, which has been performed off-Broadway, in regional theatre and at over four hundred colleges across the country. (http://www.lindanievespowell.com/#!about/cbga)

Nunez, Sigrid (1951-)

Born in New York City, Nunez is the author of six novels and a 2011 memoir about her year living with Susan Sontag in the 1970s, first as an assistant and then as the live-in girlfriend of Sontag's son. She is a fellow of the American Academy of Arts and Sciences. Nunez has taught at Amherst College, Princeton, Smith College, Boston University, Vassar, Columbia University and the New School, among other institutions. (http://www.sigridnunez.com/)

Nutt, Frances Tysen (1896?-?)

A descendant of Thys Barentsen, one of the original settlers of Staten Island, and the daughter of local developer and philanthropist, David J. Tysen (1841-1928), Nutt based her novel, *Three Fields to Cross*, on old family

documents. The Lake-Tysen House, which had been in her family for years, was moved from Tysens Lane to Richmondtown in 1962.
(Richard B. Dickenson. *Holden's Staten Island.* New York: Center for Migration Studies, 2002)

Odets, Clifford (July 18, 1906-August 14, 1963)
One of the major figures of the American theatre, Odets was a successful screenwriter and director as well as an iconic playwright. After dropping out of high school Odets took up acting with a passion and became a founding member of the highly influential Group Theatre in the 1920s. Taking up playwriting in the 1930s, Odets achieved national renown with such plays as *Waiting for Lefty* and *Golden Boy*, even as his works began to be heavily influenced by his growing Marxism. He moved to Hollywood in the 1930s and spent the remainder of his career there, working in film, most notably writing the screenplay for *The Sweet Smell of Success* (United Artists, 1957), starring Tony Curtis and Burt Lancaster.
(*Contemporary Authors Online.* Detroit: Gale, 2001, accessed 5 May, 2015)

O'Neill, Joseph (February 23, 1964-)
Of Irish birth, O'Neill spent most of his life abroad, eventually settling in New York where he writes and teaches and plays cricket at Walker Park with the Staten Island Cricket Club. His 2008 novel, *Netherland*, was received with critical acclaim and won the PEN/Faulkner award.
(*Contemporary Authors Online.* Detroit: Gale, 2009, accessed 28 March, 2015)

Penncavage, Michael
An author and editor, Penncavage won a 2008 Derringer Award for his story *The Cost of Doing Business.*
(Author bio from book)

Petersen, David
When the author's twin brother, Kenny, was murdered in the doorway of his Great Kills apartment in 1985, David Petersen left Staten Island, married and raised three girls in Hazlet, New Jersey.
(Author bio from book)

Petrosini, Dan
A successful entrepreneur and adjunct college professor, the author lived in Brooklyn and Staten Island until his twenties, an experience which inspired the characters in the book annotated here.
(https://www.smashwords.com/interview/danpetrosini)

Pinto, K.T.

Born in Brooklyn, the author grew up an avid reader of science fiction and in her teen years wrote an unpublished romance series that eventually comprised twenty-five books. The book profiled here began as a break from the author's alternate history vampire series. She works as a sex educator at an adult superstore in Staten Island where she runs workshops and plans events "...that are probably a lot more exciting than the meeting you were stuck in today."
(http://www.ktpinto.com/)

Powell, Dawn (August 24, 1896/7-November 15, 1965)

After suffering from an unhappy childhood in small town Ohio, Powell came to New York City during World War I. The city would serve as setting and locale for most of her prolific output of short stories, novels and plays. Although admired by a discriminating subset of the reading public, and beloved by fellow writers, Powell's works never achieved commercial success, but recent years have seen a revival of interest. Powell had a special place in her heart for Staten Island, having gone there on her first date with her husband and returning there frequently. She published her amusing recollections of the island in an October 1965 *Esquire* magazine article entitled *Staten Island, I Love You!*.
(http://www.loa.org/dawnpowell/)

Randisi, Robert (August 24, 1951-)

A former New York City police officer, the author is an award-winning writer of private eye mysteries and western novels.
(*Contemporary Authors Online*. Detroit: Gale, 2015, accessed 9 March, 2015)

Reigada, Flora

As a child growing up with her family at 120 Vanderbilt Avenue in Clifton, Flora Reigada was inspired by a fifth grade writing assignment at P.S. 16 to become a writer. As an adult, she became an award-winning newspaper columnist for the *Star-Advocate* in Titusville, Florida. For many years she and her husband were a writer/photographer team for the *Florida Today* newspaper. The author maintains a website, http://simemories.com/ that includes many family photos from old Staten Island.
(http://www.goodreads.com/author/show/871210.Flora_Reigada)

Rendelstein, Jill Ellen

Rendelstein graduated with a Master in Fine Arts from American University. She has taught writing at George Washington University,

American University, and Northern Virginia Community College, and tutored students for more than a decade. Jill has also written for publications such as *The World & I* magazine and *The Washington Times* newspaper. She has worked as an editor and proofreader for various print and web publications and runs her own business as a creative writing tutor and editor.
(http://jrwritingadvantage.com/about.cfm)

Reynolds, D(ewey) B. (?)
    The author resides in his hometown of Kansas City, Missouri, where he has written for several local magazines and newspapers. He once appeared on the Sally Jessy Raphael Show to speak about his experience growing up in an abusive foster home.
(Author bio from book)

Robb, J.D., see Robertson, Eleanor Marie

Robertson, Eleanor Marie [J.D. Robb, pseud.]. (October 10, 1950-)
    Better known by her other pseudonym, Nora Roberts, this immensely successful author has written over two hundred novels, mostly in the romance genre, but has also published fifty novels in her *In Death* mystery series under the pseudonym J.D. Robb. She was the first person inducted into the Romance Writers of America Hall of Fame.
(*Contemporary Authors Online*. Detroit: Gale, 2015, accessed 27 March, 2015)

Rozan, S(hira) J(udith) (1950-)
    A Bronx native, Rozan was a successful architect before pursuing a career as a writer of mystery and detective fiction. Her works have garnered several prestigious awards, including two Shamus Award from the Private Eye Writers of America and the Edgar Allan Poe Award from the Mystery Writers of America.
(*Contemporary Authors Online*. Detroit: Gale, 2013, accessed 27 March, 2015)

Russo, Daniel
    A computer programmer who was born and raised in Staten Island, the story featured in *Dark Tales from Elder Regions* was his first published work.
(Author bio from book)

Sampson, John (September 11, 1908-April 30, 2010)
    Born into an old shipping family in Liverpool, England, Sampson immigrated to the United States with his parents and sister when he was a

boy, settling on Steele Avenue in New Dorp, where he lived until he was in his 90s. He attended the former P.S. 9 (now New Dorp Park) and then P.S. 8 in Great Kills, during which time he started his own newspaper, the *New Dorp Star*, which he continued publishing until 1924. Soon after he began attending Curtis High School he was forced to withdraw because of fears of a tuberculosis outbreak, and he never again underwent formal education, although he took correspondence courses in journalism and remained a voracious reader and book collector for the rest of his life. In 1925, he joined the *Staten Island Advance*, where he worked for three years as an assistant city editor, covering local news, deaths and the Staten Island waterfront. He next moved on to the *New York American*, where he worked as ship reporter, a position which allowed him to interview countless luminaries from the worlds of politics, film, literature and sports. For the rest of his career Sampson worked for several different British newspapers in London and New York City. Sampson never married, but spent his free time traveling throughout the world and indulging his love of reading, while being active with the Staten Island Historical Society and the New Dorp Civic Association. In his retirement he wrote eight novels and a book of aphorisms, and took on a new role as revisionist historian, giving lectures and writing articles about the shortcomings of Winston Churchill. Sampson's papers were donated to the College of Staten Island in 2008.
(John Sampson Papers, Archives and Special Collections, Department of the Library, College of Staten Island, CUNY, Staten Island, New York)

Sholl, Anna McClure [Geoffrey Corson, pseud.]. (1868-April 1, 1956)
    Anna McClure Sholl was the author of twelve novels and numerous short stories, essays and reviews that appeared in national publications. The novel annotated here, *Blue Blood and Red* (sold under the title *Carmichael* in Great Britain) won the 1915 international prize of the Lyceum Club of London for the best novel of the year written by a woman. An accomplished painter, Sholl's works were regularly exhibited in New York galleries. She was one of a select number of guests at Mark Twain's seventieth birthday dinner at Delmonico's. Sholl was a member of the Staten Island Institute of Arts and Sciences and resided at 1807 Richmond Road.
(New York Times, 3 April 1956, pg 29)

Smith, F(rancis) Hopkinson (October 23, 1838 – April 7, 1915)
    A descendant of a signer of the Declaration of Independence, Smith was a self-taught mechanical engineer and contractor in New York City, who worked on numerous projects for the federal government, including

the foundation for the Statue of Liberty. A talented artist, Smith won several prestigious awards for his work, including the Order of Medjidieh from the Ottoman sultan, an admirer. Smith began his writing career at the age of forty-five, when he was asked by his publisher to describe a series of watercolors being prepared for publication. His first foray a success, Smith turned to fiction, his novels finding worldwide popularity.
(New York Times, April 8, 1915)

Skewes, John
Skewes worked for Disney and other major studios as an artist and illustrator. It was at Disney where he met co-author Michael Mullin.
(http://larrygetslost.com/about.html)

Smith, Martin Cruz (November 3, 1942-)
An award-winning mystery writer, Martin Cruz Smith (originally named Martin William Smith) has written almost one hundred novels, including seven that feature Arkady Renko, the Russian protagonist of *Gorky Park*, which was number one on the *New York Times* bestseller list for two weeks in 1981.
(*Contemporary Authors Online*. Detroit: Gale, 2014, accessed 5 May, 2015)

Smith, Patricia (1955-)
A College of Staten Island professor, Smith is the author of six acclaimed volumes of poetry. She is married to author Bruce DeSilva.
(Author bio from book)

Spellman, Francis Cardinal (May 4, 1889-December 2, 1967)
Appointed Catholic Archbishop of New York in 1939 and raised to the Cardinalate in 1946, Spellman reigned during a momentous era in the American Church. He participated in the Second Vatican Council, voted in three conclaves and played an active part in public affairs. In addition to *The Foundling*, which was a national bestseller, Spellman wrote several volumes of poetry.
(American National Biography Online, http://www.anb.org/articles/08/08-01438.html)

Spiers, A(ugustus) M(ansfield) (1871-?)
A florist who resided in New Dorp at one time, all that is known of Spiers is that he moved to Macon, Georgia.
(William T. Davis and Charles W. Leng. *Staten Island and its People*. New York: Lewis Historical Publishing Co., 1929)

Spollen, Anne (February 19, 1958-)

A native Staten Islander, Anne Spollen's poems and short stories have appeared in a number of collections and anthologies. In addition to *The Shape of Water*, which received a National Book Nomination, she has written one other novel, and is currently working on a book of essays exploring the effect that drug addiction has had on her family.

(*Contemporary Authors Online*. Detroit: Gale, 2011, accessed 17 March, 2015)

St. Jean, Catherine Avery

In addition to a successful and groundbreaking career in advertising and business, the author is a certified New York State teacher with a Masters in Childhood Education. An avid biker and hiker, the author maintained part of the Greenbelt's blue trail before retiring and moving to Florida. She is also listed as being the executive producer for the short film *Willowbrook*, which depicted a young doctor's experience at the Willowbrook State School in the 1960s.

(Author website,
http://catherinestjeanportfolio.blogspot.com/2010/06/about-me.html)

Stone, Robert (August 21, 1937-January 10, 2015)

Born in Brooklyn to a "…family of Scottish Presbyterians and Irish Catholics who made their living as tugboat workers in New York harbor," Stone served in the Navy and afterwards was acquainted with the Beat Poets and Ken Kesey's Merry Pranksters. His critically-acclaimed works have won several awards, including a National Book Award and the John Dos Passos Prize and have been finalists for the Pulitzer Prize, The PEN/Faulkner Award and the National Book Award.

(*Contemporary Authors Online*. Detroit: Gale, 2014, accessed 13 March, 2015)

Telford, Robert S.

Robert Telford attended Kent State University, served in World War II, and earned his bachelor of theatre arts degree from the Pasadena School of Theatre. He has acted in and directed off-Broadway plays and worked for the American Negro Theatre with such luminaries as Frank Silvera, Maxwell Glanville, and Sidney Poitier. Telford currently lives in New York City.

(Author bio from book)

Temple, W(illard) H(enry). (December 18, 1912-November 1982)

The author of novels and short stories, Boston University houses a collection of his papers.

(Howard Gottleib Archival Research Center,
http://hgar-srv3.bu.edu/collections/collection?id=122866)

Wallis, Geraldine. [Hope Campbell, pseud.]. (June 17, 1925-?)
Born in Seattle, Mrs. Wallis was, in addition to being an author, an actress on radio, television and stage under several pseudonyms. One of her novels, *Why Not Join the Giraffes?*, was adapted into a three act play by James Reach and another novel, *Mystery at Fire Island*, was adapted into a television special for CBS in 1981.
(*Contemporary Authors Online*. Detroit: Gale, 2001, accessed 17 March, 2015)

Wanglund, Colleen
An online book and film reviewer, the author is an aficionado of Asian horror, who has published a novella *Fukushuu: Damaged Woman of Violence*.
(Author bio from book)

Weisgard, Leonard (Joseph) (December 13, 1916-January 14, 2000)
The illustrator and author of numerous children's books, Weisgard won the Caldecott Medal for Illustration in 1947 for *The Little Island*, written by Margaret Wise Brown. He and his family resided in Denmark for the last thirty-one years of his life.
(*Contemporary Authors Online*. Detroit: Gale, 2001, accessed 17 March, 2015)

Weiss, Ed
Raised in Brooklyn Heights, the author was inspired to write *Peter Pigeon of Snug Harbor* when he saw a pigeon sitting on the back of the Staten Island Ferry, staring at the island. Weiss, an artist, was the creator of the *Forgotten History of Staten Island*, a multi-disciplinary (involving performance, painting, written narratives, a blog, and outdoor installations) art project about the unreliability of history, and which still maintains a website for the project at https://fhsi.wordpress.com/. Weiss moved to Baltimore in 2011.
(Author bio, http://www.msac.org/artists/edward-weiss#/0)

Wheat, Carolyn (August 8, 1946-)
The author worked for years as an attorney for the New York City Police Department, and used her experience there as fodder for a series of mystery novels featuring attorney Cassandra "Cass" Jameson.
(*Contemporary Authors Online*. Detroit: Gale, 2005, accessed 17 March, 2015)

Westlake, Donald E(dwin) (July 12, 1933-December 31, 2008)
Born in Brooklyn, Westlake wrote over a hundred novels and non-fiction books. A three time winner of the Edgar Award (in three different categories), the author was made a Grand Master of the Mystery Writers of America, their highest honor. Many of his works have been adapted for film.
(Author website, http://www.donaldwestlake.com/)

Whitehead, Jeffrey
Raised in a small town near Allentown, Pennsylvania, Whitehead's novel was based on stories told by his grandparents, who had grown up on Staten Island during the Depression. Whitehead is currently the Director of the Study Abroad program at his alma mater, the University of Pittsburgh.
(Pitt magazine, University of Pittsburgh,
http://www.pittmag.pitt.edu/winter2005/bookshelf.html)

Whitney, Phyllis A(yame) (September 9, 1903-February 8, 2008)
Born in Yokohama, Japan, to American parents, Whitney lived in Japan, China, and the Philippines until the death of her father when she was fifteen. While she began selling stories to magazines right after high school, it wasn't until 1941 that she found a publisher for her first novel, *A Place for Ann*. That would prove to be the beginning of a highly successful writing career, which saw the publication of over seventy five novels for both young adults and adults. Whitney would live in Staten Island for over twenty years with her second husband, Lovell Jahnke, residing in homes on Fort Hill Circle in St. George and on Constance Avenue in Westerleigh. The author donated a small collection of her papers to the College of Staten Island in 2008.
(Phyllis A. Whitney Collection, Archives & Special Collections, Department of the Library, College of Staten Island, CUNY, Staten Island, New York)

Wilder, Elyzabeth Gregory
Wilder is a graduate of the dramatic writing program at New York University, where she was a Tisch Dramatic Writing Fellow. As playwright-in-residence at the Alabama Shakespeare Festival, Elyzabeth developed the curriculum for Playwright in the Classroom, a program aimed at inspiring more high school students to write plays. Currently, Wilder is the Tennessee Williams Playwright-in-Residence at Sewanee: The University of the South.
(http://www.wilderwriting.net/bio.htm)

Wylly, Phillips
Born on Staten Island, the author broke into the television industry in its early days, working as editor, director and interviewer for RKO and NBC, where he would go on to cover major events such as Grace Kelly's wedding and interview such figures as Carl Sandberg, Sophia Loren and Jacqueline Kennedy. Moving to Hollywood, he worked as a production executive for many major films and television series, including *Roots*. The material for *Staten Island* originated with the stories of Mr. Wylly's father, who told his son about the bootleggers who plied the Atlantic Coast during Prohibition. Mr. Wylly also wrote a sequel, *Hollywood's Best* which continues the story in California
(http://pwylly-statenislandthenovel.blogspot.com/)

Yockey, Ross (November 11, 1943-April 13, 2008)
Ross Yockey was a writer, author and television journalist for stations in New York and New Orleans, where he was born. Yockey won an Emmy Award in the 1970s for his documentary *Hide Them or Help Them*, which exposed institutional mistreatment of the developmentally disabled. He is the author of many books in several different genres, including biography, art, local history, inspirational, sociology, and political satire. Yockey also had a footnote in New Orleans DA Jim Garrison's famous investigation of the JFK assassination, which Yockey- then a reporter for the *New Orleans States Item*- supported by reprinting leaks from Garrison about Clay Shaw's reputed links to the CIA, Jack Ruby and Lee Harvey Oswald.
(*Contemporary Authors Online*. Detroit: Gale, 2006, accessed 17 March, 2015)

Youngblood, Shay (1959-)
A one-time Staten Island resident, Youngblood has authored two novels and a collection of short fiction.
(Author bio from book)

Zindel, Paul (May 15, 1936-March 27, 2003)
A best-selling author, whose young adult novels have become a part of middle school and high school curricula, Zindel won the 1971 Pulitzer Prize for Drama for his 1964 play *The Effect of Gamma Rays on Man-in-the-Moon Marigolds* which was subsequently adapted for film (20th Century Fox, 1972), starring Paul Newman and Joanne Woodward. Born in Stapleton, Zindel's father abandoned the family, causing his mother to try disparate money-making schemes to support them, and forcing them to move frequently, finally settling on Glen Street in Travis. The influence of his impoverished and peripatetic youth upon his writing is evident, as was his time as a

teenaged tuberculosis patient in a sanatorium. He graduated from Port Richmond High School and Wagner College, where he took a play-writing course taught by playwright Edward Albee. After graduating, he worked as a chemistry teacher at Tottenville High School for almost a decade, during which time he began publishing immensely successful novels for young people, most notably *The Pigman*, which he wrote while living in Horrmann Castle. After winning the Pulitzer, Zindel moved to Hollywood to write screenplays but came back East after six years. Although he never again resided in Staten Island, Zindel retained a close relationship with the island, speaking to students and providing aid and encouragement to local cultural groups. He is buried in Moravian Cemetery.

(*Staten Island Advance*, Friday, March 28, 2003)

Appendix A
Miscellaneous

The following works, while not meriting inclusion in a list of fictional works set in Staten Island, deserve to be mentioned either to give recognition to what Staten Island content they do have, or to definitively disassociate the work from a mistaken reputation as a Staten Island book.

G.I. Joe, a Real American Hero. New York: Marvel Comics, 1982-1994.

This popular comic book series featured a secretive military unit whose headquarters, The Pit, was located in a multi-story, high-tech underground bunker concealed beneath the Chaplain's Assistants motor pool at Fort Wadsworth. Once discovered by the terrorist organization, C.O.B.R.A., Staten Island was the scene of espionage, firefights and pitched battles involving tanks and air strikes, until The Pit was finally destroyed and the Joe team relocated.

Helprin, Mark. *In Sunlight and Shadow.* New York: Houghton, Mifflin Harcourt, 2012. 705pp.

Although only one chapter of this epic novel takes place on Staten Island, the driving romance begins on the Ferry, which the protagonist was riding in order to visit an aunt on Staten Island, a place described as an almost rural exile, where an interreligious couple had moved as a refuge from family disapproval.

Neressian, Arthur. *The Swing Voter of Staten Island.* New York: Akashic Books, 2007. 277pp.

This book proposes an alternative history in which dirty bombs destroyed New York City in 1970, after which the federal government recreated a bastardized version of it in the Nevada Desert. The ersatz city is torn apart by revolutionary and gang violence and Staten Island is buried in toxic waste. In a sort of mini Electoral College, each borough has one vote in the Presidential election, with the entire city's votes going to the candidate who wins the most boroughs. The borough president of replacement Staten Island is the wild card.

Smith, Thorne. *The Bishop's Jaegers*. Garden City, N.Y.: Sun Dial Press, 1932. 311pp.

    Although often advertised by booksellers as taking place on the Staten Island ferry, a significant portion of this sex farce actually takes place on a ferry to New Jersey, from which a collection of comical New York types get cast adrift and marooned on a nudist colony, where they engage in an adventure of self-discovery.

Stansbury, Charles Frederick. *A Kittiwake of the Great Kills*. New York: The Grafton Press, 1904. 221pp.

    Although contemporary critics regarded these intimate tales of animal life as a satire or elaborate jest, the author appears to have been a genuine and passionate naturalist who dedicated this book to those who "...maintain that Animals have rights." And although there is no explicit Staten Island content, the fact that the author is known to have written a detailed article about the oysters of Great Kills Harbor would indicate that Staten Island is the setting for some of these unique stories in which animals, from birds to mice to cats, are the protagonists.

Tosches, Nick. *Trinities*. New York: St. Martin's, 1994. 456pp.

    Although sometimes advertised by booksellers as having Staten Island content, due to a dust jacket mention, this epic novel about inter-ethnic conflict between organized crime groups contains only two short local scenes depicting a mafia conference at the Castleton Avenue home of one of the Mafia Dons.

Wells, H(erbert) G(eorge). The War in the Air. New York: Macmillan, 1908. 395pp.

    In this military science fiction novel, an armada of Imperial German airships attack New York City. Though the city government meekly surrenders to overwhelming force, citizen militias rise up and manage to down one airship, which crashes in Staten Island. Because police control over the island's unruly, polyglot population had become lax in recent years, almost everyone owned guns, which they used to fight and overcome the crew of the airship, but not before many citizens and villas were destroyed.

Wilner, Herbert. *All the Little Heroes*. New York: Bobbs-Merrill Company, Inc; A Subsidiary of Howard W. Sams & Co., Inc., 1966. 487pp.

    Although frequently advertised as a Staten Island book, the local content consists solely of an ambiguous death at a Staten Island beach bungalow witnessed by one of a group of Brooklyn boys.

Zindel, Paul. *And Miss Reardon Drinks a Little.* New York: Dramatists Play Service, 1971. 53pp.
    This short play, which explores the strained relationship between three sisters, takes place in "the New York Metropolitan area" but makes mention of a handful of Staten Island place names.

Zindel, Paul. *The Ladies Should Be in Bed.* New York: Dramatists Play Service, 1973. 21pp.
    A group of women gather together at the Howard Avenue home of one of the ladies for a game of cards. They decide to play a cruel prank on the young man who is the caretaker of the old convent across the street. Suspecting him to be a homosexual, they call up the parents of the teens he is socializing with and anonymously tell them that the man is abusing their children. (Zindel himself was the caretaker at Horrmann Castle on Howard Avenue for a time). Several Staten Island locales and institutions are mentioned, but it's notable that the ladies pass judgment on the socioeconomic status of several neighborhoods: Theresa Place in Silver Lake is slummy but not as slummy as some; Slosson Avenue is well-to-do; and Van Duzer Street has lots of "shanty Irish".

Zindel, Paul. *The Pigman and Me.* New York: HarperCollins, 1991. 168pp.
    While described as a memoir, this book reads as a novel and describes the man, Nonno Frankie Vivona, who was Zindel's inspiration for *The Pigman* when he and his family lived in Travis.

Appendix B
Annotated Works Listed Chronologically

1896-1950

108.   Smith, F(rancis) Hopkinson. *Tom Grogan*. New York: Houghton Mifflin, 1896. 247pp.

82.   Mills, W(eymar) Jay. *Through the Gates of Old Romance*. Philadelphia: J.B. Lippincott Company, 1903. 281pp.

26.   Daulton, Agnes Warner McClelland. *Fritzi; or, The Princess Perhaps*. New York: Century Co., 1908. 417pp.

5.   Baker, Etta Anthony. *Captain of the 'S.I.G.'s'*. Boston: Little, Brown and Company, 1911. 323pp.

6.   Baker, Etta Anthony. *Miss Mystery*. Boston: Little, Brown & Co., 1913. 370pp.

41.   England, George Allan. *The Air Trust*. Illustrations by John Sloan. St. Louis: Phil Wagner, 1915. 333pp.

107.   Sholl, Anna McClure [Geoffrey Corson, pseud.]. *Blue Blood and Red*. New York: Henry Holt, 1915. 395pp.

23.   Burleigh, Cecil [Harry Moore, pseud.]. *The Liberty Boys at Staten Island*. The Liberty Boys of "76", No. 900. New York: Frank Tousey- Publisher, March 29, 1918. 18pp.

54.   Holding, Elisabeth Sanxay. *The Unlit Lamp; a Story of Inter-Actions*. New York: E.P. Dutton, 1922. 334pp.

42.   Forgione, Louis. *Reamer Lou*. New York: E.P. Dutton, 1924. 279pp.

112.   Spiers, A(ugustus) M(ansfield). *Nell of Narragansett Bay*. Boston: The Stratford Co., 1925. 294pp.

45.   Gilman, Mildred. *Headlines*. New York: Horace Liveright, 1928. 309pp.

120.   Weisgard, Leonard. *Suki, the Siamese Pussy*. New York: Thomas Nelson and Sons, 1937. 32pp.

88.   Nathan, Robert. *Journey of Tapiola*. Decorations by Georg Salter. New York: Alfred A. Knopf, 1938. 121pp.

32.   DuBois, Theodora. *Death Tears a Comic Strip*. Boston: Houghton Mifflin, 1939. 235pp.

63.   Kolff, Cornelius G. *The Haven of Wooden Shoes*. Staten Island, N.Y.: Richmond Borough Publishing & Printing, 1939. 20pp.

64.   Kolff, Cornelius G. *Staten Island Fairies*. Staten Island, N.Y.: Richmond Borough Publishing Company, 1939. 48pp.

118.   Temple, W(illard) H(enry). "The Eighth-Grade Picnic; A Staten Island Story," in *Picnic Adventures*. Edited by Elizabeth L. Gilman. New York: Farrar and Rinehart, 1940. 192pp. pgs 90-107.

93.   Odets, Clifford. *Clash by Night*. New York: Random House, 1942. 242pp.

9.   Bowles, Jane. *Two Serious Ladies*. New York: Alfred A. Knopf, 1943. 271pp.

92.   Nutt, Frances Tysen. *Three Fields to Cross*. New York: Stephen-Paul Publishers, 1947. 368pp.

33.   DuBois, Theodora. *The Devil and Destiny*. New York: Lancer Books, 1948. 271pp.

125.   Whitney, Phyllis A(yama). *Ever After*. Boston: Houghton Mifflin, 1948. 279pp.

30.   De Sylvia, Josephine [Sylvia Dee, pseud.]. *Dear Guest and Ghost*. New York: Macmillan, 1950. 259pp.

35.   DuBois, Theodora. *High Tension*. Garden City, N.Y.: Published for the Crime Club by Doubleday, 1950. 224pp.

1951-1970

34.   DuBois, Theodora. *Fowl Play*. Garden City, N.Y.: Published for the Crime Club by Doubleday & Company, Inc., 1951. 189pp.

38.   DuBois, Theodora. *Solution T-25*. New York: Modern Literary Editions Publishing Company, 1951. 221pp.

85.   Mowat, Grace Helen. *Broken Barrier; A Romance of Staten Island and the Province of New Brunswick*. Fredericton, N.B.: University Press of New Brunswick, 1951. 182pp.

111.   Spellman, Francis Cardinal. *The Foundling*. New York: Charles Scribner's Sons, 1951. 304pp.

126.   Whitney, Phyllis A(yame). *The Island of Dark Woods*. Illustrated by Al Fiorentino. Philadelphia: Westminster Press, 1951. 190pp.

36.   DuBois, Theodora. *The Listener*. Garden City, N.Y.: Published for the Crime Club by Doubleday and Company, Inc., 1953. 192pp.

129.   Whitney, Phyllis A(yame). *Step to the Music*. New York: Thomas Y. Crowell, 1953. 256pp.

37.   DuBois, Theodora. *Seeing Red*. Garden City, N.Y.: Published for the Crime Club by Doubleday & Co., Inc., 1954. 187pp.

98.   Powell, Dawn. *The Wicked Pavilion*. Boston: Houghton Mifflin, 1954. 306pp.

127.   Whitney, Phyllis A(yame). *The Quicksilver Pool*. New York: Ace Books, 1955. 319pp.

40.   Earle, Olive L. *White Patch*. Illustrated by Olive L. Earle. New York: William Morrow, 1958. 64pp.

128.   Whitney, Phyllis A(yame). *Secret of the Emerald Star*. Illustrated by Alex Stein. Philadelphia: Westminster Press, 1964. 233pp.

51. Harrington, Joseph. *The Last Known Address.* New York: J.B. Lippincott, 1965. 190pp.

67. Ledbetter, Gladys Manée. *A Wideness in God's Mercy.* New York: Vantage Press, 1965. 445pp.

122. Westlake, Donald. *The Fugitive Pigeon.* New York: Random House, 1965. 172pp.

141. Zindel, Paul. *The Pigman.* New York: Harper and Row, 1968, 182pp.

139. Zindel, Paul. *My Darling, My Hamburger.* New York: Harper and Row, 1969. 168pp.

39. Du Bois, William Pène. *Call Me Bandicoot.* New York: Harper & Row, 1970. 63pp.

138. Zindel, Paul. *I Never Loved Your Mind.* New York: Harper and Row, 1970. 181pp.

1971-2000

119. Wallis, Geraldine. [Hope Campbell, pseud.]. *No More Trains to Tottenville.* New York: McCall Publishing Company, 1971. 170pp.

81. Millman, John. *Christmas Eve and Other Stories.* Brooklyn, N.Y.: Pageant-Poseidon, Ltd., 1972. 90pp.

75. MacKellar, William. *Alfie and Me and the Ghost of Peter Stuyvesant.* Illustrated by David K. Stone. New York: Dodd, Mead & Company, 1974. 150pp.

140. Zindel, Paul. *Pardon Me, You're Stepping on my Eyeball.* New York: Harper and Row, 1976. 262pp.

135. Zindel, Paul. *Confessions of a Teenage Baboon.* New York: Harper and Row, 1977. 154pp.

99. Randisi, Robert. *The Disappearance of Penny.* New York: Charter, 1980. 234pp.

142. Zindel, Paul. *The Pigman's Legacy.* New York: Harper and Row, 1980. 183pp.

109. Smith, Martin Cruz. *Gorky Park.* New York: Random House, 1981. 365pp.

136. Zindel, Paul. *The Girl Who Wanted a Boy.* New York: Harper and Row, 1981. 148pp.

65. Kuczkir, Mary and Roberta Anderson [Fern Michaels, pseud.]. *Cinders to Satin.* New York: Ballantine Books, 1984. 499pp.

137. Zindel, Paul. *Harry and Hortense at Hormone High.* New York: Harper and Row, 1984. 151pp.

44. Gallerne, Gilbert [Gilles Bergal, pseud.]. *Cauchemar á Staten Island.* Paris: Fleuve Noir, 1986. 156pp.

29. DeStefano, Anthony [Anthony John, pseud.]. *The Judas Voice.* New York: Jove Books, 1989. 329pp.

105. Sampson, John. *O, Call Back Yesterday.* Castleton, Vt.: Thornfield Press, 1989. 197pp.

133. Zindel, Paul. *Amulets Against the Dragon Forces.* New York: Dramatists Play Services, 1989. 80pp.

50. Harper, Karen [Caryn Cameron, pseud.]. *Liberty's Lady.* Toronto: Harlequin, 1990. 297pp.

89. Nielsen, Alfred. *The Summer of the Paymaster.* New York: W.W. Norton, 1990. 379pp.

47. Goldsborough, Robert. *Silver Spire.* New York: Bantam Books, 1992. 216pp.

116. Stone, Robert. *Outerbridge Reach.* New York: Houghton Mifflin, 1992. 409pp.

134.   Zindel, Paul. *Attack of the Killer Fishsticks*. New York: A Bantam Skylark Book, 1993. 117pp.

53.   Hoff, B.J. *Winds of Graystone Manor*. Minneapolis, Minn: Bethany House Publishers, 1995. 318pp.

123.   Wheat, Carolyn. *Fresh Kills*. New York: A Berkley Prime Crime, published by the Berkley Publishing Group, 1995. 236pp.

2.   Adinolfi, JoAnn. *Tina's Diner*. New York: Simon & Schuster Books for Young Readers, 1997. 29pp.

106.   Sampson, John. *Up at Lighthouse Hill*. Hinesburg, Vt.: Thornfield Press, 1999. 203pp.

143.   Zindel, Paul. *Rats*. New York: Hyperion, 1999. 203pp.

101.   Rendelstein, Jill Ellen. *Staten Doll*. (Master's thesis). Washington D.C.: American University, 2000. 98pp.

2001-2015

91.   Nunez, Sigrid. *For Rouenna*. New York: Farrar, Straus and Giroux, 2001. 230pp.

78.   Mercaldo, David, Ph.D. *Ferry*. Fairfax, Va: Xulon Press, 2002. 196pp.

12.   Brown, Tracy. *Black; A Street Tale*. Columbus, Ohio: Triple Crown Publications, 2003. 182pp.

62.   Kingsbury, Karen. *One Tuesday Morning*. Grand Rapids, Mich.: Zondervan, 2003. 352pp.

83.   Modern, Tom. *Richmondtown*. Baltimore: PublishAmerica, 2003. 161pp.

115.   St. Jean, Catherine Avery. *A Staten Island Ferry Tale*. Illustrated by Paul J. Frahm. Xlibris, 2003. 32pp.

132.   Yockey, Ross. *Diva Gate; A Novel in Three Acts.* (Master's thesis). Charlotte, N.Car.: Queens University of Charlotte, 2003. 271pp.

14.   Brown, Tracy. *Dime Piece.* Columbus, Ohio: Triple Crown Publications, 2004. 186pp.

61.   Kingsbury, Karen. *Beyond Tuesday Morning.* Grand Rapids, Mich.: Zondervan, 2004. 316pp.

77.   McMahon, Judi. *Someone to Watch Over Me.* Xlibris, 2004. 417pp.

95.   Petersen, David. *Never Say Never.* New York: iUniverse, 2004. 213pp.

100.   Reigada, Flora. *The Face Behind the Veil.* Bloomington, Ind.: AuthorHouse, 2004. 613pp.

104.   Rozan, S(hira) J(udith). *Absent Friends.* New York: Delacorte Press, 2004. 367pp.

124.   Whitehead, Jeffrey. *The Scorpion's Weather.* Baltimore: PublishAmerica, 2004. 257pp.

130.   Wilder, Elyzabeth Gregory. *Fresh Kills.* London: Methuen Publishing Limited, 2004. 63pp.

4.   Amessé, Susan. *Kissing Brendan Callahan.* New Milford, Conn.: A Deborah Brodie Book, Roaring Brook Press, 2005. 149pp.

13.   Brown, Tracy. *Criminal Minded.* New York: St. Martin's Griffin, 2005. 292pp.

7.   Bauch, Jonathan. *Permanent Record.* (Master's thesis). Las Vegas, Nev.: University of Nevada, Las Vegas, 2006. 150pp.

8.   Bettinger, Keith. *Fighting Crime with "Some" Day and Lenny; or What Happens When Dragnet Meets Car 54 Where Are You?.* Taylorville, Ill.: Oak Tree Press, 2006. 115pp.

60.   Khoudari, Amy S. *Looking in the Shadows; The Life of Alice Austen.* Lincoln, Neb: iUniverse, 2006. 149pp.

66.   Latka, John. *Staten Island Memoirs*. Bloomington, Ind.: AuthorHouse, 2006. 576pp.

79.   Mercaldo, David, Ph.D. *Seamstress*. n.l.: Crown Oak Press, 2006. 188pp.

87.   Nadelson, Reggie. *Fresh Kills*. New York: Walker and Co., 2006. 343pp.

131.   Wylly, Phillips. *Staten Island*. College Station, Tex.: Virtualbookworm.com Publishing Inc., 2006. 652pp.

18.   Brown, Tracy. *White Lines*. New York: St. Martin's Griffin, 2007. 497pp.

25.   Coston, Alicia. *She's Killin' Me*. Virginia Beach, Va.: Indigo Press, 2007. 381pp.

17.   Brown, Tracy. *Twisted*. New York: St. Martin's Griffin, 2008. 338pp.

28.   DeCandido, Keith R(obert) A(ndreassi) *Four Walls*. New York: Pocket Star, 2008. 334pp.

70.   Loehfelm, Bill. *Fresh Kills*. New York: G.P. Putnam's Sons, 2008. 326pp.

80.   Mila, Paul J. *Fireworks*. Bloomington, Ind.: AuthorHouse, 2008. 270pp.

90.   Nieves-Powell, Linda. *Free Style*. New York: Atria, 2008. 262pp.

94.   O'Neill, Joseph. *Netherland*. New York: Pantheon Books, 2008. 256pp.

113.   Spollen, Anne. *The Shape of Water*. Woodbury, Minn.: Flux, 2008. 305pp.

121.   Weiss, Ed. *Peter Pigeon of Snug Harbor*. Staten Island, N.Y.: Rocky Hollow Press, 2008. 89pp.

15. Brown, Tracy. "Flirting with Disaster" in *Flirt*. New York: St. Martin's Griffin, 2009. 195pp. pgs 6-72.

16. Brown, Tracy. *Snapped*. New York: St. Martin's Griffin, 2009. 361pp.

43. Friedman, Robin. *The Importance of Wings*. Watertown, Mass.: Charlesbridge, 2009. 170pp.

52. Hellstrom, Christopher. *Fresh Kills*. n.l.: Third Eve Books, 2009. 111pp.

68. Loehfelm, Bill. *Bloodroot*. New York: G.P. Putnam's Sons, 2009. 326pp.

46. Goldfarb, Aaron. "Health: Staten Island," in *The CheatSheet*. CreateSpace, 2010. 165pp. pgs 75-88.

48. Grayson, Richard. *Victory Boulevard*. New York: Art Pants, 2010. 110pp.

86. Mullin, Michael and John Skewes. *Larry Gets Lost in New York City*. Illustrated by John Skewes. Seattle, Wash.: Sasquatch Books, 2010. 30pp.

11. Brown, Tracy. *Aftermath*. New York: St. Martin's Griffin, 2011. 452pp.

69. Loehfelm, Bill. *The Devil She Knows*. New York: Sarah Crichton Books; Farrar, Straus and Giroux, 2011. 322pp.

74. Lynch, Lee. "Dumb Bunny" in *Best Lesbian Romance 2012*. Edited by Radclyffe. San Francisco, Cal.: Cleis, 2011. 195pp. pgs 139-155.

97. Pinto, K.T. *Sto's House Presents: Beer with a Mutant Chaser*. Howell, N.J.: Dark House, 2011. 167pp.

102. Reynolds, D(ewey) B. *Master of Plagues*. CreateSpace.com, 2011. 257pp.

114.   St. Jean, Catherine Avery. *Caleb Takes a Ride on the Staten Island Ferry.* Illustrated by Paul J. Frahm. CreateSpace, 2011. 24pp.

19.   Brown, Tracy. *White Lines II: Sunny.* New York: St. Martin's Griffin, 2012. 290pp.

1.   Abbruzzi, Patrick. *Nothing to Report.* CreateSpace, 2012. 327pp.

3.   Ambrose, Dominic. *Nickel Fare.* New York: Ferrandina Press, 2012. 225pp.

59.   Kelter, Lawrence. *Our Honored Dead.* n.l.: F Street Books, 2012. 256pp.

76.   Marino, Kelly. *Into the Hourglass.* CreateSpace, 2012. 263pp.

84.   Morris, Mitzi. *Poetic Justice.* New York: Colloquial Media, 2012. 319pp.

110.   Smith, Patricia, ed. *Staten Island Noir.* New York: Akashic Books, 2012. 252pp.

117.   Telford, Robert S. *Between Two Wars.* Bloomington, Ind.: Trafford, 2012. 213pp.

10.   Brett, R. *Hypocrisy.* College Station, Tex.: Virtualbookworm.com, 2013. 244pp.

22.   Burke, Jessica and Anthony Burdge. *The Friendly Horror and Other Weird Tales.* Staten Island: Myth Ink Books, 2013. 146pp.

27.   Davis, J.T. *New York Stories; And Other Potentially Libelous Tales of the 1970s.* CreateSpace, 2013. 504pp.

31.   Drew, K. *Wolf at the Door.* Tallahassee, Fla: Dreamspinner Press, 2013. 191pp.

55.   Hopkins, George R. *Letters from the Dead.* Outskirts Press, 2013. 304pp.

71. Longfellow, Ki. *The Girl in the Next Room A Sam Russo Mystery; Case 3*. Port Orchard, Wash: EIO Books, 2013. 283pp.

72. Longfellow, Ki. *Good Dog, Bad Dog. A Sam Russo Mystery; Case 2*. Port Orchard, Wash: Eio Books, 2013. 237pp.

73. Longfellow, Ki. *Shadow Roll; A Sam Russo Mystery; Case 1*. Port Orchard, Wash: Eio Books, 2013.

96. Petrosini, Dan. *Complicit Witness*. CreateSpace, 2013. 224pp.

103. Robertson, Eleanor Marie (J.D. Robb, pseud.). "Missing in Death" in *Ritual in Death and Missing in Death*. London: Piatkus, 2013. 292pp. pgs 137-281.

21. Burdge, Anthony and Jessica Burke, eds. *Dark Tales from Elder Regions*. Staten Island: Myth Ink Books, 2014. 382pp.

24. Burtone, Gaetano J. *Only a Prayer Away*. Victoria, British Columbia: Friesen Press, 2014. 214pp.

49. Gross, Andrew. *Everything to Lose*. New York: William Morrow; An Imprint of HarperCollins Publishers, 2014. 325pp.

56. Hopkins, George R. *Random Acts of Malice*. Xlibris, 2014. 284pp.

20. Brown, Tracy. *Whites Lines III; All Falls Down*. New York: St. Martin's Griffin, 2015. 325pp.

57. Hopkins, George R. *Unholy Retribution*. CreateSpace, 2015. 294pp.

58. Joyce, Eddie. *Small Mercies*. New York: Viking, 2015. 353pp.

Index

The numbers refer to entries, not page numbers

52, 58, 64, 68, 78, 87, 89, 99, 101, 104, 138

paranormal, 21, 28, 43, 75, 82, 96, 101

Park Hill, 13, 18, 110

Pavilion Hotel, 127, 129

picture books for children, 2, 40, 86, 114, 115, 120

Police, 8, 44, 55, 56, 57, 59, 69, 108,
    120th precinct, 1, 3, 13
    122nd precinct, 29, 51, 57
    123rd precinct, 56

politics, 4, 52, 105, 108

Port Richmond High school (whether explicitly named or disguised), 13, 136, 137

Port Ivory, 49

Prince's Bay, 131, 133

prostitution, 18, 46, 70, 131, 133

Pouch Camp, 21

P.S. 5 (Huguenot), 81

P.S. 49, 107

Quarantine Station, 65 burning of, 110

Rape, 3, 11, 66, 95, 131, 139

Reformed Church, 6, 19, 100

R.H. Tugs restaurant (Livingston), 11, 55

Rendezvous bar (Targee Street), 12

Resurrection Cemetery, 21

Richmond College, 3

Richmond Parkway, 75

Richmondtown, 29, 30, 83, 105, 106, 107, 112, 119, 126

Rice, Rev. Calvin, 12

Ridgecrest Avenue, 95

Rojek, Monsignor Artur (1906-1988), 1

Rosebank, 21, 110

Rossville boat graveyard, 95, 116

Russian-Americans, 87, 96

salt grass harvesting, 112

Santa Anna, Antonio López de (1794-1876), 126

Scalia's funeral home, 70

science fiction, 38, 83, 97, 143

Secession movement, 105

www.ingramcontent.com/pod-product-compliance
Lightning Source LLC
Chambersburg PA
CBHW061041110426
42740CB00050B/2674